EUCHARISTIA

Nothing is to be rejected if it is received with
thanksgiving,
for then it is consecrated by the word of God and prayer.
(1 Tim. 4:4–5)

Eucharistia

A Study of the Eucharistic Prayer

Dennis C. Smolarski, S.J.

paulist press *new york/ramsey*

The Publisher gratefully acknowledges the use of the following materials: Excerpt from *The Sacrament of the Lord's Supper,* Revised Edition, 1981, copyright © 1972, 1976, 1979, 1980 by The United Methodist Publishing House. Used by permission; the 1974 "Guidelines for the Composition of Children's Eucharistic Prayers" and the four sample Eucharistic Prayers, used by permission of the Archdiocese of Liverpool, England Liturgy Commission; excerpts from the English translation of *Rite of Baptism for Children* © 1969, International Committee on English in the Liturgy, Inc. (ICEL); excerpts from the English translation of *Rite of Anointing and Pastoral Care of the Sick,* © 1973, ICEL. All rights reserved; excerpts from the introduction (pp. 62–63), the "short version" of the adult Eucharistic Prayer, and the "Eucharistic Prayer Particularly for the Young People I" all taken from D.S. Amalorpavadass, *Towards Indigenisation in the Liturgy* (1974). Used by permission of the National Biblical Catechetical and Liturgical Center, Bangalore, India; excerpts from *The Book of Common Prayer,* copyright © 1979 by The Church Pension Fund. All rights reserved. Used by permission of the Church Hymnal Corporation.

NIHIL OBSTAT
Rev. Francis A. DeDomenico, S.T.L.
Censor Librorum

IMPRIMATUR
Most Reverend Peter L. Gerety, D.D.
Archbishop of Newark

May 19, 1982

IMPRIMI POTEST
V. Rev. William J. Wood, S.J.
Provincial for Education
California Province, Society of Jesus

March 14, 1981

CONTENTS

Section Four

THE EUCHARISTIC PRAYER: AN ANALYSIS OF COMPONENT PARTS

Section Five

NON-STRUCTURAL COMMENTS, CONSIDERATIONS, CONCERNS

Section Six

CONCLUSION

Appendices

Acknowledgments

An author or a speaker always runs the risk of omitting someone when acknowledging special individuals. Thus, authors and speakers may possibly, yet inadvertently, slight someone they never intended to omit, but rather merely forgot about due to human weakness. I preface these acknowledgments by saying that I hope I have not succumbed to such human weakness.

A previous version of this work was submitted as a thesis for the Master of Sacred Theology degree in 1979 at the Jesuit School of Theology at Berkeley, California. The director of my research was James Empereur, S.J.; John Boyle, S.J. and Richard Hill, S.J. graciously served as official readers. To these men I offer a special word of thanks. In addition, I would like to thank Lyndon Farwell, S.J., Robert Hovda, Melissa Kay, Lawrence Madden, S.J., John Mossi, S.J., Michael Moynahan, S.J., Carlos Sevilla, S.J., Kenneth Smits, O.F.M.Cap., and Paul Soukup, S.J. who all read the manuscript in one of its many versions and offered valuable comments. I would also like to thank my many Jesuit brothers, especially in the California Province, who over the years have endured my rantings and ravings on matters liturgical, concerning both Eastern and Western rites, and have put up with me and shown me love in return, even in spite of myself.

to my parents,

Genevieve and Chester,

who taught me the meaning of thanks, praise, and love

Section One

INTRODUCTION

A Note from the Author

Language and Gender

1. A conscious effort was made to use non-sexist language as much as possible without doing damage to the train of thought, or to the English language, or by using an inordinate number of "he/she" 's. In referring to God the Creator, I retained the use of the term "Father," because it is biblical, was used by Jesus and St. Paul in reference to God, and has been in common use by both Christians and Jews for centuries. This is not to say that I view God as *male*, however. As Joachim Jeremias has pointed out, the qualities associated with a Jewish father around the time of Christ might be more properly associated with a mother nowadays (Jeremias [2], p. 18).

The Term "Presider"

2. I have deferred to suggestions and have employed the word "presider," rather than "celebrant," "president," or priest, to denote the one who presides over the Eucharist and proclaims the Eucharistic Prayer. There is some precedent for this in the writings of Ignatius of Antioch (IgMag. 6) and Justin Martyr (*1 Apol.* 65:3, 5; 67:5). It is hoped that this usage will enable us even more to realize that the entire assembly celebrates the Eucharist, that each person present is truly a con-celebrant, and that the role of the priest is to preside over a communal act of worship.

Method of Referencing

3. Throughout the text, references are given in simple, abbreviated form using only the author's last name (if necessary), and page number of his work. Complete reference information can be obtained by then checking the bibliography.

Chapter One
SYNOPSIS AND OVERVIEW

The world has gone through much change since the first satellite was sent into space in 1958, and no aspect of human life has escaped some sort of change and some questioning about its role. Even a person's simple faith in God has been subjected to much examination and purification. Parallel with the examination of human beliefs has been the change in the modes and attitudes involved in Christian worship, a worship which is normally centered around the celebration of the Eucharist—the Lord's Supper, the Mass or Holy Communion. The central prayer of the Christian Communion service is the Eucharistic Prayer, also known as the Canon or Anaphora, which is the great thanksgiving prayer by which the offerings of bread and wine become the sacrament of the Lord's Body and Blood, and which is commonly called the "prayer of consecration." In recent years, there has been much discussion concerning the Eucharistic Prayer, especially regarding the use of a variety of such prayers instead of only a limited number.[1]

The renewal in the forms of Christian worship has included, in many Churches, the introduction of additional Eucharistic Prayers as alternatives to the standard one(s) previously in use. Since the introduction of the vernacular into Roman Catholic services in 1964, a total of eight new Eucharistic Prayers have been added to the centuries-old Roman Canon by the Holy See. Three of these prayers were introduced in 1969 as general alternatives to the Roman Canon. Two more were introduced in 1975 as experimental thematic prayers with the theme of Reconciliation, and the other three were also introduced in 1975 for Masses with Children, having been specifically written with children in mind. In addition, national Catholic bishops' conferences can propose other compositions to the Holy See for approval.[2] Episcopalian priests have also recently been given the opportunity of using new Eucharistic Prayers through the approval of the 1979 *Book of Common Prayer*, and numerous other Western Christian Churches have joined the ancient practice of the Eastern Christian Churches in allowing a variety of Eucharistic Prayers. In composing new prayers, Church authorities have been concerned with preserving the tradition and heritage of the Church with regard to the Eucharistic Prayer, yet attempting to compose prayers which would at the same time speak to contemporary men and women. In other words, they have attempted to reintroduce prayers which are, in the words of Edward Kilmartin, "integrally modern and radically conservative" (p. 268).

Many people, however, feel that these concessions by Church officials only scratch the surface of what they regard as a real problem in Christian worship today. They feel that the official prayers still are too few in number and do not really speak to most people or touch most people where they need to be touched. Quite often, it seems desirable to have a Eucharistic Prayer which reflects the general mood of the liturgy or the feast, along the lines of the recent Roman Catholic Reconciliation Eucharistic Prayers mentioned above. However, because of the limited number of authorized prayers, such thematic expression is not possible in most official church liturgies (cf. *Liturgie et vie chrétienne* [July–Sept. 1974]).

To satisfy this felt need for more prayers, numerous experimental, unauthorized texts have appeared in recent years, each containing a number of Eucharistic Prayers. Among these may be noted *The Experimental Liturgy Book, Possible Patterns,* and *Bread, Blessed and Broken.* However, some of the Eucharistic Prayers contained in these collections are not up to the standards that many competent liturgists, theologians, and Church authorities would like them to possess. The recently composed official prayers have so far been fairly faithful to the tradition of the Eucharistic Prayer (in fact, too tradition-bound for some critics), while allowing some changes in what scholars consider nonessential parts. But a number of people fear that some of the readily available unauthorized texts may have varied a little too much from the tradition of the Christian Community for these prayers to be used at Christian Eucharistic services (cf. *Notitiae,* "Aberrazioni").

Before continuing any further, it may be helpful to give a brief description of the "parts" of a Eucharistic Prayer. Scholars generally agree that the Eucharistic Prayer finds its origins in Jewish prayer forms, and in the next two chapters I will present a synopsis of this development from the Jewish forms into the distinctively Christian form of prayer for a distinctively Christian worship service. In the course of this development, a certain structure also came into existence, based generally on the Jewish grace after meals, the *birkat ha-mazon,* but having its own peculiarities. By the third century (to which the earliest Eucharistic Prayers that we have discovered date), all prayers have more or less the same basic structure with the same basic parts or subsections, and this structure varies only slightly from the structure of most Eucharistic Prayers in use today.

The typical modern Eucharistic Prayer has the following components and order, sometimes referred to as the "Eastern" or Antiochian order (for other orders, see Davies).[3] After a *dialogue* of greeting and invitation to prayer, it begins with a *stylized introduction* in imitation of Jewish prayer forms. This introduction leads into the *proclamation* or *motive* section (sometimes termed the "anamnesis" in a general use of that term). This proclamation usually praises God the Father for various events in the history of salvation and often includes praise for the wonders of creation. Oftentimes this proclamation is interrupted by the prophetic hymn, the *Sanctus* or *Holy, Holy.* If a Eucharistic Prayer does contain the *Sanctus,* then the part of the prayer which precedes the *Sanctus* is usually called the *Preface.* The proclamation section typically leads into the *Institution Narrative* or the formal recounting of the words and actions of Christ at the Last Supper. However, in those prayers influenced by an ancient Egyptian structure, a *Consecratory Epiclesis* or invocation of the Spirit to sanctify the bread and wine immediately precedes the Institution Narrative (cf. Vagaggini, pp. 67–70, 140, 158; Kavanaugh [3], pp. 9–11).

After the Institution Narrative, there frequently follows some sort of *memorial acclamation* by the congregation in acclamatory style. After this, the celebrant continues with the *memorial (anamnesis)-offertory-invocation (epiclesis)* part of the prayer. This section is a statement that the community is obedient to the command of the Lord to "do this in memory of me," and therefore does remember the Lord's death and resurrection as they unite themselves to his offering to God the Father. It also asks the Father to send the Spirit upon the elements of bread and wine (and on the people present) to change them so that all who partake of the elements may enjoy the Spirit's fruits of unity and peace. This descent of the Spirit is seen to be a sign that the Eucharist being celebrated is acceptable to the Father. Often there follow prayers of *intercession,* sometimes expressing communion with the hierarchy, the saints, the living and the dead. The entire prayer is then concluded with the final *doxology,* or trinitarian statement of praise given to the Father, through the Son, with the Spirit, and assented to by the assembly with its *Amen.*

Some authors suggest that a clearer subdivision of the Eucharistic Prayer would exist if a twofold distinction were made, *memorial* and *supplication,* rather than the numerous divisions used above. In such a twofold division, the *memorial* section would include as sub-sections everything from the stylized introduction to the memorial (anamnesis)-offertory section, and the *supplication* would include the invocation (epiclesis) and the intercessions. Such a division would have the advantage of seeing the proclamation, the Institution Narrative, and the memorial (anamnesis)-offertory as all basically connected together and all subsections of a larger "memorial" division (cf. below, Chapter 8, section B). This way of dividing the Eucharistic Prayer would have practical consequences when evaluating, for example, where a congregational acclamation should occur.

Of the various parts of a Eucharistic Prayer mentioned above, it is obvious that not all sections carry the same importance. In Chapter 11 there will be a section dealing with the relative importance of various sections of the Eucharistic Prayer. However, in general, we might be able to say that what has remained fairly constant in Eucharistic Prayers throughout the ages can be considered more essential than those sections which have varied widely. With regard to composition of new prayers, both official and unauthorized, authors try to change the non-essentials while preserving the essentials. However, the average Christian may still be led to ask, "What is essential in a Eucharistic Prayer?"

In an attempt to clarify the "essentials" of the Eucharistic Prayer, the Roman Catholic Church has issued guidelines with regard to the composition of new prayers. In the summer of 1973, the Holy See issued a letter concerning the use of newly composed Eucharistic Prayers (named *Eucharistiae Participationem*). One of the major concerns of this letter was that new prayers may not be up to proper theological and liturgical standards. However, the letter did allow the composition of new prayers for special celebrations, as long as they were submitted to the Holy See for approval prior to actual use.

In a clarifying statement regarding the structure and contents of such newly composed prayers for use by Roman rite Catholics, the periodical *Notitiae* (a publication of the Congregation for Divine Worship) contained a short commentary in the April 1975 issue. In this commentary, we see that the Holy See wishes newly composed prayers to contain the following:

1. a Consecratory Epiclesis preceding the Institution Narrative;
2. the words of Christ identical to the form already used in the present official prayers;
3. mention of the sacrificial character of the Mass, and expression of the belief in the real presence after the Institution Narrative;
4. mention of the Blessed Virgin;
5. a place to mention the Pope and the local ordinary.

One should not interpret this commentary as suggesting that the five parts mentioned are the primary parts or most important sections of the Eucharistic Prayer, as far as the Roman Curia is concerned. These five points are five pastoral options that the Holy See wished to legislate for the new Eucharistic Prayers in the Roman rite, points which probably did not occur in many Eucharistic Prayers composed before the commentary was issued, and which seemed desirable, from a pastoral point of view, for Catholics of the Roman rite.

The same commentary also makes a distinction with regard to the reasons for which new prayers may be written. New Eucharistic Prayers may be composed for special events or circumstances, but not for special groups of individuals (with the sole exception of children, for pedagogical reasons).

A similar but more extensive commentary was issued a few months earlier by the Liverpool (England) Roman Catholic Archdiocese, specifically regarding Eucharistic Prayers for Children. This commentary gave general theological and liturgical requirements for all Eucharistic Prayers, and then gave specific pastoral recommendations and adaptations for each age group from six to sixteen years old. In addition, four sample Eucharistic Prayers were composed by the diocese as models for future development (cf. Appendix B).

We thus see that there is opportunity in many Churches to create new prayers for worship, provided they conform to certain norms. As we have just seen, the Roman Catholic Church is open to such new prayers, but, at the same time, is concerned about establishing norms and criteria for new prayers, whether or not they are ever used in liturgical celebrations. However, even after looking at a given set of norms, a person may still be inclined to ask, "How can I tell an *epiclesis* from an *anamnesis* from a *doxology*, and what is so special about these parts that a Eucharistic Prayer should have to contain all of them?"

Much has been written in the past two decades concerning the Eucharist and the Eucharistic Prayer. Many of the articles and books recently published on these topics are excellent reference works, authored by well-known and competent liturgical scholars. However, a person having questions and interested in this subject would be hard-pressed to locate the best of these works, and then to try to synthesize what the "experts" say about the Eucharist and the Eucharistic Prayer. Part of this problem is due to the great amount of material available and their numerous locations; part is due to different authors being concerned with different aspects or parts of the Eucharist or Eucharistic Prayer; and part is due to the various authors disagreeing among themselves. The purpose of this work is to examine the Eucharistic Prayer and to see what contemporary liturgists and theologians have to say in their recent publications about this prayer which is so central to Christian worship.

In compiling my background information for this work, I have tried to consult the major authors and the major articles and publications issued in the past two decades, and to incorporate the primary points made, wherever useful. As a result, this work is in the form of a compendium or digest of some of the best recent literature about the structure and nature of the Eucharistic Prayer. Thus, it can serve as a summary of the many recent articles and publications which have appeared and which have attempted to aid the modern Christian's understanding of what actually happens when Christians assemble together as a community and celebrate the Sacrament of the Eucharist.

Having examined many of the official and unofficial Eucharistic Prayers which have appeared in the last ten years or so, it seems more and more evident to me that the composition of new Eucharistic Prayers is an art form closely related to other types of literary composition. Great prayers are not written overnight. They are expressions of love which come from the depths of the human heart. Because they are prayers, they can never fully be captured in written words. Because they are composed of words, they must be evaluated as any other piece of literature should be.

There are many Eucharistic Prayers in circulation among Christian communities today, both authorized and unauthorized, and more compositions will surely appear in the future. Even a cursory examination of these prayers reveals that not all of them are of the same quality. These texts now available must be examined for their merits and failings. What should be looked for? What should be avoided? What is necessary in a Eucharistic Prayer and why? What may be dispensed with? It is up to serious liturgists, scholars, poets and committed Christians to read about and to understand the nature of the Eucharistic Prayer, and then to apply themselves to the task of evaluating, and even (if permitted to do so by competent ecclesiastical officials, such as in the Episcopal Church) composing, new prayers which are truly expressive of contemporary faith, concerns, and needs.

Section Two

FROM JEWISH MEAL PRAYERS TO CHRISTIAN EUCHARIST

Chapter Two
HEBREW ORIGINS

In the biblical descriptions of the Last Supper, we are told that the Lord Jesus took bread and said a prayer of blessing over the bread. He then broke the bread and shared it with the disciples present. Thus these four actions—taking, blessing, breaking and sharing—are what liturgically constitute what we commonly term "the Liturgy of the Eucharist." During the Preparation of the Gifts, the presider *takes* the bread and wine and places them on the altar. He then *blesses* God by praying the Eucharistic Prayer over the bread and wine. Next the celebrant *breaks* the bread, and then, at Communion time, he *shares* the sanctified elements with the communicants.

We see, then, that in its proper context, the Eucharistic Prayer is primarily a prayer of blessing. As a prayer of blessing, it finds its origins in the "berakah" (pronounced "b'ra-KHAH" with plural "berakoth"), a Jewish prayer-form consisting essentially of a "blessing" of God. When a Jew pronounced a "blessing," he would offer praise to God as Creator of all things. Since God had been blessed and thanked, the person or object which was the motive for the prayer of blessing was thus made holy, since this person or object was the reason why praise and thanks had been given to God (cf. Kilmartin, p. 273, note 18a). The typical "berakah" consists of three main parts: the stylized beginning, the statement of the motive for the praise, and, in the longer versions, the concluding statement which would return to a theme of praise and blessing again (cf. Lash, pp. 80–83; Audet, p. 646; Talley [1], p. 117). This last concluding statement is called the *"chatimah"* or "seal." An example of such a berakah is the following:

> Blessed are you, LORD, our God, king of the universe!
> You have sanctified us by your commandments
>   and have taught us about eating unleavened bread.

Longer berakoth would be capped or "sealed" with a *"chatimah"* such as:

> Blessed be you, LORD, who give us food to eat!

Longer berakoth also frequently contained a proclamatory section. After the initial statement of praise, the person who pronounced the blessing occasionally went into a more or less lengthy proclamation of the Lord's many blessings to Israel, even in spite of Israel's unfaithfulness to the Lord.

Besides constituting the usual daily graces before and after meals, berakoth also occur throughout the ritual of the Passover meal. After certain of the prescribed berakoth at the Passover, the person who pronounced them could also add his own commentary. It was in this context that the Lord Jesus instituted the Eucharist at the Last Supper. Some scholars suggest that Jesus pronounced the prescribed Jewish ritual blessings over the bread and wine, and then added his own comments to these blessings, comments which concluded with the statements: "This is my Body . . . This is my Blood" (cf. Jeremias, pp. 55–62, 218–37; Bouyer, p. 102).

The Gospels also record that Jesus told his disciples to repeat his actions at the Last Supper, "as a memorial of me." This command to remember him in a special meal was carried out literally by the early Christians who broke bread and shared a cup after saying certain ritual prayers of blessing—prayers which originally were probably quite close to the usual Jewish meal blessings.

The typical Jewish meal prayers or graces were of two types— a short berakah over the bread at the beginning of a meal and a longer berakah after the meal—called the *"birkat ha-mazon"* or "blessing for food." At the Passover meal, this last grace was also embellished and lengthened by prayers referring to a cup of wine, called the cup of Elijah. It seems that at the Last Supper itself, these two blessings spoken by Christ were in fact separated by the regular meal (cf. "after supper," 1 Cor. 11:25, Lk. 22:20).

The question that is raised and is really unanswerable is this: Where did the Christian Eucharistic Prayer come from? What Jewish prayers, if any, formed the basis of our Eucharistic Prayer? Unfortunately, the only early texts related to the Eucharist are the Synoptic Gospels, the First Letter of Paul to the Corinthians, possibly chapters 9 and 10 in the ancient Christian document known as the *Didache,* written most probably around 100 A.D. (almost all scholars agree that it is definitely before 150 A.D.), and then finally, the Eucharistic Prayer of Hippolytus, usually dated around 216. After the year 200, the texts are more common and more or less have the same structure. But we are at a loss to know exactly what prayers were actually used and what were the prayer forms for the period between 30 and 200 A.D.

Many theories have been proposed for explaining the origins of the Eucharistic Prayer. However, most of the recent writers suggest that the Christian Eucharistic Prayer is historically developed from the Jewish grace after meals—the *birkat ha-mazon*—as it existed around the time of Christ (cf. Audet, Daniélou, pp. 331–38, Kilmartin, Ligier, Ligier in Sheppard, Talley [1] & [2]), rather than descending from the prayers in the Passover Seder ritual, even though the Passover remains the original context of the Last Supper. We might now look at this prayer as it is conjectured to have existed at that time.

    I Blessed are you, LORD, our God,
       king of the universe.
       For you feed us and the whole world
       by your goodness, grace, tenderness and mercy.
       Blessed are you who give food to all.

    II We give you thanks, LORD our God,
       for giving us as our heritage
       a desirable, good and ample land,
       the covenant, and the Torah, life and food.

       [Insertion on Hanukkah and Purim]

       And for all your blessing we give you thanks
       and we bless your name continually and for ever.
       Blessed are you, LORD, for the earth and for food.

    III Have mercy, LORD our God, on Israel your people,
       on Jerusalem, your city, and on your temple,
       on your dwelling-place,
       and on Zion, the abiding-place of your glory,
       and on the great and holy house
       over which your Name has been invoked.
       And in our days, restore to its place
       the royalty of the house of David
       and build Jerusalem soon.

       [Invocation insertion on Sabbath and Feasts]

       Blessed be you, LORD, who build Jerusalem.

       Amen.

                    (cf. Ligier in Sheppard, p. 128)

As we see, this prayer is divided into three sections—the first is a berakah in typical form blessing God for the works of creation, the second is a "berakah which is joined to the immediately preceding berakah" (cf. Kadushin, p. 71) and is introduced by the words "we give you thanks" (literally "we acknowledge you" or "we confess you" since Hebrew has no real word for giving thanks; cf. Ledogar, p. 587). This second section concentrates on thanksgiving for redemptive actions. The final section is a petition. Since the time of Christ, a fourth berakah has been added to the *birkat ha-mazon* and each of the other three berakoth somewhat expanded.

It may also be good at this point to examine the text of the two tri-partite prayers found in the *Didache* (chapters 9 and 10). The first prayer is prescribed to be said before the meal and the second after all have eaten. (Note: indented lines are conjectured by scholars to be congregational responses.)

I We give thanks to you, our Father,
   for the holy vine of David your servant,
   which you made known to us through your servant
      Jesus.
      To you be glory for ever.
We give thanks to you, our Father,
   for the life and knowledge
   which you made known to us through your servant
      Jesus.
      To you be glory for ever.
As this broken bread was scattered over the hills,
and was brought together and made one,
so may your Church be gathered together
from the ends of the earth into your kingdom.
      For yours is the glory and the power,
      through Jesus Christ, for ever and ever.

II We give you thanks, holy Father,
>   for your holy Name which you made to pitch-tent
>>   in our hearts,
>   and for the knowledge, faith, and immortality
>   which you made known to us through your servant
>>   Jesus.
>>>   To you be glory for ever.
>   All-powerful Lord, you created all things for your
>>   Name's sake,
>   and you gave all people food [meat] and drink to
>>   enjoy,
>   so that they might thank you.
>   To us you have given spiritual food and drink
>   and also eternal life
>   through your servant.
>   So, above all, we thank you for your mighty power.
>>>   To you be glory for ever.
>   Remember, Lord, your Church.
>   Deliver her from all evil, perfect her in your love.
>   Make her holy
>   and gather her from the four winds
>   into your kingdom which you have prepared for
>>   her.
>>>   For yours is the power and the glory,
>>>   for ever and ever.

Both of the prayers of the *Didache* are tri-partite in structure and exhibit certain characteristics in common with the *birkat ha-mazon*. Thanksgiving is common to all three prayers. The last section of both *Didache* prayers is a petition for the Church, corresponding to the last section of the *birkat ha-mazon* which is a prayer for the people of God, Israel, and for the deliverance of Jerusalem. There is an inversion of the themes of thanksgiving and praise for creation in the second *Didache* prayer, which otherwise would follow the pattern of the *birkat ha-mazon*. If a person retains the use of the word Church (*ekklēsia*), a word appearing in the Hebrew scriptures as *Qahal,* and omits the references to Jesus, the *Didache* prayers can be seen as perfectly good Jewish meal prayers, based on the pattern of the *birkat ha-mazon* (cf. Talley [1], p. 125).

Scholars have pointed out many other connections between the tri-partite *birkat ha-mazon,* scriptural references, the *Didache* prayers, and the Christian Eucharistic Prayer, and some of these connections will be good for us to examine:

1. The Last Supper accounts in Matthew and Mark state that Jesus *blessed* the bread, but *gave thanks* for the wine. This would correspond to the typical berakah ("blessing") over the bread at the beginning of a meal, but also to the *birkat ha-mazon* at the end, which is sometimes known by the key word used in the second section—"thanks" (cf. Talley [1], p. 124).

2. The triple structure of the *birkat ha-mazon* corresponds to the general thrust of most Eucharistic Prayers—praise for creation, thanksgiving for benefits and the wonders of God recorded in Scripture, supplication for needs (cf. Talley [1] and [2]; more on this subject in the next chapter).

3. The *birkat ha-mazon* provided for insertions, especially in the second and third parts, on the feasts of Hanukkah and Purim, which recalled the institution of the feast. Such a custom and structure could have been easily adapted by early Christians who inserted a commemoration of Christ and his life and death, of the Last Supper and of his command to repeat a meal in his memory.

4. The triple structure of the *birkat ha-mazon* is found duplicated in some ancient Eucharistic Prayer texts, particularly the Anaphora of Addai and Mari—which is divided into three "g'hanata" each of which ends with a doxology. We also have seen the resemblance between it and the prayers in the *Didache* (cf. Talley [1], p. 131).

5. The phrase in the middle section, "and for all your blessings, we give you thanks," occurs in a number of early mid-Eastern Eucharistic Prayers.

6. The third section ends with an Amen, which has been considered an important part of the Eucharistic Prayer since early times. This response is less frequent in Jewish prayers and the Passover ritual than we might be inclined to think at first, so its inclusion in the Eucharistic Prayer may be due to its existence in this section of the *birkat ha-mazon*.

These connections and parallels given here are, of course, very sketchy and brief, but they serve to give some validation to the thesis of the origin of our Christian Eucharist in the Jewish meal prayers. Yet, since we do not possess actual texts from the first century, any hypothesis of any scholar will always remain pure conjecture.

Chapter Three
TRANSITION

The very earliest Eucharists may have been connected to actual meals, in which case the blessing of the bread would have been separated from the blessing of the cup of wine. However, if the problems mentioned by Paul in his First Letter to the Corinthians (1 Cor. 11) were in any way typical, very early it probably seemed wise to separate the fellowship meal from the ritual action which recalled the Last Supper. In this case, the prayers used gradually were combined to include a reference both to the bread and to the wine.

Another early development seems to have been the rise of the motive of thanksgiving from the second section of the *birkat ha-mazon* to overwhelm the first theme of blessing. In fact, even the normal invitation to the *birkat ha-mazon*, "Let us bless [the LORD] [our God]" changed to the Christian invitation to the Eucharistic Prayer, "Let us give thanks to the Lord (our God)" (Sheppard, p. 144).[4]

The four Institution Narratives in Scripture provide a hint at both of these two early developments in Eucharistic practices. The accounts found in Matthew (26:26–28) and Mark (14:22–24) are basically the same. They both suggest seven actions: taking bread, saying a blessing, breaking bread, distributing the broken bread, taking a cup of wine, giving thanks, distributing

21

the cup. Some scholars (though not all) would suggest that these two accounts represent the earliest liturgical tradition, especially when one compares them with Luke's account (22:19–20) and Paul's quotation (1 Cor. 11:23–25). Luke and Paul seem to have somewhat contracted and changed the accounts of Matthew and Mark. First of all, in Luke and Paul there is only one mention of prayer, and it occurs before the breaking of the bread. It is now "give thanks" rather than "said a blessing." The three separate actions concerning the cup mentioned in Matthew and Mark are omitted in Luke and Paul, and only the words of Christ over the cup are mentioned. These differences in the Scripture texts thus correspond to the two above-mentioned early developments in the Christian celebration of the Eucharist: (1) the predominance of "thanksgiving" over "blessing" which eventually gave rise to the title of "Eucharist," and (2) the compacted structure of the Eucharistic Celebration which involved *one* prayer and *one* distribution (rather than repeating the actions over the cup as in Matthew and Mark, texts which possibly represent a very early form of the Christian Eucharist involving two prayers and two distributions possibly separated by a meal). This second development probably accompanied the gradual separation of the Christian Eucharist from regular meals.

These two developments gave rise to a single prayer with two major emphases, praise-thanksgiving and intercession. At various times in history, one or the other seemed to dominate. For example, the Hippolytus Canon (Appendix A) has almost a minimal intercession section, but a long thanksgiving section. The Common Preface with the Roman Canon combination of the Tridentine Missal had a minimal thanksgiving section but many intercessions.

In his examination of the *birkat ha-mazon* and recent writings on berakoth and early Eucharistic Prayers, Dr. Thomas Talley, an Episcopalian priest, posits some very interesting conclusions concerning the development of the importance of thanksgiving in early Eucharistic Prayers. The basic Jewish structure of the *birkat ha-mazon*, as we have seen, is threefold: blessing (for creation), thanksgiving (for redemption), supplication (for present needs) (cf. Talley [1], pp. 129, 136; [2], p. 317). The early Christians saw the overwhelming importance of the thanksgiving for redemption, especially for redemption through Christ. This eventually led to an omission of "blessing," and the rise to prominence of "thanksgiving," eliding both creation and redemption together. This, Talley suggests, is what happened in the *Didache* prayers, where the primary verb is "thanks," even though the prayers retain a threefold division. This is also what occurs in the Eucharistic Prayer in Hippolytus, which basically has two motifs—thanksgiving and supplication (i.e., bi-partite). There is no praise or blessing for creation (and thus, some would suggest, no need for a *Sanctus*, which is best suited as a creation acclamation; cf. below, Chapter 6, section C; Talley [1], pp. 129–30; [2], p. 318). When the original Jewish influence was restored in some early Eucharistic Prayers (such as the prayer of Addai and Mari), instead of returning to a first motif of "blessing," the Christian community used a different verb, "praise," so that the Christian pattern of prayer became "praise, thanksgiving, supplication" (Talley, [1], p. 136). Hence, the principal verbs in Christian meal (Eucharistic) prayers became verbs of praise and thanks, rather than the Jewish verb of blessing. The result of this is that Christian Eucharistic Prayers begin usually with "It is truly right and just to give you thanks and praise . . ." rather than the Jewish form, "Blessed are you, LORD . . ."

The major verbs of praise found in the early Christian Eucharistic Prayers are also found in the psalms and in other places in the Hebrew Scriptures (Ps. 18:3; 2 Sam. 22:4) and also in Christian Scriptures (2 Thess. 1:3) (cf. Ledogar [2]). As will be mentioned below, praise of God was seen by Jews and early Christians alike as a joy to be able to do—God's gift to us for us to return to him (cf. Roman Missal, Weekday Preface IV [Preface 40 in English editions]).

In his research and writings, Talley has tried to clarify some of the ambiguities raised in the late 1950's when Jean-Paul Audet did his (very valuable) work on the influence of the Jewish *berakoth* on the Christian Eucharistic Prayer, for Audet also seemed to suggest the equivalence of many different verbs, three of which were praise, blessing and thanks (cf. below, Chapter 14, section D). According to Talley, basically the Christian Eucharistic Prayer is a "thanksgiving," rather than a "blessing," because of the early Christian innate sense of the priority of the redemptive work of Christ and the thanksgiving which should respond to it.

Talley's writings are interesting as a background to other discussions which occur later in this work. He sees the bi-partite structure (thanksgiving and supplication) still evident in some prayers in the Roman tradition (e.g., the Roman Canon, where the thanksgiving consists of everything before the *Sanctus*, and the supplication includes all the rest, including the Institution Narrative, which structurally becomes subordinate to a sanctification petition, and thus itself part of the supplication section). In the classical Eastern prayers, the tri-partite structure remained, and so the section before the *Sanctus* was devoted to the praise of God as Creator, and the first part of the section after the *Sanctus* was a thanksgiving for the redemptive work performed by Jesus, a thanksgiving which included the Institution Narrative (as part of the works to be remembered). Finally, the memorial of Christ's death and resurrection leads to a petition for sanctification by the Spirit and the intercessory-supplication section. This tri-partite structure also employs a good Trinitarian economic balance in prayer, for the praise of creation deals with the Father, the thanks for redemption remembers the Son, and the supplication for needs begins by invoking the Spirit upon the elements and the people. Talley suggests that the Roman tradition, working with a bi-partite structure, could not easily assimilate this economic manifestation of the Trinity into its structure, and so the prayer tradition of the Roman rite lacked explicit reference to the Spirit for many centuries ([2] p. 344).

Another point for discussion recently is the origin of the Institution Narrative, or narrative of the Last Supper and the institution of the Eucharist. As was mentioned above, the *birkat ha-mazon* allows for the inclusion of an institution narrative on the feasts of Purim and Hanukkah. It also allows for an inclusion of an invocation in the third section, and, historically, the Institution Narrative has been found in many different places in the Eucharistic Prayer.

Some authors suggest that the Institution Narrative occurred originally in a Eucharistic Celebration not in the Eucharistic Prayer, but rather as "words of distribution" after a Eucharistic Prayer had been prayed (cf. Kilmartin, p. 274). Then, as Christian prayers very early began to include more and more references to the redemptive works of Christ, especially the event of his death and resurrection, the Institution Narrative *became absorbed into* the Eucharistic Prayer from its original position following it, as a justifying reason for remembering Christ and performing the sacred meal rites with bread and wine (cf. Talley [1], p. 130). This had a beneficial effect of uniting past, present and future together around a core literary section of the Eucharistic Prayer. As Talley writes (basing his thoughts on Ligier):

> This [inclusion of the Institution Narrative in the Eucharistic Prayer] had the effect of bringing a present focus to the past orientation of the thanksgiving which extended to the supplication as well, directing its future orientation toward present action in the development of the epiclesis. ([1], p. 130)

This thesis suggests that the Institution Narrative *always* occurred in the course of the Eucharistic Celebration, but originally
it functioned differently—accompanying the distribution of the
elements of bread and wine, after they had been consecrated by a
more Jewish style Eucharistic Prayer (lacking an Institution Narrative), such as the prayers shown above from the *Didache* (cf.
Keifer [4], p. 16). It is also conceivable that after the Institution
Narrative found a place within Eucharistic Prayers, older, more
Jewish forms of such Christian Eucharistic meal prayers, still
lacking an Institution Narrative, were seen as and were instinc-
tively felt to be less suitable for the Christian Eucharist.

Some other authors would go even further and suggest that
very early Eucharists did not have the Institution Narrative anywhere in the course of the celebration. They suggest that the
eventual inclusion of the Institution Narrative in early Eucharistic Prayers may have been necessitated by the removal of the
celebrating community from the very early Christians' experience
of eating a meal in memory of Christ. As the gatherings of
Christians became further and further removed, both historically
and culturally, from the experience of the early disciples sharing
a meal in the presence of the risen Christ and from the Jewish
milieu in which the original Christians lived, some constant vocal
reminder was needed at the center of their worship service to
recall to their memories the reason why they gathered to partake
of a loaf of bread and a cup of wine—hence, the Institution
Narrative (cf. Guzie, 115).

However, this second thesis, although accepted by some
scholars, still has difficulty dealing with the liturgical nature of
the four scriptural Institution Narratives unless the conjectured
very early Eucharists without any Institution Narrative existed
for only about twenty years or so after Christ's death. As an
example, 1 Corinthians was written about 56 or 57 A.D., and if
Paul had "received" the Institution Narrative he passed on—a

very "liturgically" sounding narrative already bearing marks of simplification from the narratives which appear in Matthew and Mark—then we are speaking of only the period between around 30 A.D. and 45 or 50 A.D. where some Eucharists (possibly) did not have any Institution Narrative at all.

As we saw in the previous chapter, the *Didache* does give prayers which some scholars suggest are early forms of the Eucharistic Prayer, closer in format to the *birkat ha-mazon* (cf. Kilmartin, pp. 276–77), even though they lack Institution Narratives with a repetition of the Lord's words. However, other scholars would disagree with this evaluation of the *Didache* and suggest that the prayers found there were used at so-called "agape-meals," that is, fellowship meals which were *not* "Eucharists" in our contemporary understanding of the term "Eucharist." These scholars base their distinctions on the distinction seemingly found in the writings of Ignatius of Antioch (cf. IgSmyrnaeans 8) and in the *Apostolic Tradition* of Hippolytus (Chapters 25–26 in Botte's numbering). Still other scholars argue that the modern distinction between the Eucharist and agape-meal is actually a misreading of ancient texts such as Ignatius, and that such a distinction would not have been made in the first two centuries. Therefore, any meal celebrated during that time in Christ's memory, which included bread, wine, and a prayer of thanksgiving recited by an acknowledged leader of the community, would be a Eucharist in our modern sense of the term (cf. Kilmartin, Dix, Empereur, Keifer [4], p. 16). There is a larger discussion of the use and omission of the Institution Narrative in the Eucharistic Prayer in a later section (Chapter 11, section C).

There are many other points and details which could be mentioned regarding Jewish practices and the Christian Eucharistic Prayer. There is the obvious relationship to the Passover meal—the Seder service. There is the influence from the Synagogue service prayers, especially seen in the eventual inclusion of the *Sanctus* into the Eucharistic Prayer along with other words and phrases (cf. Bouyer). There is also the importance of the Eucharistic Prayer and the Eucharist itself in Christianity, an importance which is paralleled by the *Shema* in Judaism, that is, the quote from Deuteronomy (Dt. 6:4), "Hear, O Israel, the Lord is our God, the Lord alone." Thus, in looking at our Christian Eucharistic Prayer in relationship to our Jewish ancestors, we might make three concluding statements of comparison:

1. The Eucharistic Prayer is (probably) *derived* in form and structure from the normal Jewish grace after meals, the *birkat ha-mazon.*

2. The Eucharistic Prayer, and the Eucharist in general, is probably *influenced* by other Jewish prayers and feasts, especially the rites of Passover, for some of its contents, context, and expressions (cf. Bouyer, especially regarding the *Tefillah,* the Eighteen Benedictions).

3. The Eucharistic Prayer may play the same *role* in Christian services as the recitation of the *Shema,* which in contemporary Jewish services is a climactic moment and is often recited by Jews aside from their liturgical services.

By the beginning of the third century, the Eucharistic Prayer became a prayer-form in its own right. From that time, almost all texts we possess betray the same basic structure, content and form, starting with the Eucharistic Prayer of Hippolytus to the recent compositions found in the revised liturgical books. That structure and content will be the subject of Section Four.

Having examined the Jewish and early Christian meal prayers, and before concluding this chapter, it may be good to briefly speak about the psychology of the berakah in order to better understand the spirit behind the Eucharistic Prayer.

One may be misled by literal translations of Hebrew berakoth. The usual beginning is: "Blessed are you, LORD our God, king of the universe, who sanctified us by your commandments and has commanded us to . . ." (Barukh atta, YHWH, Elohenu,

malekh ha-alom, asher kadshonu b'mitzvosov, v'tzivonu al . . .).
The initial word *Barukh* is variously translated as "blessed," or
"praised," and the divine name YHWH is never pronounced,
Adonai (Lord) or *Hashem* (The Name) being used instead. But
the Rabbinic midrash on the berakah would suggest that what is
actually being intended is more like this in English:

> You, Lord of Creation, are acknowledged as our God of
> justice and mercy, the arbiter of all existence, who set us
> aside in a special relation to you by reason of the *mitz-
> vot* (covenant of Sinai) and set for us a divine impera-
> tive to . . .

The *"mitzvot"* or commandments were seen as a privilege given
to the Jews by their God, a privilege not given to any other
people. It was a joy to be able to fulfill such a commandment, and
the berakah uttered while fulfilling a command and thus interpreting a human action was a sincere act of worship (cf. Kadushin, pp. 64–69).

I would suggest that a similar psychology was operative
among early Christians, especially Jewish converts. It was a privilege for them to fulfill the command of Christ, "Do this in
memory of me." It was worship. It was a joy. This psychology, or,
we might say, spirituality, which was the background for their
communal action fulfilling Christ's command, was the primary
thing operative in this ritual. Words, though important, were
almost secondary. These early Christians were filled with the
Spirit of the risen Lord and the Spirit gave them words to speak.
Their role was to be receptive to the Spirit and faithful to God's
command.

This stance, this posture before the Lord, for these early
Christians, was highly influenced by their Jewish religious heritage. As a result, great reverence, awe, and wonder filled their

hearts as they pronounced the words of their prayers. They approached, in prayer, the God who had approached them first in Christ. And through their Eucharistic Prayer, God again was approaching them as food and drink—nourishment in their journey toward him.

Section Three

INTERCONNECTIONS: EUCHARIST, CHURCH, THEOLOGY

Chapter Four
THE EUCHARISTIC LITURGY, THE EPISCOPACY AND ECCLESIOLOGY

The Eucharist has been called the "sign of unity and bond of charity" (Augustine, *In Joannis* 26:13) for Christians, and so any discussion of the Eucharist would really be incomplete without at least a brief mention of the two other major focal points of Christian unity, that is, the office of bishop, and the Church itself. On the other hand, any discussion of Church, or bishop, or the Eucharist, especially when such a discussion (inevitably) touches on the practice of the Christian community in the early centuries, is going to be filled with debated issues, uncertain practices, unclear history, divergent customs and structures, and a modern day simplification of some very complex topics. Let it be said here that the topic of this chapter could easily be turned into a major work by itself, and thus any attempt to simplify the actual situations will of necessity lead to omissions. Yet, it was felt that there should be at least some mention of the interconnection between the episcopacy, ecclesiology and the Eucharist, so that our discussion of the Eucharist and the Eucharistic Prayer is not isolated and seen outside of its proper context.

Since Christians are a continuation of the Israelites of old, it is important for Christians to remember that God did not deal with the Israelites as individuals, or even as a group of individuals, but as a people—a people who had definite bounds, who had laws, who had customs. On occasion, one meets Christians who act as if Christianity could exist separated from some external unifying element or visible structure, i.e., a Church. I, for one, do not think that this is possible, especially since, among other reasons, the human creature has rarely been able to form "non-structured" groups throughout history. Moreover, such a thesis and practice has been denied from the earliest times of Christianity.

The ancient structure of the Church has been one based on the existence in the Church of a ministry of service—that is, the existence in the Church of a group of individuals who were both leaders and servants, a group which relatively early developed in some parts of Asia Minor into the three-tiered structure of deacons, presbyters (priests) and bishops (cf. Brown, *Priest and Bishop*). A further refinement of this structure of Church ministry viewed the bishop, that is, that Church leader entrusted with the ministry of "over-sight" (i.e., the *episkopos*, from *epi* = over, and *skopos* = one who sees), as a central focal point for the organization and life of the local "incarnation" of the one Church of Christ.

The early history, evolution and development of the grades of ministers in the Church is a subject that contemporary authors are helping to clarify. As Father Raymond Brown and other scholars point out, it seems that during the first two centuries of the Christian era, there were two major competing ministerial structures (among others), one of Jewish origin—the council of elders (or presbyters), and the other of Greek origin—the overseer and his assistants (or bishop and deacons). Different communities employed different structures, some communities augmented the basic leadership group with other ministers (e.g.

confessors, teachers, prophets, preachers, etc.), different communities may have assigned different ministers the same function, and various communities employed different methods to induct new individuals into the ranks of the ministers. For example, the Christian Scriptures speak primarily (or exclusively) about bishops and deacons in some places (Acts, Phil, 1 Tim) and primarily (or exclusively) about presbyters in other places (Tit, Jas). The *Didache* speaks about other types of ministry and seems to indicate that presiding at the Eucharist was *not* an exclusive right of bishops or presbyters (cf. prophets in 10:7). The *Apostolic Tradition* of Hippolytus speaks about ordination rites for bishops, presbyters and deacons, but then seems to indicate that if a "confessor" has suffered for the faith, he is *not* ordained to the presbyterate, but merely takes his place with those already ordained. Even St. Ignatius of Antioch (who died around 107 A.D.), the great advocate of the schema of ministry presently used by most "hierarchical" Churches (i.e. the three-fold division of bishop, presbyter, and deacon), is not consistent in all his letters in the use of these terms, thereby suggesting to some scholars that even though Ignatius found great comfort in the structure of ministry as employed in Antioch, insisted on the authority of the bishop where there was one, and advocated the adoption of this structure elsewhere (with the same importance and authority he gave to the various ranks), nevertheless, not all the communities he wrote to employed this same structure. (It is noteworthy to many that in the letter of Ignatius to the Romans, *nothing* is mentioned about Church leaders and their authority, a topic which is very forcefully presented in the other writings of Ignatius!) Two points are important to remember from an analysis of the data from this time in the history of the Church. First, the Church ministry derived from the ministry of the Apostles *was continued* in the various communities (although possibly differently in different places and possibly given varying importance). Second, the different structures over many years *eventually developed*, merged, and unified into the three-tiered structure of bishop, presbyter and deacon mentioned above.

Once the Church's ministerial structure became more or less standardized, and once specific functions were assigned to the different ranks, we see a development in the role assigned to the bishop (such developments could even have been significantly influenced by strong bishops such as Ignatius of Antioch). In the local Church's life in this early stage of Church history, the bishop became the key minister of all liturgical rites. He was the one who presided over Christian initiation and "sealed" the catechumens with the oil of chrism. He was the one who presided over the Eucharist. He was the one who reconciled penitents. He was the one who was seen as the visible representative of the Lord for the local community of Christians. The priests (presbyters) were his assistants in this ministry and performed these major rites of Christianity when he could not be present. The presbyters together formed the college of priests or "presbyterium" of the local Church—united to each other and to their bishop. The deacons were assistants to the bishops and, in their absence, to the priests, but it was the bishop who, in some sense, embodied the local Church in himself. (A further discussion of the use of and distinction between the words "priest" and "presbyter" occurs below in Chapter 16, section A. Also cf. *Apostolic Tradition* of Hippolytus, sections II, VII.)

Because of this, the Eucharist also came to be seen as a special sign of unity, uniting all Christians together, under the united pastoral responsibility of one bishop (cf. Ignatius of Antioch, "There is really one only flesh of our Lord, one only cup to unite us in his blood, one only altar, as there is one only bishop" [IgPhil. 4]). The bishops of various cities kept communion among themselves, and this "college" of bishops in communion with each other is what united the Church as a whole in the early centuries. Very early, the Church, the Eucharist, and the bishop almost became interchangeable when speaking and thinking about Church unity. Even today, "excommunication" implies both being severed from the unity of the Church and being denied access to the Eucharist.

The view of the unity of the Church being bound up with communion with a local bishop is not an outmoded model of the Church either. It is this ecclesiology that is really the basis behind many practices in the Roman Catholic Church today, for one example. This type of Eucharistic-episcopal ecclesiology is the basis of many inter-denominational discussions on ministry, the Church, orders, and the Eucharist (cf. Documents of Chambesy, 1977 meeting). In one sense, this view of communion is what "keeps the Roman Catholic Church in existence" when a Pope dies—that is, the communion of individuals with a local bishop who is in communion with other bishops. To explain further, let me use an example previously used by Nicholas Lash (p. 186, note 34): I am a Roman Catholic. My "Roman Catholic-ness" is expressed by my communion with a local bishop, who, in turn, is in communion with the Bishop of Rome (and with other bishops in communion with the Bishop of Rome). At the basis of my being a Roman Catholic, however, is my communion with the local bishop, rather than my immediate communion with the Bishop of Rome. This communion with a local bishop is at one and the same time a sign, a test, and a manifestation of my membership in the Roman Catholic Church. I express this communion primarily by a unity of faith and love, based on a common experience of being joined to Christ and of the paschal mystery of his death and rising. On a practical and external level, this communion is also expressed by my compliance with the directives of the local bishop (and also the directives of the Holy See, but only when they have been promulgated by the local bishop). A similar type of unity exists in other Churches which retain an episcopal structure, such as the Orthodox, Anglican, and Methodist Churches.

The rule of the bishop (exercising the office of the apostles) over a local Church in imitation of a shepherd caring for his flock has been a prominent characterization of the Church from apostolic times (cf. Letters of St. Ignatius of Antioch). In continuity with this model of Church government, an individual presbyter exercises his ministry only in communion with, and with the authority of, the local bishop. By himself, the individual presbyter is only an assistant to the bishop, yet one who is authorized to perform certain functions in helping the bishop carry out his ministry of service and over-sight for the community.[5]

A prominent strain of very early ecclesiology seems to view the Christian community as a group of people united to their local leader—the bishop—who in some sense was a representative to the community of Christ himself and who himself was united to the bishops of other communities. This view seems to have grown rapidly and won favor eventually through most of the Christian world. Ignatius of Antioch, around the year 100, wrote to the Smyrnaeans: "Only that Eucharist is valid (*bebaia*—proper, firm, legal), which is offered by the bishop or by one designated by him" (IgSmyr. 8; cf. IgMagn. 3, 7, 13; IgPhil. 3; IgTrall. 2; IgEph. 1, 5–6).[6]

The tension between varying approaches to the Eucharist, the Church and the episcopacy inevitably causes tensions in many areas. Sometimes these areas are obvious, and sometimes they are evident only upon reflection. One area of tension which is sometimes overlooked is in the matter of receiving the Eucharistic elements and what is termed "Intercommunion" or reception of the Eucharist by members of different Christian communions.

If we approach the Eucharist primarily as a sign of unity already achieved, then only those who are in ecclesial unity with the local bishop with whom the priest/presider has communion should be permitted to receive Communion. This (more ancient) view is the prevalent view operative in Roman Catholic legislation permitting only Catholics to receive Communion at a Catholic Eucharist (with minor exceptions).[7]

Another viewpoint is that which sees the Eucharist in its "sacramental" or ontological dimension, as the reality of the Body and Blood of Christ. This viewpoint prompts some Christians to ask why we should prohibit anyone from receiving Communion who professes belief in this sacramental presence of Christ. This position represents the dynamic present in Roman Catholic law which permits Catholics (in special situations) to receive Communion from Orthodox priests, and non-Catholics who hold the Catholic Eucharistic belief to receive Communion in Catholic churches (in special situations). This is also the dynamic present in the writings of contemporary theologians who suggest that divorced and remarried Catholics should be allowed to frequent the Eucharist. They argue that no one should be denied the food of life (even though remarried individuals have not followed Church law and tradition, with regard to their marital status, and, in that way, have severed their communion with the local bishop) (cf. Seasoltz, pp. 110–111).

We should remember, however, that the two views just presented represent two extremes on a spectrum, and theologians and ordinary Christians hold many other views, which usually fall somewhere in between these two. Both of these viewpoints have merits, both represent truths, but both views also do not *quite* blend with the other, and thus they lead to opposing practices. I am not attempting to resolve any of these difficulties at this time, however. The Eucharist is too large a topic to be discussed only in terms of black and white issues and practices. It only seems natural that varying approaches to the Eucharist will have varying consequences with respect to ecclesiology, since the two are so intertwined in meaning. It would seem that the varying practices should be considered in terms of what is desirable at the moment for greater emphasis.

I have tried to make a few important connections in this

chapter, connections usually overlooked when discussing the Eucharist, ministry and episcopacy, or ecclesiology separately. Time and time again throughout history, religious writings point out that the community called the *"Church"* most perfectly expresses who it is and most fully realizes its true nature when it celebrates the *Eucharist,* especially when it is presided over by the local *bishop.* In celebrating the central sacrament of ecclesial life—the *Eucharist*—we must express and remember that the local *Church* is related not only credally and ritually with other Churches, but also *personally* through the local presider (priest or bishop) who himself is a member of a college of presbyters or *bishops.* This *personal* aspect is what is most important and most basic in all our relations with Christ the Lord, but it is also what is frequently most overlooked in speaking about the meaning of the hierarchical structure of the Church and our relationship to it. Yet, the hierarchy makes most sense only when seen as the *personal* thread joining the fabric of the Christian Church together into one seamless robe of Christ. This *personal* aspect may become even clearer if one recalls any experience of a European-style "extended family" structure. Many Americans become overwhelmed when welcomed into a family based on the old-world idea of a "family." Two total strangers can be considered as close as brothers and sisters just because they know individuals who, in turn, know individuals who are brothers or sisters, or cousins in such an extended family. Such it is, or should be, with the Church and the episcopacy.

The three aspects in Christian life of Church, the Episcopacy, and the Eucharist have been so interwoven throughout history and in theology that any discussion of one without the other, it seems to me, really leads to an incomplete view of the Church and the totality of Christ's continued incarnation in the world today. We must keep this fact in mind as we further examine the Eucharistic Prayer of our sacrament of unity.

Chapter Five

THE MEANING OF THE EUCHARISTIC PRAYER IN THE HISTORY OF SACRAMENTAL AND EUCHARISTIC THEOLOGY

Scholars and theologians tell us that the Eucharistic Prayer is the central prayer of the Eucharistic Liturgy (cf. *IGMR*, section 54). But why? Is there any theological or historical reason for this? Before examining the prayer in depth, let us take a moment and consider the position that the Eucharistic Prayer has played in the history of the Liturgy of the Eucharist, and also the classical Western theological evaluation of this role.

The Eucharistic Prayer, as mentioned before, corresponds to the prayer of blessing pronounced by Christ at the Last Supper. At the least, then, we should say that after the Eucharistic Prayer has been prayed, the bread and wine are to be considered "blessed." The relationship of these blessed elements to the faith-community and to Christ himself has been explained in many different ways through the ages, probably the most well-known of which is by use of the term "transubstantiation," as used by the

Roman Catholic Church in the Council of Trent (in the sixteenth century). However, what any explanation of the new relationship and reality is trying to articulate is this: the elements, after the Eucharistic Prayer has been prayed, are now considered to have a different meaning and a new reality for the faith-community present. Something more will be mentioned below concerning the relationship between "transubstantiation" and the text of the Eucharistic Prayer.

In classical Western theological terms, at least from Thomas Aquinas, the Eucharistic Prayer is considered the "form" of the Sacrament of the Eucharist, and the bread and wine are considered the "matter." The terms "matter" and "form" find their origin in Aristotelean metaphysics where the same terms are used to subdivide physical realities in order to account for both continuity (or similarities) and change (or differences). Sometimes the determination of the sacramental form of the Eucharist has been further narrowed down, due to "minimalistic" theological tendencies, limiting the "form" to only the words of Christ, "This is my Body . . . this is my Blood," which occur within the Eucharistic Prayer. Such was the case in the Decree for the Armenians of the Council of Florence (in the fifteenth century) which defined the matter and form (as then understood) for all the sacraments.

In general, then, when speaking about the "form" or verbal formula of a sacrament, we are speaking about those words which contextualize the objects present, or the action taking place, which itself is considered the "matter" or material, visible aspect of the sacrament or sacramental action. So, for example, in the Sacrament of Baptism, the action of immersing a catechumen in water is contextualized by the words, "I baptize you in the name of the Father . . ." (or, for the East, "The servant of God is baptized in the name of the Father . . ."). In the celebration of Ordination, the imposition of hands is accompanied (or followed) by a prayer of consecration—both, however, constitute the sacramental experience. The audible, verbal aspects are linked to the visible, material action and the union of the two comprise the sacramental experience. As Augustine said, "Accedit verbum ad elementum et fit sacramentum" (The word is joined to the element and a sacrament is constituted) (*Super Joann.* LXXX on 15:3, PL 35:1840).

In Baptism, Confirmation, and the Anointing of the Sick, the "form" is associated with an action performed on an individual, and not with the object administered to the individual. However, in the Eucharist, the important formulae have, historically, been attached to the Eucharistic Prayer over the elements of bread and wine. The formula of administering the consecrated elements seems to have been considered secondary and minor.

Thus it is that the Eucharistic Prayer is the main "contextualizing" formulation for the Sacrament of the Eucharist. And, as in other sacraments, this formula is what makes the Sacrament become what it is to be. To do this *properly*, it should be worded *unambiguously*. To explain this a bit further, let me briefly anticipate a later discussion on the "moment of consecration."[8]

The "moment of consecration" is that point of the Eucharistic Prayer at which the elements of bread and wine can be considered "changed." This point is determined usually by the words spoken at the chosen point of the prayer, and in the history of Christian Liturgy, two traditions have been prominent. In both traditions, however, explicit reference is made by the wording of the prayer to the bread and wine present and to the relationship they are said to have to the Christian community present at the Eucharist (cf. McKenna [2], pp. 48–189).

The Western tradition, following St. John Chrysostom, has held that the main emphasis should be put on the words of Christ contained in the Eucharistic Prayer, "This is my Body . . . this is my Blood." This is what is found in Chrysostom's speech:

> The priest acts as the representative of Christ when he
> pronounces those words, but the power and grace are

God's. "This is my Body," he says. These words transform the offerings before him. (*In proditione Judae.*
Hom. 1:6, PG 49:380)

However, the Eastern tradition, following St. Cyril of Jerusalem,
says that the *epiclesis* is the primary moment in the Eucharist,
i.e., the invocation of the Holy Spirit to change the bread and
wine into Christ's Body and Blood. This we see in the following
excerpts from his "Mystagogic Catechesis":

> . . . the bread and wine of the Eucharist before the holy
> invocation of the adorable Trinity was simple bread and
> wine, while after the invocation the Bread becomes the
> Body of Christ, and the Wine the Blood of Christ (I, 7)
> . . . the Bread of the Eucharist, after the invocation of
> the Holy Spirit, is mere bread no longer, but the Body of
> Christ (III, 3) . . . we call upon the merciful God to send
> forth His Holy Spirit upon the gifts lying before Him,
> that He may make the Bread the Body of Christ, and the
> Wine the Blood of Christ, for whatsoever the Holy Spirit
> has touched is sanctified and changed (V, 7).

In both traditions, the words used, i.e., the formula, unambiguously relate the action and material elements to the faith of
the community gathered. Both traditions, when concretized in
Eucharistic Prayers, express (unambiguously) the community's
belief that the ritual meal taking place is important because the
community considers that the bread and wine have some relationship to Christ's Body and Blood. Note, however, that the two
traditions clash as to the "moment of consecration," but they do
coincide as to the purpose of praying the Eucharistic Prayer over
bread and wine.

As was mentioned at the beginning of this chapter, the
Eucharistic Prayer results in the "blessing" of the bread and wine,
so that they can be considered by the assembled faith-community

(in some way) as the Body and Blood of Christ. This transformation has been traditionally called, in Roman Catholic theology, "transubstantiation." In 1965, Pope Paul VI issued an encyclical letter entitled *Mysterium Fidei* in which he discussed the mystery of the Eucharist and the various methods of explaining this mystery which seemed to be current during that period. As could be expected, he reaffirmed the traditional Roman Catholic position and readvocated the use of the term "transubstantiation" to describe what "happens" in the Eucharist to the elements of bread and wine. I do not wish to discuss, in any detail, transubstantiation or any other theory of Eucharistic transformation. My purpose in raising the topic is only to point out how such theological questions can affect discussions concerning Eucharistic Prayers.

We should all be aware of the way that beliefs influence the reading or writing of any texts, and particularly Eucharistic Prayers. It has been a standard principle of hermeneutics to take documents at face value—they mean what they say (cf. Keifer [2]). However, one might be inclined to wonder, "What do they really say?" Frequently, contemporary individuals approach ancient works with unknown and hidden biases which they do not realize they possess until these biases are pointed out to them. As a result of the biases, there is a tendency to read certain contemporary positions into ancient writings which never originally possessed such positions. In fact, the original positions of the ancient writings may have even been in opposition to a given modern position thought to be contained therein.

To be more concrete, let me give this example. If a person takes almost any ancient Eucharistic Prayer, or even some of the modern compositions of the more traditional Churches, he can read the prayers as being perfectly consistent with the Roman Catholic doctrine of transubstantiation, even though transubstantiation probably was not in the minds of the ancients, and is almost definitely not in the mind of many modern non-Catholics.

In addition, one's Eucharistic theology can influence the wording of one's Eucharistic Prayer. As we saw above, the 1975 Vatican Letter on Eucharistic Prayers emphasized that a Consecratory Epiclesis should precede the Institution Narrative, and that after the Narrative, the prayer should express the belief in the real presence of Christ in the elements of bread and wine. The Consecratory Epiclesis before the Institution Narrative plays an interesting psychological role in Roman rite Eucharistic Prayers. It invokes the Holy Spirit in anticipation, and is usually so worded as to imply that the "change" takes place after the invocation, that is, at the Institution Narrative or Consecratory Words of Christ. The stress on expressing the belief in the real presence of Christ after the Institution Narrative caps off and encloses the Institution Narrative, pointing to it as *"the"* moment of the Eucharistic Prayer. This is a very obvious example of one's theology influencing the expressions one uses in a Eucharistic Prayer (cf. Keifer [5], p. 15).

The writings of the great Fathers of the Church in the first few centuries all express the belief that a change does take place in the elements of bread and wine (cf. Cyril of Jerusalem quoted above). But most of them are equally insistent that a corresponding change should take place in the Christian as well. "You are what you receive." How theologians explain any "change" in the Eucharistic elements is really secondary to the Christian belief that, by our partaking of the bread and wine, we are brought into contact with the risen Lord and are fulfilling the command of Christ expressed in the sixth chapter of St. John's Gospel: "Unless you eat my Flesh and drink my Blood you shall not have life within you."

Therefore, in conclusion and summary, let us review the main points of this chapter. The Eucharistic Prayer is the central verbal formulation of the Sacrament of the Eucharist. Its purpose is to be the prayer of blessing corresponding to the prayers of blessing used by Jesus at the Last Supper. As that prayer of blessing, its composition can be and is influenced by different theological positions, for example, positions regarding the "moment of consecration," or the mode of the presence of Christ in the elements of bread and wine. Yet, in any case, the Eucharistic Prayer should perform its function as the main contextualizing formulation, or sacramental "form," of the Sacrament of the Eucharist as well as possible. Problems arise when the sacramental form does not express what it *should* express, in clear enough terms.

With this background concerning the purpose of the Eucharistic Prayer, and having discussed the historical literary genre of the Eucharistic Prayer as *prayer* descended from the Jewish berakah form, let us now examine the Eucharistic Prayer as to its components and see better what should and what should not be present in it.

Section Four

THE EUCHARISTIC PRAYER: AN ANALYSIS OF COMPONENT PARTS

Chapter Six
INTRODUCTION AND PATRICENTRIC PROCLAMATION

a. Addressee of Eucharistic Prayers

Eucharistic Prayers are traditionally addressed to God the Father. They are viewed as prayers of the Body of Christ present in the world today, addressed to the Father, prompted by the Spirit. In an extraordinarily early reference to a Eucharistic celebration, Justin Martyr, writing about the year 150 A.D., says this:

> Then bread and a cup of water and of mixed wine are brought to him who presides over the brethren, and he takes them and offers praise and glory *to the Father of all in the name of the Son and of the Holy Spirit,* and gives thanks at some length that we have been deemed worthy of these things from him. (1 *Apol.* 65:3; italics added).

All throughout Christian history, it has been repeatedly maintained that Christians pray through Christ to the Father (cf. Rom. 1:8; 2 Cor. 1:5; 3:4; Heb. 13:15; 1 Pet. 2:5). The Council of Hippo in 393 forbade the direct addressing of Christ in prayer. Even though in private prayer it may be legitimate to pray to Christ or

the Holy Spirit, nevertheless, in public worship, the basics of our
faith as expressed throughout history and recorded in the Hebrew
and Christian Scriptures should be preserved. These basics proclaim that it is the Father who hears all prayers and grants our
requests (cf. Podhradsky, p. 194).

On occasion, one may find an official Eucharistic Prayer with
certain parts addressed to Christ, or even to the Spirit. Such
occurs with some of the prayers in the Maronite Rite of the
Catholic Church, where the anamnesis-offertory is often addressed to Christ. This may have crept into the presider's prayer
due to analogy with the responses of the people which are usually
directed to Christ. Some contemporary prayers have even been
written with the first section addressed to the Father, the middle
addressed to the Son, and the final section addressed to the Spirit
(cf. Hoey, Eucharistic Prayer number 625). In all such cases,
these practices seem to be inconsistent with the traditional format of Christian prayer, that is, the Christian community prays to
the Father, through the Son, with and in the Spirit.[9]

b. **Introductory Dialogue and Stylized Beginning**

Eucharistic Prayers have traditionally begun with at least a
threefold set of greetings and responses. In the Western tradition
these greetings and responses have been: "The Lord be with you."
R. "And with your spirit" (or in the commonly used ICET
translation, "And also with you"). "Lift up your hearts." R. "We
lift them up to the Lord." "Let us give thanks to the Lord our
God." R. "It is right and just" (or, in ICET translation, "It is right
to give him thanks and praise"). In the Byzantine tradition, the
first greeting is changed to the Pauline-Trinitarian greeting, "The
grace of our Lord Jesus Christ, the love of God the Father, and the
communion of the Holy Spirit be with you all" (2 Cor. 13:13).
This Pauline greeting is also an alternative given in the Episcopal
Book of Common Prayer. In addition, some of the Eastern traditions add other greetings or admonitions (sometimes spoken by

the deacon or others, as in the Byzantine rite) before the normal preface dialogue begins. The dialogue itself is very ancient. It first appears in the text of the Eucharistic Prayer of Hippolytus (cf. Appendix A). As was mentioned in Chapter 3, the greeting, "Let us give thanks to the Lord our God," seems to be a very slight modification of the normal Jewish invitation to grace after meals, probably influenced by the predominance of "thanks" over "blessing" in Christian prayers.[10]

The beginning of the body of the Eucharistic Prayer has traditionally tried to capitalize on the last response of the people and tried to reinforce it. This is probably clearer in the original liturgical language (e.g., Greek, Latin, etc.) and some modern European languages than in English. For example, in Latin the last response of the people is: "Dignum et justum est," and the body of the Eucharistic Prayer (i.e., the preface) begins, "Vere dignum et justum est, aequum et salutare . . ." In German, the last response is: "Das ist würdig und recht," and the preface begins, "In Wahrheit ist es würdig und recht . . ." In Polish, the last response is: "Godne to i sprawiedliwe," and the body of the Eucharistic Prayer begins, "Zaprawdę godne to i sprawiedliwe . . ." Due to the English language, the impact of the initial "vere" (truly!) is very weak in most translations and thus is practically overlooked, compared with the impact it has in other languages. So, in English, the beginning of the Eucharistic Prayer has usually been similar to the following: "It is truly right to give you thanks and praise, all-powerful Father . . ." "Father, all-powerful and ever-living God, we do well to give you thanks . . ." "Father, we thank you and we praise you . . ."[11]

c. The Proclamation: Motive for Thanks and Praise

The stylized introduction logically leads to the question, "Why give God the Father thanks and praise?" The next section of the Eucharistic Prayer—the proclamation—attempts to answer that question. In this section the presider praises and gives thanks to God the Father for his many wonders (*magnalia Dei*) and his many blessings given to people throughout recorded history.

This section is probably the most changeable one of Eucharistic Prayers, for it is in this section that a given theme can be expanded and reinforced again and again. In the revised Roman Missal, the eighty-four prefaces differ precisely in this motive section in an attempt to connect the Eucharistic Prayer to the feast or season of celebration. However, in the official Roman rite, the motive section is very short, limited only to a small section of the "Preface" of the Eucharistic Prayer, that is, that section which comes before the *Sanctus* or Holy, Holy. On the other hand, in many Eastern Churches and in most contemporary prayers, the motive section extends through all of the preface and up to the Institution Narrative, in some instances omitting the *Sanctus* or Holy, Holy.

This proclamation may be unified and totally concerned with the deeds of God the Father. In some instances, however, the section before the *Sanctus* emphasizes the wonders of God mentioned in the Hebrew Scriptures and the section after the *Sanctus* is concerned with the wonders worked by Jesus (cf. Episcopal prayers 1 and 2 in Appendix A). However, since many authors see the Eucharistic Prayer as the prayer of the risen Christ alive in the world today, they advocate very little reference to the works of the Lord Jesus in the proclamation section, since it would seem self-centered or introspective (even egotistical) for Jesus to proclaim all the works *he* had done for the world.[12]

Some authors suggest that the *Sanctus* best fits as an acclamation to a "creation" section of a Eucharistic Prayer (cf. Talley [1], pp. 130, 136). Otherwise, the *Sanctus* seems almost forced into a prayer without having any real context. These authors suggest that the omission in some early Eucharistic Prayers of the *Sanctus* is due to the fact that these same Eucharistic Prayers had no real creation motif present. In an ideal Eucharistic Prayer containing a *Sanctus,* the *post-Sanctus* would deal with redemption events, and future Eucharistic Prayers could even be arranged so that after an invariable creation "preface," the major variation, describing some "salvation" event, would occur after the *Sanctus* and before the Institution Narrative (cf. Talley [2], pp. 319–20; cf. also Roman Eucharistic Prayer for Children III for an example of a variable *post-Sanctus* section).

We should also keep in mind the relative importance of what may be included in this proclamation section. Professor Emil Lengeling has stated that praise and thanksgiving for the mystery of salvation is indispensable in a Eucharistic Prayer. However, he places praise and thanksgiving for creation in his last (or optional) category (cf. below, Chapter 11, section A). (We should, however, remember that praise for creation and thanksgiving for salvation events comprised equal sections of the *birkat ha-mazon*!) On occasion, some contemporary Eucharistic Prayers overly dwell on the objects of creation—mountains, seas, birds, trees, etc.—without any reference to the saving events brought about by God the Father. From the mention of the objects of creation, such prayers immediately lead to the mention of the Lord Jesus, often giving the impression that Christ is no more significant than any other object of creation.[13] Our sacred writings mention the presence of God in our world in many different ways— created material objects, prophets and other holy women and men, salvific events, the person of Jesus Christ. Eucharistic Prayers should reflect the relative importance of these different manifestations of God as they proclaim the divine wonders in the midst of the assembled Christian community.

d. Sanctus: Holy, Holy

In the Book of Isaiah and the Book of Revelation, an apocalyptic vision is given to the reader of what the heavenly court is like. In addition to all the normal trappings of a royal court, there is also present a chorus of angels singing hymns of praise to the holiness of God. The words of their hymn are "Holy, holy, holy is Yahweh, the God of the heavenly armies. All heaven and earth are filled with his glory" (Is. 6:3; Rev. 4:8).

In the Jewish tradition and also in the early Christian tradition, the praise of God on earth was seen as a participation in the praise of God as portrayed in Isaiah and in Revelation (cf. Bouyer, p. 62). Thus, in the *Yozer*, one of the great solemn blessings in the Jewish Synagogue service, we find that the congregation joins in singing the *Sanctus* to conclude this great prayer of blessing chanted by the leader of the service. By joining in singing this hymn, the local congregation felt joined to the heavenly praise which is continually being given to God. Similarly, the early Christian Eucharistic Prayers began including this same hymn probably for the same reasons—a sign of union of the earthly praise to the eternal praise given to the Father in heaven.

The *Sanctus* thus began to be a standard feature of the Eucharistic Prayer. Almost every Eucharistic Prayer in official use up to about 1965 included the *Sanctus*. But this was not always the case. One of the most famous Eucharistic Prayers of the Patristic Age, the Hippolytus Canon, lacks a *Sanctus* (see Appendix A). Many recently written prayers similarly omit it. The argument for this practice which is given today is that the *Sanctus* breaks up the train of thought too much in the proclamation section of the Eucharistic Prayer. In addition, it is frequently not sung, and thus is another instance of a song which is only recited, and therefore really should be omitted. These arguments do have some truth to them, but they are also much too simplified to be considered without additional qualifications and considerations. Omitting the *Sanctus* omits an acclamation which can involve the people more in the Eucharistic Prayer. In some informal liturgies, the presider does most of the talking, and if he uses a prayer which lacks the *Sanctus* the congregation present becomes mere uninvolved bystanders, silently listening through the entire liturgy.

Omitting the *Sanctus* also eliminates the image that the local congregation is joining in a praise of the Father which is even wider than the Church on earth. This image seems to be a major reason why the *Sanctus* was included in early Eucharistic Prayers. The presider proclaims that the local congregation joins all those in heaven in the eternal praise of God in the very same words. Such a statement, eschatological in thrust, can help a community feel its union with the Church throughout the ages.

When the *Sanctus* is included in a Eucharistic Prayer, there are usually two additional transitional sentences which normally precede and follow it. The "lead-in" sentence usually mentions that this hymn is being (constantly) sung in heaven by angels and others, as referred to in Isaiah and Revelation. Its form, therefore, is more or less as follows: "And so, with the angels and all those in heaven, we join our voices in singing your praise: Holy . . ."[14]

The transitional sentence which follows the *Sanctus* is frequently referred to as the *"Vere Sanctus"* or *"Post-Sanctus."* The second and third Roman Eucharistic Prayers offer good examples of such transitional statements: "Lord, you are holy indeed, the fountain of all holiness . . ." "Father, you are holy indeed, and all creation rightly gives you praise." The purpose of this sentence is to serve as a link between the *Sanctus* and the continuation of the proclamation section which continues after the *Sanctus*. Frequently, this sentence also serves as a transition from the *magnalia Dei* mentioned in the Hebrew Scriptures to Christ, the "blessed" one "who comes in the name" of God the Father.

Whenever the *Sanctus* is included as part of a Eucharistic Prayer, the section of the Eucharistic Prayer which precedes it is called the "preface," as mentioned before. Thus, the preface is not something additional "tacked onto" a Eucharistic Prayer solely to introduce the *Sanctus*, but rather it is the first section of the proclamatory part of a prayer which contains a *Sanctus,* and so should be viewed as being liturgically and literarily an integral part of the entire prayer.

Some scholars (though not all) suggest that the Latin word "praefatio" (from which "preface" is derived) does not in this context imply any temporal anteriority. Rather, they contend, it is used to indicate a "solemn discourse" or proclamation and is derived from the Latin verb "praefari" which means "to proclaim." Thus, even the name "preface" indicates that this section contains a proclamation (cf. Dallen [2], p. 329).[15]

One might also note here that the Roman Eucharistic Prayer for Children III has a variable section in the "preface" and *also* in the *"post-sanctus"* and intercessions, and the accompanying document to these prayers for children suggests that translators (for the various language groups) are free to compose more such variable sections of a similar style. The bulk of this prayer remains the same, thus giving an interesting example of a prayer with both set and changeable sections. The German Catholic bishops, following a statement in the previously-mentioned 1973 Vatican letter on Eucharistic Prayers, authorized insertions into the *post-sanctus* section of Roman Eucharistic Prayers II and III for feasts and other occasions.

Chapter Seven
CHRISTOCENTRIC MEMORIAL OF THE LAST SUPPER

a. Institution Narrative

Usually the proclamation ends with the statement that the Father's greatest wonder and greatest gift to humanity was Jesus, his Son. (Some prayers based on the ancient Egyptian structure have the proclamation leading into a preliminary invocation of the Spirit, or consecratory epiclesis. This will be discussed below in Chapter 9.) From this mention of Jesus, the prayer leads into the Institution Narrative, that is, the narration of what Jesus did and said at the Last Supper. In introducing this section, many biblical statements have been used, such as, "The night he was betrayed . . ."; "The day before he suffered . . ."; "The night the Lord gave himself up . . ." The presider then narrates the actions and words of the Lord at the Institution of the Eucharist as recorded in the Christian Scriptures.

It is interesting to note that in Latin and Greek Eucharistic Prayer texts, the Institution Narrative begins usually with a *relative pronoun*, thus making the entire section a relative clause dependent on what precedes (whether it be part of the proclamation section or a petition in the form of a consecratory epiclesis).

We must grant that classical languages used relative clauses much more frequently than modern day English, sometimes giving them the importance we now associate only with main sentences in English. Nevertheless, it is also interesting to note that what has become the primary, all-important section of the Eucharistic Prayer in the piety of many Catholic priests and laity was only (linguistically) a secondary section in prayers written in Latin and Greek.

With this in mind, we see that some Latin and Greek prayers exhibit the following structure:

> It is truly right and just . . .
> to give you thanks, almighty Father, . . .
> through Jesus Christ our Lord,
> > who . . .
> > and who . . .
> > and who, on the night before he died,
> > > took bread . . .
> > > and said,
> > > > "This is my body given for you,"
> > and who, when the supper was ended,
> > > took the cup . . .
> Therefore,
> remembering his death and resurrection,
> we offer you . . .

(Also cf. below Chapter 11, section C.)

Some authors speak of the Institution Narrative (and even the proclamation section) under the title of "anamnesis," a word rich in meaning and history. Suffice it to say for now that the word implies much more than the usual English word used to translate it—"remembering." However, more will be mentioned concerning anamnesis below in section C and in Chapter 8 (especially section B). In addition, some writers use the term "Institution Narrative" to refer to *any* mention of the Last Supper and

Jesus sharing bread and wine with his apostles, no matter how vague and minimal the reference may be. More standard usage, however, suggests that this section should actually *narrate* the complete *institution* of the Eucharist, describing *what Jesus did* and *what he said,* fairly closely following the Last Supper descriptions (probably in fact early liturgical formulae) found in the Synoptic Gospels or in St. Paul.

Thus, in praying the Eucharistic Prayer, after the proclamation section which ends with the mention of Jesus, the presider next states that the Lord Jesus took bread and pronounced the blessing. As was mentioned before, God the Father was the object of Jewish meal blessings and not the food over which the blessing was prayed. Thus this next sentence normally takes on the form, "He took bread and blessed you, his Father . . ." or "He took the bread and gave you thanks and praise . . ." or "He took the bread and pronounced the blessing . . ." The presider then mentions that Jesus broke the bread and gave it to his disciples seated at table with him while stating that the bread was his "Body broken for you." Normally, both the words over the bread and also the words over the wine add the Pauline and Lucan sacrificial phrases "broken for you" and "shed for you" (cf. 1 Cor. 11:23–24; Lk. 22:19–20). These phrases also help to reinforce the Christian belief that what Christians celebrate in the Eucharist is not only the Lord's presence, but rather a presence brought about by his sacrificial death for the sins of humanity and his subsequent resurrection. On occasion, one does find Eucharistic Prayers which only have "This is my Body," or "This is my Blood," without any subsequent modifying phrase—such was the case in the Roman Canon in the Tridentine Missal before its revision in 1969. The narrative concerning the cup of wine usually parallels the narrative about the bread.

In his First Letter to the Corinthians, St. Paul narrates the "tradition" of the early Church concerning the Last Supper. This "tradition" or "that which was handed down" was very stylized and familiar to all who heard it. "I hand on to you what I myself received: that the Lord Jesus, on the night he was betrayed, took bread, and when he had given thanks, he broke the bread and said: 'This is my body for you'" (1 Cor. 11:23–24). Biblical scholars conjecture that this stylized formula was probably an early liturgical formula, and most of the Eucharistic Prayers up to recent times have followed this Pauline example by employing a stylized narrative of the Institution of the Eucharist which is not too far distant from this Pauline passage.[16]

b. Memorial Acclamation or Proclamation of Faith

Most of the Eucharistic Prayers of the Eastern Churches include numerous acclamations for the congregation. Invariably, one of these acclamations comes as a congregational response to the celebrant's narration of the Lord's command, "Do this in memory of me." In response to this, many of the Eastern Eucharistic Prayers have the congregation responding with a memorial acclamation similar to "We do remember your death, Lord Jesus. We proclaim your resurrection and we await your return." In the recent revision of Western Liturgies, many of the new official Eucharistic Prayers have included one or more acclamations in a similar style, to be recited by the congregation at some point after the Institution Narrative.

The prayers in the Roman Missal place this acclamation immediately after the words of the Lord in the Institution Narrative. The first of the more recent Roman Catholic prayers for Children's Liturgies delays this acclamation until the next major section is prayed (see Chapter 8, Section D)—Alternate Location for the Acclamation, below. Note: the other two children's prayers use a refrain repeated a number of times after the Institution Narrative).[17]

The recently composed acclamations of the revised Roman

Missal are based on a literary tradition of such acclamations as they have existed in some of the Eastern rites. This acclamation has usually been fairly short, and it succinctly commemorates the triple aspect of the paschal mystery—death, new life, parousia— in such a way that the congregation usually states that they remember Christ's death and resurrection while they await his return. This acclamation, along with numerous others in various liturgies, is usually addressed to Christ, following a principle that has developed over the ages, of the congregation praying to Christ, while the presider prays to God the Father (cf. Sheppard, pp. 200–202). It should be noted, however, that the additional repeated acclamations found in the recent Roman Children's Eucharistic Prayers neither commemorate the paschal mystery nor are addressed to Christ. They seem to perform a different purpose in the Eucharistic Prayer and should be considered as a "refrain" rather than a "memorial acclamation" (cf. below, Chapter 16, section C) (cf. Dallen [2]).

A few additional points may be noted about the memorial acclamation. In the revised Roman Missal, the Latin text has three acclamations as options, all of which are addressed to Christ. The English translation of the Missal has four acclamations—the first two being different versions of the same Latin original. The translators turned the first English option ("Christ has died . . .") into an acclamation more in the style of a proclamation of faith, rather than a short prayer to Christ.

It is also not really clear why the congreagation has traditionally prayed to Christ rather than to God the Father. Most of the acclamations of the Roman rite are addressed to Christ ("Lord, have mercy . . . Christ, have mercy . . . Praise to you, Lord Jesus Christ . . . Lamb of God . . . Lord, I am not worthy . . ."). This custom could also have a scriptural basis in that the early short acclamations are so addressed (e.g., "Maranatha" [Come, Lord Jesus]; cf. Rev. 22:20). This may also have been a way of attempting to concretize what is meant for the body of Christians to pray "through Christ," as given in the Christian Scriptures. The body of the congregation prayed to Christ. He in turn was seen to bring these prayers to his Father on behalf of his Body. In this particular case, the memorial acclamation may have been addressed to Christ in response to the presider's repetition of Christ's words, "Do this in memory of me."

If occasions demand a new acclamation, the principles and traditions which governed the more recent compositions should be kept in mind. It might be appropriate here to note that the Irish hierarchy has approved the Easter Octave acclamation of the apostle Thomas, "My Lord and my God," as an additional alternate acclamation for use in Ireland. Although this decision formalizes a practice popular among Catholics for decades, and officially tries to integrate it into the revised liturgy, one can seriously wonder how well-advised that decision was! The acclamation of St. Thomas is of a completely different form than both the historical acclamations of the Eastern Churches and the other contemporary official acclamations. In Catholic piety, this acclamation of Thomas was previously used to reinforce one's belief in the Real Presence, and it was recommended to be recited by the laity at each elevation, immediately after the words of Christ were said by the presider. With that background, it seems very ill-suited to be used as an acclamation proclaiming the paschal mystery of Christ's death and resurrection!

c. Memorial (Anamnesis)—Offertory—Invocation (Epiclesis)

After the Institution Narrative (and the Memorial Acclamation by the congregation if it occurs here) the presider continues praying the body of the Eucharistic Prayer. The next section is based on the command of Christ which the presider just narrated, "Do this in memory of me." Even though the congregation may have responded to these words through its acclamation, nevertheless, the presider, on behalf of the assembled community, prays to the Father, stating that the community is obedient to Christ's command and requesting the Father to respond to the obedience of the Church by sending the Spirit as a sign that the Church's action of thanksgiving is actually acceptable. Since this section is the explicit statement that the community is fulfilling the command of Christ to perform the Eucharist in his memory, this section is, liturgically, the central section (in relative importance) of the Eucharistic Prayer.[18]

Normally the three sub-sections—anamnesis, offertory, epiclesis—are linguistically connected with a dependent verb structure, so in some prayers it is awkward to try to distinguish one section from another. The rationale for this interdependence is this: the Lord said, "Do this in memory of me," so the presider, in the name of the community assembled in prayer, "remembers" the Lord, especially the paschal mystery of Christ's death and resurrection (anamnesis means "remembering," but also see Chapter 8, section B, below). But mere remembering is pointless unless it elicits or is accompanied by some action—specifically a union to Christ's actions. Thus we pray, "As we remember, we now do something." Christ's ultimate action was to offer himself as a sacrifice to the Father on our behalf. This sacrifice is even commemorated in the words "Body broken for you . . . Blood poured out for you." Thus our remembering is connected to an action of offering, so we word our prayer, "As we remember, we offer the Body and Blood of Christ," or, "As we remember, we unite ourselves to Christ's perfect offering of himself."

The Church has now stated in prayer that it has been faithful to Christ's command to remember him, and so it next prays that, in response, God the Father will find the Church's action acceptable and will manifest the presence of the Spirit in the gathering taking place. The primary fruit of the Spirit's presence is the unity of all who partake of the bread and wine, which are, in faith, the Body and Blood of Christ. And so, following the memorial-offertory, the celebrant prays in more or less these terms: "We pray that your Spirit will come upon us and our gifts so that all who partake of the Body and Blood of your Son may be joined in unity."[19]

Chapter Eight
PASCHAL MYSTERY— REMEMBRANCE AND RESPONSE

a. Memorial (Anamnesis)

As was mentioned in the previous chapter, the anamnesis is motivated by the recitation of the Lord's words, "Do this in memory of me." It has traditionally mentioned the paschal mystery of Christ's death and resurrection, but it has also on occasion included other events in his life, such as the passion, the ascension, and the enthronement at the Father's side in glory. In some contemporary prayers, sometimes a theme or significant event in Christ's life is mentioned, in this manner, "Father, remembering your Son's life of love (joy, service), how lovingly he died for us . . ."

For the reasons mentioned in the previous chapter, usually the verb of remembrance has occurred in participial form, i.e., "remembering" or "in memory of," rather than the indicative form, "we remember," although there are some traditions in which the verb of remembering is the major independent verb.

b. Use of the Term "Anamnesis"

More often than not, the term "anamnesis" is reserved to the small section which comes immediately after the Institution Narrative, and such is the usage here. However this practice is not uniform. Some authors include the "offertory" as part of the anamnesis since both are usually grammatically intertwined (cf. Davies). Others, such as Nicholas Lash (pp. 83–84), tend to use anamnesis more broadly to include the Proclamation section and the Institution Narrative, since these sections are also a "remembrance."

However, no matter what it includes, anamnesis invariably connotes much more than the English words "remembrance" and "memorial." Anamnesis is used to convey a Hebrew concept of "active" or "effective" memorial (for want of better English words)—*zikkaron* in Hebrew. This concept is best exemplified in the following instruction, taken from the Jewish Passover ritual:

> In every generation each person should regard himself as though he, personally, came out of Egypt. That is what the Scripture means when it says: "And you shall tell your son on that day: 'It is because of what the Lord did for *me* when *I* left Egypt' " (Ex. 13:8). It was not only our forefathers whom the Holy One, Blessed be He, redeemed from slavery, but He redeemed us, too, with them. As the Holy Scriptures say: "He brought *us* out of there in order to lead *us* to, and give *us*, this land which He had promised to our forefathers" (Deut. 6:23).

In our "remembering" we are actually making the event remembered present because of our action of remembering. This is a significant part of the meaning of *zikkaron* or anamnesis.

In these words we have, ultimately, a double time framework—the present time in which we do the "remembering" and the past time in which the event "remembered" (first) existed (historically). However, *zikkaron* and anamnesis also indicate that by our remembering, we, in the present, enter into the meaning of the event, as if we were present in the time of the (historical) event. The event becomes "incarnated" in the present through symbolic action (and not merely "reincarnated") (cf. Fulco, p. 9). The meaning and implications of the event are alive, "active," and "effective" for us today. Our liturgical memorial is not a remembrance of an event that does not and cannot affect us today. Quite the opposite. Our remembering makes real in our present-day lives the event which chronologically took place in the past. In the case of the Christian Eucharist, our remembering makes real the event of the death-resurrection of Jesus our Lord.

Perhaps looking at two examples from the Scriptures may help us gain a deeper insight into the meaning of *zikkaron* or anamnesis:

> Yahweh our God made a covenant with us at Horeb. It was not with our fathers that Yahweh made this covenant, but with us, with us who are here, all living today. (Deut. 5:2–3)

As we can see, this scriptural passage seems to be the basis of the section given above which was taken from the Jewish Passover ritual. The basic meaning of *zikkaron* is found in this passage: past event—present reality.

> When we were baptized in Christ Jesus, we were baptized in his death; in other words, when we were baptized we went into the tomb with him and joined him in death, so that as Christ was raised from the dead by the Father's glory, we too might live a new life. (Rom. 6:3–4)

Again we see that in this passage, Paul seems to be using the basic idea involved in *zikkaron* to convey to his readers the meaning of the events of baptism.

A correct understanding of anamnesis and *zikkaron* has many consequences, some of which are very important. For example, in the meaning of these words, Christians may come to a deeper (and united) understanding of what we mean when we speak about "presence" with regard to the Eucharist, and what relationship the Eucharist has with the death of Jesus on Calvary. As J. Frank Henderson says in a recent article:

> Rediscovery of the biblical notion of *zikkaron*, as with other aspects of modern biblical study, is the fruit of work by scholars of many Christian traditions and has important ecumenical implications. The way in which Christ's paschal mystery becomes present in the eucharist has been a matter of controversy and division for centuries; hopefully a common acceptance of the meaning of *zikkaron* will bring the churches closer together on this point. . . . *Zikkaron* is particularly helpful in enabling us to understand the nature of liturgical participation: in the liturgy of the eucharist the salvific event of the death and resurrection of Christ is made present in such a way that the entire assembly enters into that event. (p. 24)

A correct understanding of the meaning of anamnesis and *zikkaron* may also help the way contemporary authors word the "anamnesis" section of a Eucharistic Prayer. Any wording that gives the impression that Christ's death and resurrection are just past events (with no present implications or effects) does not do justice to the full meaning of the original Greek and Hebrew words and underlying concepts (cf. "Zikkaron" in Bouyer, pp. 84–85, 104).

c. Offertory

The small section of the Eucharistic Prayer which is connected to the anamnesis is the true "offertory" of the entire Eucharistic Liturgy as far as the language expresses this concept. (However, ritually, the "offertory" takes place, in gesture, for the Roman rite at the final Doxology, even though an offering gesture is actually made at this point in the Byzantine rite.) Formerly, at least for Roman Catholics, the rite of preparation before the Eucharistic Prayer used to be called the "offertory." Even now, many contemporary extemporaneous prayers at the preparation of the gifts still emphasize "offering" selves, the bread and wine, etc., to God the Father. The more that is done, the less need there is seen for an offertory in the Eucharistic Prayer, even though theologically and liturgically the offertory of the Eucharistic Prayer is the only "offertory" possible.

This is the position that Ralph A. Keifer takes in a recent article, "Preparation of the Altar and the Gifts or Offertory?" In this article, he makes the following points:

> The appeal of the overemphasized rite of preparation suggests that there is a felt need for expressing the people's share in the act of offering. . . . If these two themes—the people's self-oblation and the recognition of the value of creation and human work—are receiving such attention outside of where they properly belong— namely, the eucharistic prayer—the fault may rest with our present eucharistic prayers . . . In the eucharistic prayer the anamnesis, or memorial, as well as the great Amen conveys the people's share in the offering—for those who have done advanced studies in liturgy. The virtual neglect of catechesis on such matters hints that this understanding is not obvious to the clergy, let alone to the laity. Perhaps the situation could in part be remedied by an acclamation at the end of the anamnesis which unambiguously expressed offering. It is interesting to note that many of the expressions in contemporary "offertory hymns" would be appropriate if they were to appear at this point in the eucharistic litur-

gy. . . . There needs to be a clearer sense of the people's offering within the eucharistic prayer. (p. 597)

After the sacrifice of Christ on the cross, the sacrifices of the Jewish covenant—animals, fruits of the earth, etc.—are no longer acceptable for Christians. Anything offered to the Father must somehow be offered in union with the offering of Christ when he gave the Father his total life and love on the "altar of the cross." Thus, first of all, we can only offer Christ to the Father, and never bread and wine. Secondly, if we wish to offer ourselves, this can only be done to the degree that we have united ourselves to Christ and share his offering to the Father. In any case, "offering" should not be thought of in terms of giving tokens to an angry God in order to appease his wrath. After Christ, offering and sacrifice mean something totally different for the committed Christian. These terms now indicate a response due to an existing love-relationship. They indicate the same type of action and response that a married person performs in supporting a spouse and family, or that a parent performs in caring for a house and raising children. Offering and sacrifice are both real terms in these situations, but neither word connotes the image of a trying to appease an angry Godhead who threatens to destroy the humble worshiper.

Sometimes the question is asked, "What exactly is offered at this point of the Eucharistic Prayer?" To this question we reply: "Christ." However, at the same time Christ is one and yet present in many different forms. It is true that in many prayers this section is so worded that reference is specifically made to the bread and cup on the altar, and so they alone seem to be offered to the Father. However, more often the reference is to the "Body and Blood of Christ," and this wording is much more pregnant with meaning. The Body of the Lord is the Body present in the bread on the altar, in the congregation assembled in prayer, and in the Church throughout the world. The Blood of Christ is that which is present in the cup on the altar, and in the sufferings of Christians everywhere. These are what are offered to the Father—the ultimate and perfect offering which is possible for the Christian. Perhaps Lash summarizes it best.

> It is misleading to say either that "we offer Christ to the Father," or that "Christ offers us to the Father." The balanced statement is to the effect that, by the grace of Christ, our self-offering to the Father, expressed and sealed by our sharing in the meal, is a participation in his self-offering to his Father on Calvary. (p. 61)

As was mentioned above, too often there is no mention of "offering" at this point of many contemporary Eucharistic Prayers. This omission leads some celebrants to extemporize prayers during the preparation of the gifts which tend to emphasize the "offering" of bread and wine. In the East, the Eucharistic Prayer is termed the "anaphora," a word meaning "oblation" or "offering." Some of the Syrian Christian Churches refer to the entire Eucharist as the *"Qurbana"* or "offering." This shows that, at least in the East, much emphasis was placed on the "offering" aspect of the Eucharist. This also shows that the concept of "offering" in the Eucharistic Prayer is not as much a medieval Western deviation of the liturgy as some would assert.

In a sequence of articles concerning the Eucharistic Prayers in the Roman Missal, Fr. Aidan Kavanaugh, O.S.B. makes the following comments about the concept of "offering" in a Eucharistic Prayer:

> More is involved in "consecration" than just the transformation of bread and wine into the sacramental body and blood of Christ. Considered liturgically, in terms of the whole Eucharistic Prayer, "consecration" is a progressive offering to the Father of the whole assembly—Christ's body which is the Church. This is the import of

the *Unde et memores:* its *offerimus* refers essentially to
the action . . . done here in Christ by the whole hierar-
chically assembled community. . . . The offering-sacri-
fice is conceived of being made not "with" the
sacrament after it has been confected; rather, the offer-
ing-sacrifice of the body of Christ which is the church
makes the sacramental body of Christ—under the forms
of food for Christian nourishment. . . . The whole
anaphora is the prayer of eucharistic offering, but the
Unde et memores makes this textually explicit in view
of the command, "Do this for the *anamnesis* of me."
[Note: The *Unde et memores* is the anamnesis prayer of
the Roman Canon.] ([2], pp. 6–7)

This faith-response of the church is explicitly directed
to the Father *not* as coming from some corporate entity
alien to him, but as the response that is identical with
that of the Son. With the Son the church maintains a
communion-identity secured in the Spirit. Such a faith-
response is . . . objectively liturgical, and takes the form
of an oblatory self-sacrifice that is eucharistic. . . . Jesus
continues to give himself only in the first person plural,
and this is expressed in the "we offer" of the church's
eucharistic anamnesis. ([3], pp. 7–8)

In line with what was said in the previous chapter in section
C concerning the unity of this section of the Eucharistic Prayer,
especially the concepts of memorial and offering, let me again
mention that, traditionally, these two concepts have been linked
together by a dependent verb structure so that "offering" becomes the principal verb in this section and "remembering"
depends on it. In a recent article, Thomas Talley puts forward the
position that this type of structure is still important in our
contemporary prayers. In this article, he is reacting against Eucharistic Prayer B in the *Book of Common Prayer* of the Episcopal

Church (pp. 367–69). In that prayer, the concepts of remembering and offering are separate. The people's acclamation is construed as being the entire "memorial" section of the Eucharistic Prayer, and the priest continues after this acclamation with the words, "And we offer our sacrifice of praise. . . ." In reaction to this, Dr. Talley says:

> This division in the assignment of anamnesis and oblation represents, I fear, at least a first step toward that opposition of memorial and sacrifice which has been so unproductive since the sixteenth century. In the classic anaphoras from the *Apostolic Tradition* in the third century to the new compositions of the twentieth, it has been one of the more remarkable regularities that memorial and oblation have been so intimately related and intertwined that one could conceive the Eucharist as one over against the other only by deliberately rejecting the clear insistence of liturgical texts that it is the one only insofar as it is the other. . . . If we are to have such memorial acclamations, then the following presidential prayer should reiterate the content of the anamnesis so that it will be clear that it is only in relation to the memorial of the paschal mystery that oblation is made. (p. 323)

d. Alternate Location for the Acclamation

In the first of the new Roman Eucharistic Prayers for Children and in many other contemporary prayers, the memorial acclamation of the congregation (previous chapter, section B) occurs at this point in the Eucharistic Prayer, after the memorial-offertory has been proclaimed by the presider. Some of the arguments for choosing one location over the other were presented in the previous chapter (section B and footnote 17), but it may be good to recall the reasons for placing an acclamation here instead of after the words of Christ.

One major argument given is that the people should not anticipate what the presider is to say, and this is precisely what does happen when the memorial acclamation is in the earlier location (cf. Kavanaugh [3], p. 12). However, a counter-argument to this is that the creed is oftentimes recited prior to the Eucharistic Prayer and, in it, the entire congregation recites the triple mystery of Christ's death, rising and second coming. For Roman Catholics and certain other groups of Christians, perhaps a more forceful reason for postponing the acclamation may be of a more pedagogical nature. It would be good for many Christians to de-emphasize the Institution Narrative in order to give a better balance to other parts of the Eucharistic Prayer and to the Eucharistic Prayer considered as a whole.[20] One way to give a better balance is to try to connect the anamnesis section to the Institution Narrative as much as possible, thereby relating the actions of the Last Supper to the paschal mystery proclaimed in the anamnesis. After the presider has made the audible connection, the congregation can re-emphasize the same paschal mystery in their acclamation. The acclamation in the earlier place may be all right if it were not for the "baggage" most Catholics carry with them of past one-sided piety which can distort a balanced picture and appreciation of the Eucharistic Prayer as a whole (cf. Keifer [5], p. 15).

Still another major reason for including the acclamation at this point lies with the structural breakdown of the Eucharistic Prayer. As mentioned previously in Chapters 1, 2 and 3, the invocation (epiclesis) section begins the supplication section of the Eucharistic Prayer. Thus *everything* previous to the invocation is memorial (sometimes, for convenience, subdivided into praise for creation and thanksgiving for redemption, or even into further subdivisions). Since it is basically *memorial*, the unity of this memorial proclamation should be kept intact as much as possible. After an acclamation at this point of the prayer, it may be appropriate even for the presider to change his arm gestures from the *orans* prayer position (arms extended) to the imposition of hands gesture over the bread, wine and assembly as he prays the epiclesis beginning the intercessions (we will say more on the gestures below in Chapter 12).

Chapter Nine
PNEUMATOCENTRIC MOTIF: THE SPIRIT—GIVER OF LIFE

Invocation (Epiclesis)

As was mentioned above, following the offertory is the invocation of the Spirit. The longer Jewish berakoth allowed the inclusion of petitions, and, as we saw, the third section of the *birkat ha-mazon* was petitionary. In the Christian Eucharistic Prayer, the petition for the Spirit is usually the first of any that are included. However, many scholars suggest that the invocation for the Spirit should not be seen as just one of the many intercessions which form their own section later in the prayer. Nor should it even be seen as the most important or the first of the petitions. The role of the epiclesis as it has developed through the ages in the Church is much more subtle than being a simple request made of the Father.

Before looking in greater depth at the invocation in the Christian Eucharistic Prayer, let us look at some of the scriptural background for prayer petitions, completion of sacrifice, and the work of the Spirit in relation to Jesus. The invocation (epiclesis) and any form of petition is a logical movement from memorial and praise. In many prayers in the Hebrew Scriptures, a section of praise is ended by a section of petition, or these two movements become interwoven throughout the prayer. Good examples of such prayers can be seen in the prayers for the dedication of the Jerusalem temple by Solomon, found in 1 Kings 8 and in 2 Chronicles 6. In the account given in 2 Chronicles, two details are mentioned which should be pointed out—the consummation of the sacrifice by fire from heaven (2 Chr. 7:1) and the body postures of supplication which are kneeling (2 Chr. 6:13) and bowing (2 Chr. 7:3).

The prayer for the dedication is composed of memorial and petition, and asks that the sacrifice being offered be accepted by God. Its acceptance is indicated by the divine response of fire. It is offered in a bodily gesture of supplication (kneeling or bowing). Such a posture of bowing is still prescribed in the Roman Canon during the "epicletic" prayer for acceptance of the sacrifice after the Institution Narrative, and in some Eastern liturgies the presider will bow or kneel or even prostrate himself while reciting the invocation section of the Eucharistic Prayer.

The thrust of any petition is future directed, and in Christian Eucharistic Prayers, this petition becomes a prayer for the divine acceptance or completion of the sacrifice, and for the fruitful effects of that sacrifice upon those partaking of it. In the famous prayer of Jesus found in John 17, we see this plea for completion most clearly. It also appears in the theology of sacrifice espoused by the Letter to the Hebrews. An accepted Christian sacrifice leads to the outpouring of the Spirit, and this is seen particularly in the theology of St. John, where we read in the description of the death of Jesus that, "bowing his head, he gave over the spirit" (Jn. 19:30).

In a very real sense, at the same time we have a number of twofold aspects, seemingly at odds with each other, which are united in Christian petitionary prayer. In Jesus' prayer in John 17, we have a prayer for completion of the sacrifice, yet the sacrifice is already being completed. In Hebrews, Christ's sacrifice is once and for all—yet he still intercedes for us with the Father. We ask for unity in Christ, yet it is the Spirit which is given (esp. cf. Jn.

14—16). The Spirit proceeds from the Father, yet is sent by the Son. Christ is present now, yet he is still to come. All these various poles come together in the psychological background which has given rise to the invocation (epiclesis) in Christian Eucharistic Prayers.

As was mentioned above, the essential content of the invocation is a petition for the divine response to the Church's obedience to Christ's command, an obedience which was expressed in the anamnesis-offertory. But, throughout the New Testament, the divine response to the prayer of Christians in their attempt to know the Lord Jesus is linked with the activity of the Spirit. As J. Tillard asserts, in the New Testament Jesus comes to individuals only through the Spirit (cf. Ryan [1], p. 168).

For this reason, the petition for divine response is usually worded in terms of a petition for the Spirit. (Exceptions, of course, do occur, such as the Roman Canon which words the request for divine response in images found in the Hebrew Scriptures rather than in pneumatic images.) In full form, the invocation comprises three sections: (1) a petition for the working of the Spirit, (2) a description of the effects of his working as the change of the bread and wine into Christ's Body and Blood, and (3) the statement of the reason for which the Spirit has been invoked (that is, the statement of the "fruit" of the invocation), which is the unity of all who believe in Christ (and thus, who partake of the bread and cup) (cf. Davies, pp. 15–16; Albertine, p. 200).

Thus it is that the invocation, rather than just "happening" to fall in a Eucharistic Prayer after the memorial-offertory, is intimately related to and derived from the community's action of remembering. This relationship is frequently overlooked, as an examination of some of the contemporary Eucharistic Prayers will reveal. As a result, many such prayers immensely downplay the role of the invocation, and if a reference to the Spirit is made, it is usually seen as one of many petitions and intercessions. One of the most recent studies on the Eucharistic Epiclesis, by John H. McKenna, C.M. (article and book, both published in 1975) tries to evaluate both extremes of views on the importance of the invocation in a very careful and scholarly manner. His research and conclusions have been taken into account in this section and in later sections which deal with the epiclesis.

A number of authors have tried in one form or another to explain or describe more fully the unity which exists between the memorial (anamnesis) and the invocation (epiclesis). One explanation is that mere remembering (anamnesis) is useless without the Spirit to give it life (epiclesis). Thus, some authors reason, for example, that the Church administers Confirmation to give life to the commemorative initiation action of washing which Baptism enacts. However, other authors reason differently. Looking at mystics such as Augustine, who saw the presence of God in the action of remembering, these authors argue that an epiclesis should be viewed more as a prayer that the praying community will realize even more the workings of the Spirit in its midst, since it is only by the already-present Spirit that the Christian community is able to pray to the Father or to remember God's deeds in the first place. Thus, even though we may phrase our prayer in terms which ask for the Spirit to come, we actually are asking the help of the Father to realize all that the Spirit has done and continues to do in the community even as we remember what Christ has done for us in the past. The Spirit is present in our remembering of Christ's life—we petition that we may appreciate that presence (cf. Mitchell, pp. 477–79).

In a complete epiclesis there are two distinct requests made of the Spirit as was mentioned above. The first request, which is actually more a description of the Spirit's action, is that the Spirit "come upon these gifts so that they may be the Body and Blood" of Jesus the Lord. The second request, which is the request for the "fruit" of the invocation, is that "all who partake of this bread and cup may become one body in Christ." The first request is sometimes termed the "consecratory" aspect and the second, the "Communion" aspect of the epiclesis. In prayers based on an old Egyptian structure, and in other traditions thought to have a similar structure such as the Roman Catholic Eucharistic Prayers (however, cf. Albertine for a contrary opinion), these two requests are separated into two different epicleses, one occurring before the Institution Narrative and the other after the anamnesis-offertory. In the Roman practice the first "consecratory epiclesis" is accompanied by an imposition of hands over the bread and wine (cf. also below for more on the imposition of hands and gestures during the Eucharistic Prayer, Chapter 12, section B).

Although most writers speak of the "consecratory" aspect of the epiclesis, a recent article written by Joseph H. Crehan, S.J., suggests that perhaps a different term should be used instead. He suggests that this aspect of the epiclesis should be termed "establishing." He suggests that only the Institution Narrative with the words of Christ can "consecrate," but that the writings of the Fathers suggest that the Holy Spirit is necessary so that the consecrated elements can be recognized, i.e., established, in the community as the Body and Blood of Christ. He suggests that this "establishing" by the Holy Spirit is something separate from a "consecration" by Christ. Such an explanation would be consistent with the formulation of certain ancient Eucharistic Prayers, such as the Byzantine version of the prayer of Basil the Great, whose epiclesis reads thus:

> We implore you . . . to make your Holy Spirit come down upon us and upon these . . . gifts . . . to bless and sanctify them and to show that this bread is, indeed, the precious Body of . . . Christ, and to show that this cup is, indeed, the precious Blood of . . . Christ, which was shed for the life of the world, and to unite with one another all of us who partake of this one Bread and Cup in the fellowship of the Holy Spirit.

If Crehan's theory gains acceptance, it would seem to go a long way in reducing the traditional East-West differences mentioned elsewhere in interpreting the moment of consecration and in interpreting the differences in the roles and importance of the Institution Narrative and the epiclesis.

As was asserted above, it seems that these two petitions (consecratory and Communion) are really two aspects of the same basic request (however, cf. Appendix C, Introduction, for a contrary opinion). For this reason, the practice of "splitting" the epiclesis into two separate invocations seems to hyphenate the working of the Spirit and to destroy the unity of the Spirit's action. The Spirit makes the Body of Christ present in a given community and that Body is marked by a divine unity. The action of the Spirit which leads a community to realize that the bread and wine have been changed will be the same action which will lead the community to realize that "since the bread is one, all who partake of it form one Body in Christ" (1 Cor. 10:17) (cf. Talley [2], p. 324).[21]

Chapter Ten
INTERCEDING FOR CHRIST'S CHURCH AND CONCLUSION

a. Intercessions

As a logical consequence of the request for unity in the epiclesis, various members of the Church are mentioned (if they are saints), or prayed for (if they are alive or recently dead) to express that the unity requested does in fact exist in some degree. These intercessory prayers express the concern of the local community for the more universal community of Christians. It shows that the local community is taking upon itself the work of Christ, our Mediator, who is constantly interceding for us with the Father.

In this section reference can be made to Church authorities, that is, those whom the local community depends upon for its authentic sacramental life. Civil authorities can also be mentioned, along with other classes of people and other community concerns.[22]

The Intercessions may include what Lengeling calls "the expression of communion with the local Church and the Church universal," a part which he calls integral to the prayer. Thus, the complete omission of the Intercessions should not be done lightly. In a joint statement between Anglicans and Catholics (Dec. 31, 1971), we read: "In the Eucharistic Prayer the Church continues to . . . entreat the benefits of [Christ's] passion on behalf of the whole Church. . . ." Commenting on this listing of what occurs in a Eucharistic Prayer, J. B. Ryan states: "If any of these are omitted in an EP, that EP is an incomplete expression of the Church's *minimal* understanding of the Eucharist. That is why the omission of intercessory prayer from the EP . . . cannot be undertaken lightly" (Ryan [1], pp. 182–83).

A healthy balance should be maintained concerning the number and length of the Intercessions in future Eucharistic Prayers. Some presiders regularly omit the General Intercessions concluding the Liturgy of the Word and include all petitions and intercessions during the Eucharistic Prayer. Besides being a misunderstanding of the place of intercession in the Eucharistic Prayer, this practice tends to lengthen the Eucharistic Prayer to such a degree that it tends to be unrecognizable as a single unit. On the other hand, as was mentioned above, many contemporary prayers omit any intercessory prayer altogether. This practice entirely overlooks the origins of the Eucharistic Prayer in the *birkat ha-mazon*, the last third of which is an intercessory section. It is hard to say what should be included in the intercessions of a Eucharistic Prayer. The historical evidence is contradictory as to what or who should be commemorated in the Eucharistic Prayer and what or who should be commemorated in the General Intercessions which usually conclude the Liturgy of the Word. Scholars do not seem to give any more hints, either. At times, the Eucharistic Prayer can be very specific, for the Roman Missal allows commemorations *by name* for deceased persons, for married couples (Roman Canon), for newly baptized Christians, and for newly professed religious. Yet, throughout the history of Eucharistic Prayers, the Intercessions therein have more often tended to contain *general* classes of Christians, such as "widows, orphans, virgins, monks, nuns," whereas the Intercessions at the end of the Liturgy of the Word tend to be more specific. Perhaps this is due to the fact that if the Eucharistic Prayer was written down and meant to be repeated, the text should be general enough to be used at almost any celebration of the Eucharist. It would seem that the consensus of scholars is that the Eucharistic Prayer should have some Intercessions in it, yet the Intercessions should not overshadow (by length or by style) the thanksgiving and praise aspects of the prayer as a whole, and any Intercessions should not duplicate the General Intercessions which occur earlier in the Liturgy.

b. Doxological Transition

The doxology (see next section) is a statement that praise and thanks are given "through Christ, and with him, and in him," to God the Father. Usually some transitional statement is needed to get from the Intercessions to the doxology without doing damage to the literary form of the doxology. Frequently some experimental Eucharistic Prayers state "All this we ask: through him, . . ." using the traditional doxology of the Roman Canon. However, this practice grammatically makes no sense whatsoever, for the doxology states that praise and glory is given through Christ, and such a transition changes the meaning to say that the preceding Intercessions are made through Christ. When such a transition occurs, the "glory and honor" section of the doxology is left to stand on its own which it cannot do literarily. Therefore, some type of transitional sentence should precede the doxology and end with some reference to Christ.[23]

c. Doxology

The doxology is the last section which appears in each berakah, the return to the initial theme of praise. It is a final statement that glory, praise and honor is given to the Father through the Son and in the unity of the Spirit. All three persons of the Trinity are usually mentioned, and many contemporary prayers seem to use the doxology of the Roman Catholic official prayers either intact, or with only slight modifications.

d. Amen

"*Amen*" is one of three Hebrew words (along with *Alleluia* and *Hosanna*) which we retain for regular use in the Christian liturgy. It is derived from the Hebrew root which indicates *reality* or *truth* and thus has the meaning "so be it," "so it is," "it is true," "I agree." In our Judaic-Christian religious history and Scriptures, Amen is used frequently as a conclusion to affirm what preceded, or as a response to indicate agreement with what another person spoke. It is in this latter context that Paul writes concerning the use of "Amen" to a charismatic prayer of thanksgiving (perhaps even an early Eucharistic Prayer) in his First Letter to the Corinthians (1 Cor. 14:16). Here Paul bemoans the fact that others present could not assent and say Amen to prayers which they could not understand.

In a seemingly unusual use of the word in the Book of Revelation, the author of the book calls Christ himself the Amen (i.e., Truth) (Rev. 3:14), who says, "I stand at the door and knock. . . . I will eat with him and he with me" (Rev. 3:20), a possible reference to the Eucharist.

As mentioned in Chapter 2, the Amen ended the *birkat hamazon* (as it appeared at the time of Christ) and was an opportunity for those at dinner to join and unite themselves in the graces after meals spoken by the head of the house. The practice of concluding the Eucharistic Prayer with an Amen seems to have continued from this early start almost immediately. In two extraordinary references by Justin Martyr (died around 165) he mentions the "Amen" being made by the assembly to the prayers and thanksgiving at the Eucharist:

> When he has finished the prayers and the thanksgiving,
> all the people present give their assent by saying,

"Amen." Amen is Hebrew for "So be it." And when the
president has given thanks and all the people have assented, those whom we call deacons give to each one
present a portion of bread. . . . (1 *Apol.* 65:3, 4,5)

The president likewise offers prayers and thanksgivings
to the best of his ability, and the people assent, saying
the Amen. (1 *Apol.* 67:5)

St. Jerome (died around 420) mentions that the "Amen" thun-
dered in the Churches of Rome and caused pagan temples to
tremble (*In Epist. ad Galat.* 2, praef., PL 26:381). All texts of
ancient Eucharistic Prayers include the Amen, and in the earliest
prayers this simple response is the *only* response which the
assembly makes to the Eucharistic Prayer (aside from the responses in the introductory dialogue) (cf. Hippolytus Canon, Appendix A).

In recent liturgical writings, this Amen is usually called the
"Great Amen," for it is *the* acclamation of the entire Eucharistic
Liturgy. All other responses by the assembly throughout the
Eucharistic Liturgy are really secondary, compared to this accla-
mation which sums up and affirms the entire preceding prayer,
which itself is the central prayer of the Eucharistic celebration.

Too often, in practice, this acclamation gets lost in the
shuffle. Instead of being the climax, it becomes an afterthought.
The Eucharistic Prayer should really build up to a climax with
the doxology and Amen, which is an affirmation of a biblical
truth that all glory is given to God the Father through Christ (cf.
2 Cor. 1:20). However, given Roman Catholic piety based on
theological emphases during the past few centuries, the words of
Christ still remain the high point for most people in the Eucharistic Prayer, and everything after it is deemed negligible. In Roman
Catholic Churches, the congregation usually changes postures
from kneeling during the Eucharistic Prayer to standing for the

Lord's Prayer, and so, frequently, the Amen is also lost in the rumble of this posture change. As a result, in a number of places, the congregation has begun to recite the final doxology along with the presider in order to make a meaningful final acclamation to the Eucharistic Prayer (possibly in imitation of the practice at concelebrations). However, this practice has its own drawbacks as well (although there are some Eastern Christian Eucharistic Prayers in which it is normal for the entire assembly to say the concluding doxology). This practice turns the linguistic conclusion to a prayer by one person into a response for all, and the doxological conclusion as it now exists is not really well-suited for this function. In addition, when the entire congregation does say the complete doxology, the Amen still seems to get overlooked (cf. *Notitiae* 14 [1978], 4[whole num. 143–44], pp. 304–05, Inaest. Donum #7).[24]

There is no easy solution to this difficulty of giving the Amen the emphasis it deserves. On Sundays and major feasts, the normal practice should be to sing the Amen with enough repetitions to make it truly a "Great Amen." Some composers have included other words of affirmation (with authorization from the 1972 U.S. Roman Catholic "Bishops' Committee on the Liturgy" document, "Music in Catholic Worship," section 58). In these cases, one finds such words as "Alleluia," "for ever and ever," and "Praise the Lord," included with a series of repeated Amens to lengthen this acclamation and give it more significance.

This practice of giving more emphasis to the Amen is commendable and should be encouraged. However, it should not be limited only to Sundays and major feasts. Even the most simple liturgies (e.g., 6 A.M. weekday Masses) could profitably employ a sung *a capella* Amen (cf. "Music in Catholic Worship," section 54). Other helps should also be used to emphasize this climactic moment. For example, even the presider's gestures should be such as to give significance to this final acclamation. In the Roman rite, the presider is to lift up the bread and cup in a gesture of offering

to emphasize the words of the doxology, "Through [Christ] . . .
all glory . . . is yours, almighty Father. . . ." These gifts should be
held high enough to indicate that this action is not merely a
"showing" of the gifts to the assembly, or an insignficant ritualis-
tic gesture, but a climactic part of the prayer. In addition, the
presider should *continue* to hold the gifts high until well into the
Great Amen (or throughout it and even *past* it, if the version is
short enough). Especially if the Amen is spoken, it would be well
for the presider to continue to hold the gifts raised for a moment
or two in silence, and then slowly lower them, and then pause
another moment before inviting the assembly to stand and pray
the Lord's Prayer.

c. **Sample Eucharistic Prayer**

In order to exemplify the various sections of a Eucharistic
Prayer as discussed above, and to give the reader an opportunity
to see a contemporary Eucharistic Prayer with the subsections
indicated, the following prayer is given as an example.

Introductory Dialogue

> The Lord be with you.
> R. And also with you.
>
> Lift up your hearts.
> R. We lift them up to the Lord.
>
> Let us give thanks to the Lord our God.
> R. It is right to give him thanks and praise.

Stylized Beginning

> Father, it is right and just
> that we give you thanks and praise
> through Jesus Christ our Lord,

Proclamation

> for through him
> you have again shown us your great love.

> Father, you chose us to be your people
> and throughout every age we have
>   turned from you.

> But you sent your prophets to us
>   again and again,
> and we repented,
> and you took us back.

Sanctus

> Father, we are left speechless.
> We can only join our voices
>   to all those in heaven
> and together proclaim your glory:

>   Holy, holy, holy Lord . . .

Proclamation Cont'd (Post-Sanctus)

> Father, you called Abraham
> and told him to leave his land
>   and follow your call.
> He obeyed and you blessed him.

> Throughout history you have called
>   men and women to yourself.
> Some have listened—many have not.

> Then you sent your Son,
>   like us in all things.

He again showed us your love
    and your concern,
and how we all can respond to your call.

To show how great was your love
he gave up his life on the
    altar of the cross.

Institution Narrative

On the night before his death,
he took bread and gave you
    thanks and praise.
He broke the bread, gave it to
    his disciples, and said:

Take this, all of you, and eat it:
This is my Body which will be
    given up for you.

When supper was ended, he took the cup.
Again he gave you thanks and praise,
gave the cup to his disciples and said:

Take this, all of you, and
    drink from it:
This is the cup of my Blood,
the Blood of the new and everlasting
    covenant.
It will be shed for you and for
    all,
so that sins may be forgiven.

Do this in memory of me.

Memorial Acclamation

> Let us proclaim the mystery of faith:

>> We remember your death, Lord Jesus.
>> We proclaim your resurrection.
>> We eagerly await your coming.

Anamnesis

>> Father, remembering all your Son
>>> did for us,
>> his death, his resurrection
>>> and his glorification,

Offertory

>> we unite ourselves to his sacrifice,
>> and again offer you
>>> the Body and Blood of Christ.

Epiclesis

>> We pray that you will again
>>> send us your Spirit
>> so that our offering may be in truth
>> the Body and Blood of your Son
>> and that all who partake of them
>> may be united
>> in the union your Son so dearly
>>> prayed for.

Intercessions

>> We pray that we may always
>>> express the love you showed us

as we work with our brothers
    and sisters in need.

We pray for all our Church leaders,
    especially N. our bishop
and all who minister to the needs
    of your chosen people.

We pray for our sick brothers and
    sisters.
We pray for all those who seek
    your presence.

Doxological transition

We pray that we may always
    proclaim your presence
to all we meet,
so that all people may come to know you,
the one true God,
and him whom you sent, Jesus Christ.

Doxology

For,
through him, with him, in him,
in the unity of the Holy Spirit,
all glory and honor is yours,
Almighty Father,
for ever and ever.

Amen

Amen.

Chapter Eleven
COMPONENT SUBSECTIONS: RELATIVE IMPORTANCE AND POSSIBLE OMISSIONS

a. Relative Importance of the Component Parts of the Eucharistic Prayer

Although opinions vary as to what the "essential" parts of a Eucharistic Prayer are, it seems that most liturgical writers would, for the most part, agree with the fourfold classification given by Prof. Emil Lengeling (of the University of Münster, Germany) (cf. *Questiones Liturgiques* 53[1972], p. 251).

Class one: Indispensable

1. praise and thanksgiving for the mystery of salvation
2. the institution narrative
3. the anamnesis (remembrance of the paschal mystery)
4. the doxology

Class two: Integral but not indispensable

1. mention of the sacrificial character
2. epiclesis
3. expression of communion with the local Church and the Church universal.

Class three: Parts which would not be omitted in principle, but whose presence may be limited

1. Sanctus
2. expression of communion with the heavenly liturgy
3. communion of the saints
4. remembrance of the living and dead

Class four: Parts not necessary at all, but which may be included and may even be desirable at times

1. praise and thanksgiving for the works of creation
2. prayer for the acceptance of the sacrifice
3. mention of present concerns
4. responses of the community

   If we place the sub-sections of a Eucharistic Prayer in a chart in the order they usually appear, noting the relative importance as given by Lengeling, we obtain the following diagram (brackets indicate section titles not specifically mentioned):

Introductory Dialogue	[1]
Stylized beginning	[1]
Proclamation	[1]
Praise for the mystery of salvation	(1)
Praise for the works of creation	(4)
Communion with the heavenly liturgy	(3)
Sanctus	(3)
Consecratory Epiclesis	(2)
Institution Narrative	(1)
Memorial Acclamation	(4)
Anamnesis	(1)
Offertory	[2]
Mention of sacrificial character	(2)

Epiclesis	(2)
Prayer for the acceptance of the sacrifice	(4)
Intercessions	[2]
Communion with the Church local and universal	(2)
Communion of the saints	(3)
Remembrance of the living	(3)
Remembrance of the dead	(3)
Mention of present concerns	(4)
Doxology	(1)
Amen	[1]

b. **Omissions of Major Sections in the Eucharistic Prayer, and the Underlying Operative Theology: Praise or Consecration**

The question is inevitably raised when examining a list of subsections of a Eucharistic Prayer (and their relative importance), "How important is this section *really?* What 'happens' if it is omitted?" The next two sections will deal specifically with the omission of the Institution Narrative and of the Epiclesis (or Invocation), but it would be good to speak a moment about sometimes unconscious, yet operative, theological presuppositions which influence discussions about omissions in Eucharistic Prayers.

The two extremes of the spectrum which describe the purpose of the Eucharistic Prayer are, on the one hand, a prayer of consecration which effects the "real presence" in the gifts of bread and wine, and, on the other hand, a memorial prayer of praise and thanks. The first view places major emphasis on the *part* of the prayer which is consecratory and after which exists the "real presence" of Christ in the elements (however that presence is understood in the different Christian traditions). The other view sees the prayer more as a whole, and puts major emphasis on grateful praise of God for all God's mighty works remembered in the prayer.

In recent centuries, the Eucharistic Prayer has been seen as primarily a prayer for consecrating the bread and wine. However, as we have seen, in its literary form, the Eucharistic Prayer is primarily a prayer of praise and thanksgiving to God the Father. Some modern authors (e.g., Guzie) conjecture that very early in the Christian era there was a shift in emphasis in the Eucharist from the action taking place (giving thanks), to the objects present (bread and wine). Even in the old Roman Missal, the central part of the Canon was termed "infra actione," showing that, in some sense, the Eucharistic Prayer was always considered as an "action."

If, for some reason, certain contemporary Eucharistic Prayers must be very short, at least some portion of the prayer should be devoted to the praise of God, for this prayer is primarily a blessing of the Father for his many gifts. The fact that the original concern of apostolic age Christians was to perform an action of thanksgiving should not be relegated to a secondary place no matter how short a Eucharistic Prayer needs to be. In the not too distant past, if a celebrant using the Roman Missal prayed a Eucharistic Prayer composed of the common preface and the Roman Canon, this prayer possessed no proclamation section at all. No reason was included as to why God should be praised. All that was mentioned was that it was right to praise and thank the Father. That was a far cry from the Canon of Hippolytus and other early prayers.

Quite often, discussions regarding the Institution Narrative and the Epiclesis are speaking with the background of a theology of consecration, and so the arguments deal more with what is needed to produce *real presence* than with what adds to the prayer as a memorial prayer of thanks and praise (cf. discussion of "moment of consecration" in Chapter 5; Keifer [4], p. 16). Recent writers are trying to emphasize the memorial aspect (anamnesis) of the Eucharistic Prayer more and more using the Hebrew concept of *zikkaron* spoken about above (cf. Chapter 8, section B). In this biblical concept, some scholars see a new view developing in trying to explain presence and the Eucharist, a view that enjoys the consensus of theologians of various traditions.

In considering the omission of the Institution Narrative and of the epiclesis, arguments will frequently be presupposing a theology of consecration, a theology which is considered somewhat outmoded today. However, this viewpoint must not be *totally* ignored in trying to move and develop newer theological opinions, for it is this theology of consecration which is very operative in the minds of most priests and laity today, at least in the Catholic tradition.

c. Omission of the Institution Narrative

There are two celebrated instances of ancient Eucharistic Prayers omitting the Institution Narrative—one is the Syrian Prayer of Addai and Mari, and the other is an Ethiopian Eucharistic Prayer. A few years ago, Dom B. Botte seemed to argue convincingly that both these prayers originally had Institution Narratives which had been lost in all existing manuscripts. However, more recent scholars are re-evaluating Botte's position (cf. Cutrone, Dix [p. 198 note], Kilmartin. However, cf. Talley [1], p. 134, for an opinion supportive of Botte).

Some authors today argue that the command of Jesus was to "do this in memory of me." He did not command Christians to narrate what he did, but just to repeat his actions in his memory. Therefore, although a prayer of blessing is necessary, since that is what the Lord did, some contemporary liturgists argue that we need not include in such a prayer a narrative of what Jesus did, but only need to have some sort of reference to the fact of the Last Supper. Some authors have similarly come to the conclusion that the very earliest Eucharistic Prayers did not include any narration of what happened at the Last Supper (i.e., Institution Narrative containing "words of consecration") (cf. Guzie, p. 115; Kilmartin, p. 276). However, some of these same authors will suggest that the Institution Narrative did occur somewhere in the course of the Eucharistic celebration, even though outside of the Eucharistic Prayer. In this sense, the Institution Narrative was "non-consecratory." It was used, it is suggested, as a formula for the distribution of the elements (cf. Kilmartin, p. 274). This thesis is supported by the presence and literary style of the Institution Narrative in 1 Corinthians 11, where Paul "hands on what I myself received," and then proceeds to narrate a very stylized account of the institution of the Eucharist—so stylized that most agree it must have been used frequently and repeatedly in some worship context. As was mentioned above in Chapter 3, the Institution Narrative probably became drawn into the early Eucharistic Prayers because of the primary importance that the early Christian community felt belonged to the thanksgiving for the works of redemption through Jesus, and the necessity for an explicit reason for remembering Christ (cf. above, Chapter 3; Talley [1], p. 130; Keifer [4], pp. 16–17).

Ralph Keifer (cf. [4]) also suggests that originally the Institution Narrative within Eucharistic Prayers may have only played the role of being a reminder of why the Eucharist was being celebrated, i.e., a true Narrative of the Institution of the Eucharist. At that time in history, the entire prayer was considered consecratory. Only later did the consecratory aspect become narrowly associated with the words of Christ said during the Institution Narrative. It was at this time that the Institution Narrative became less a part of the great thanksgiving (which was its original function; cf. above, Chapter 7, section A), and, in the minds of many believers, more of a semi-independent set of "words of consecration" (pp. 16–17).

In contemporary times, some Protestant usages place the Institution Narrative outside of the Eucharistic Prayer proper, and use the Narrative to preface the entire Liturgy of the Eucharist, thereby explaining the reason for its structure, or they use the Narrative to accompany the breaking of the bread (cf. *Word and*

Action, pp. 79ff.). In this position, some call it the "Gospel Warrant" for the Eucharistic Prayer, fraction, and Communion actions which follow. Many (myself included) feel, however, that such a departure from long-standing tradition is premature for most Christian communities, and, since the inclusion of the Institution Narrative has the overwhelming tradition of the Church to back it (only two exceptions found so far in ancient liturgies), contemporary Eucharistic Prayers should also include it. Even as recent as 1972, Lengeling includes the Institution Narrative as an indispensable part of the Eucharistic Prayer (cf. also Chapter 5).

The inclusion of the Institution Narrative can be viewed as an authentic early development of Christian practice, a development prompted by the inspiration of the Holy Spirit to keep the Christian community ever mindful of and ever faithful to its roots and origin. There were a number of such developments in the early centuries of the Church in almost every area of Christian life (and developments continue to occur even up to the present time as well). For example, in the first few centuries, the structure of ministry developed and became standardized, the major ritual actions (sacraments) became more and more concretized, and the theological understanding of the nature of Christ and of the Holy Spirit became developed and defined through conciliar acts. All areas of early Christian existence were touched by the Spirit and grew according to the guiding hand of God. Most Christians consider that such developments were good and necessary to keep Christians ever in touch with Christ and true to his message. In most cases, no one would consider reverting to a previous doctrinal formulation or to an earlier practice, after a period of growth, without serious considerations. To do that would be antiquarianism, rather than (a healthy) traditionalism.

In keeping with this, it seems to me that we should not lightly consider omitting the Institution Narrative from contemporary Eucharistic Prayers simply because very early Eucharistic

Prayers (probably) did not contain such a narrative (although the celebration they were used at may have had other ways of contextualizing what was happening), nor should we reduce the Institution Narrative to a simple reference to the Last Supper for the same reason. In particular, some Christian communities may even have legislation which makes such an innovation a very serious act. For example, the Roman Catholic Church considers the words of Christ in the Institution Narrative as the "form" of the sacrament, having been thus defined by the Council of Florence in 1450 (cf. Chapter 5). Thus, if a Roman Catholic priest used a Eucharistic Prayer which lacked an Institution Narrative, according to present Roman Catholic legislation, the service would *not* be a (juridically) valid Eucharist (in addition to being illicit), regardless of the historical conjectures mentioned in Chapter 3. This position is paralleled by other legislation regarding the validity of other sacraments, such as requiring the trinitarian formula for Baptism. In the case of Baptism, the formula "in the name of the Lord Jesus" is not considered valid for Baptism in the Roman Catholic Church, even though the biblical and historical evidence suggests that non-trinitarian and non-declarative formulas were actually used.[25] Juridically, an invalid act is to be repeated, since the first act is considered so defective in content as to nullify any hoped-for results. No doubt this legislation betrays an operative theology of consecration, but it is still the binding legislation for Roman Catholics.

There are many things which need to be considered when introducing any major changes (or omissions) into the contemporary structure of our Eucharistic Prayers. A pastoral judgment must be made in the light of the piety of a local community. A theological judgment must be made in the light of the contemporary understanding of Christianity. A liturgical judgment must be made in the light of the function that the various parts of the Eucharistic Prayer play in expressing our relationship to our God. On the one hand, we must not make ill-advised changes, without considering the major implications. Yet, on the other hand, we must also consider that some of the contemporary *suggestions* for future Eucharistic Prayers may actually be inspired by the Spirit and may lead to valid future *developments*—especially when those suggestions are based on a renewed understanding of and emphasis on the importance of anamnesis (*zikkaron*) and thanks in the Eucharistic Prayer. The Eucharistic Prayer can be considered a prayer of consecration only because it is first a prayer of thankful praise and remembrance. The Institution Narrative plays an important role because it is part of this remembrance and (as mentioned in Chapter 5) it helps to contextualize the action and the elements present. Yet it must itself be seen in the context of the entire Eucharistic Prayer.

d. Omission of the Invocation (Epiclesis)

There are many more authors who downplay the necessity of an epiclesis in comparison to those who permit the omission of the Institution Narrative. In fact, many contemporary prayers, even though they might have some reference to the Spirit (usually asking for the unity of Christians and therefore a "Communion epiclesis"), seemingly in an effort to move away from a theology of consecration, omit any reference to the Spirit sanctifying the bread and wine on the altar (i.e., a "consecratory epiclesis") (cf. Mossi). Often the authors of such prayers use the official Roman Catholic prayers as models, and since the Roman prayers split the epiclesis, the contemporary prayers often omit the first (consecratory) epiclesis and use only a remnant of the second (Communion) epiclesis instead, rather than recombining both aspects of a complete epiclesis into one.

It seems to me that this practice is unfortunate, especially for ecumenical purposes. The Eastern Orthodox Church in particular holds that the epiclesis is essential, since it is only by the power of the Spirit that any prayer becomes effective (this is consistent with their generally high regard for the action of the Spirit in

contrast to classical Western theologians). Thus, especially because of the way the epiclesis is worded in the Anaphora of St.
John Chrysostom, and due to the writings of some Church Fathers, particularly Cyril of Jerusalem (cf. above, Chapter 5), the
Orthodox hold that if a Eucharistic Prayer does not include, in
some form, a petition for the Spirit to transform the bread and
wine into the Body and Blood of Christ, the Eucharist is not
celebrated since an essential aspect is ignored. As one Orthodox
author puts it, the epiclesis is an expression of faith by the
assembled community that more is happening than a mere human commemoration of past deeds and events. The epiclesis, as a
prayer, expresses the belief that God is the source of all change
and that the Father hears the petitions of those who pray to him.
Rather than being something secondary, the epiclesis becomes
something essential (cf. Meyerdorff, p. 50; also Ryan [2] for a
very recent statement of East-West differences concerning the
Spirit and their liturgical implications). (As can be seen, these
arguments remain on the level of a theology of consecration,
although there is some concern for the memorial aspect of the
prayer.)

Even if one's theology remains on the level of "consecration," the epiclesis can help to complement the Western position
on the "moment of consecration," usually limited to the recitation of the words of Christ in the Institution Narrative. A complete epiclesis in a Eucharistic Prayer can help the faithful to view
the entire prayer as consecratory, rather than as just one particular section. However, lacking any sort of developed epiclesis, a
Eucharistic Prayer normally peaks at the Institution Narrative,
reinforcing a Western theological position which many contemporary theologians would rather see broadened. (An even better
emphasis, according to many contemporary authors, would be to
concentrate on the total *anamnesis*, however.) The downplaying
of the epiclesis is consistent with the seeming disregard of the

Holy Spirit in Western Christianity as a whole. This is seen in the Filioque controversy (which can be seen as an attempt to theologically subject and channel the Spirit through the Son). Also, even as recent as the Second Vatican Council, we have no major statement on the Holy Spirit in any decree, even though there is a whole chapter on the Mother of God.

In contrast to the position which sees the epiclesis as essential, other authors take a milder view. The prayer of Christians is, of necessity, trinitarian. A Christian prays, impulsed by the Spirit, to the Father, through the Son (cf. Rom. 1:8, Gal. 4:6). If a prayer is truly Christian, no aspect is ignored, even though it might not always be expressed. Thus, in the Eucharistic Prayer, the *evocation* of the Spirit is integral to the prayer since it is a prayer of Christians (cf. Lengeling above, section A). However, the *invocation* is only a subsidiary part, since, as a berakah, the invocation is a petition and petitions are secondary to the anamnesis of the berakoth, that is, the proclamation and memorial of God's goodness. Authors holding this position would permit the occasional or even regular omission of an epiclesis (although one could still be consistent and require the presence of some sort of epiclesis).

The epiclesis is also an occasion to introduce the ancient Jewish imposition of hands, a sign of blessing, into the Eucharistic Prayer. Such an imposition has been reintroduced into the Roman Liturgies and almost all sacramental actions as a significant symbolism in the various rites. Eliminating an epiclesis from a Eucharistic Prayer would also eliminate the possibility of using such a gesture of blessing (also cf. below, Chapter 12, section B, for more on the imposition of hands and gestures during the Eucharistic Prayer).

The frequent omission of (the consecratory part of) the epiclesis in many contemporary prayers often results in more references to the Spirit being included in prayers during the preparation of the gifts. As a result, quite often the extemporaneous prayers which occur during the preparation of the gifts contain the notions of offering and sanctification by the Spirit which properly and originally occurred within the Eucharistic Prayer.

In his recent paper on the epiclesis, Fr. John McKenna poses the question, "Is an epiclesis necessary in a Eucharistic Prayer?" To this question he gives the following discussion:

> To pose the question in terms of absolute necessity, however, is to chance tending in the direction of a sacramental minimalism. And one should build one's theology, and practice, not on the minimum required but upon the ideal or, at least, the normal. (p. 281)

While unwilling to make a "god out of any formula, be it institution narrative or epiclesis" ([2] p. 204), McKenna nonetheless suggests that the question of an epiclesis be considered in terms of a *practical* necessity.

> For it belongs to the nature of man to give some expression to his deepest beliefs and feelings or to risk having them stagnate. It is not enough simply to believe or intend something. It is necessary to express this belief or intention in some word or gesture. . . .
>
> Similarly it is a practical necessity for the eucharistic assembly to express its awareness, for instance, of the necessary intervention of the Holy Spirit and of its own need for a praying or "epiclesis" attitude. If it fails to do so, the assembly runs the risk of having this awareness stagnate or fall into the oblivion of forgetfulness. It pertains, moreover, to symbolic activity to express and deepen man's, and in this case the assembly's, beliefs and feelings. And within this symbolic activity it is usually the spoken word which possesses a value superior to the sign or action in giving voice to these beliefs.
>
> It is in view of all this that we would maintain that

an epiclesis proper is a *practical* necessity in the realization of the Eucharist. The epiclesis is not the only means of expressing the role of the Holy Spirit in the Eucharist, the total dependence of the praying assembly, the unity between "consecration" and Communion, etc. It is, however, a pre-eminent means of expressing these important aspects of the eucharistic celebration. ([2] pp. 205–06)

e. Other Omissions

The omission of the Intercessions was commented upon above in the preceding chapter along with the omission of the *Sanctus*. Except for a stylized introduction, which is universal, almost every major section (as an identifiable component part) has been omitted from some official Eucharistic Prayer presently in use, or from some ancient prayer. This is not to say that there are no essential parts of a Eucharistic Prayer. Rather, this exhibits the fact that different sections seem to be essential at different points in history and that some sections seem to compensate for others when those have been omitted. (It should be noted, however, that the paschal mystery of Christ's death and resurrection has been included in virtually every Eucharistic Prayer. When there is no post-Institution Narrative anamnesis section, the paschal mystery is usually mentioned in the pre-Institution Narrative proclamation section instead.)

On occasion, the opposite phenomenon occurs, in which the anamnesis occurs more than once, or the Eucharistic Prayer occurs in two or three sections each of which ends with its own doxology (cf. Anaphora of Addai and Mari). This practice, it seems to me, although it does follow the example of the *birkat ha-mazon,* has the major disadvantage of presenting the Eucharistic Prayer as a group of prayers, thereby destroying its unity (cf. also Chapter 16, section A).

Section Five

NON-STRUCTURAL COMMENTS, CONSIDERATIONS, CONCERNS

Chapter Twelve
THE BODY AT PRAYER: SYMBOLIC GESTURE

a. Gestures During the Eucharistic Prayer

The Roman Missal prescribes a number of gestures by the presider as he proclaims the Eucharistic Prayer. There are two genuflections during the Institution Narrative, an imposition of hands (with a sign of the cross over the bread and wine) during the first epiclesis, taking and elevating both the bread and the cup with wine during the Institution Narrative, a great elevation of the paten with the bread and the cup during the final doxology, and, in the Roman Canon, a bow of the body at the second epiclesis. In the *Book of Common Prayer* (Episcopal Church), there is a touching of all the elements during the Institution Narrative. In the Byzantine rite, the elements are pointed to (with a sort of imposition of hands) during the Institution Narrative, are raised during the offertory section of the prayer in a "great elevation," and the sign of the cross is made over them during the epiclesis. The priest also makes a few small bows and incenses the altar and gifts during the commemorations. The question can be raised as to what are really appropriate gestures (if any) during the Eucharistic Prayer.

A growing number of scholars are suggesting that the only

appropriate gesture during the Eucharistic Prayer is the ancient
gesture of prayer—arms extended with palms heavenward in the
"orantes" gesture of prayer. However, throughout the history of
Christian worship, other gestures have entered the liturgical
books, to be performed during the recitation of the Eucharistic
Prayer. Most of these gestures center around the Institution
Narrative, and in some way imitate the gestures of Christ which
are being narrated (except that usually the bread is *not* broken).
The Roman rite, especially in its recently revised form, has tried
to highlight the gesture of the imposition of hands during the
epiclesis section of the Eucharistic Prayer (see below). In addition, almost every tradition has also included some sort of gesture
of elevation or offering of the gifts heavenward in conjunction
with either the offertory section or the final doxology. But, as
mentioned above, some scholars suggest that any gesture during
the Institution Narrative is inappropriate. The Institution Narrative is recited as a part of a general remembrance of the *mirabilia
Dei*, but it is done in a context of prayer. Thus, they argue, the
proper gesture is a gesture indicating prayer, that is, arms extended.

A short comment is probably appropriate concerning the
orans or *orantes* gesture of prayer—that is, praying with arms
extended out from the sides of the body, slightly forward (at
about right angles to each other), raised about shoulder high,
with palms open facing upward. As a Christian gesture, it is
probably based on 1 Timothy 2:8, "I desire then that in every
place the men should pray, lifting holy hands, without anger or
quarreling." This Christian practice was probalby influenced by
earlier Jewish practices, for there are numerous references in the
Hebrew Scriptures, especially in the psalter, to praying with
uplifted hands (cf. 1 Kgs. 8:22, 38, 54; 2 Chr. 6:12, 13; Pss. 28:2;
44:20; 63:4; 68:31; 143:6; Is. 1:15, *et al.*). In earlier centuries, it
seems that the gestures of the people were the same as those of
the presider, the result being that especially during the Eucharis-

tic Prayer, everyone joined the presider in praying with arms extended in the *orantes* posture. This is documented both by drawings and ikons of the third to fifth centuries, and also by various writings, especially of St. John Chrysostom (*In Phil. hom.* 3, 4 [PG 52, 204]) and of St. Ambrose of Milan (*De Sacr.* VI, 4, 17). This common practice of all present extending their arms in prayer continued in some places much later. It was known to occur in Switzerland during parts of the Eucharistic Prayer until the fifteenth century and remained the practice in some monastic communities even later. It has even reoccurred in contemporary Christian groups among some charismatics (cf. Jungman [1], vol. I, p. 239).

The only other gestures that could be admitted during the Eucharistic Prayer would seem to be the imposition of hands (see below) and possibly a bowing of the body at the supplication section (cf. above, Chapter 9). Although some ritual books prescribe other gestures, especially during the Institution Narrative, these gestures tend to break up the unity of the prayer form and distract from the basic concept of the Eucharistic Prayer as prayer (cf. Perham, pp. 13–14). Thus, any gesture which is used should help the community present understand that the Eucharistic Prayer is a prayer of praise and thanks, which forms a unified whole and which brings to life in the community the mystery of the death and resurrection of Jesus Christ.

b. Imposition of Hands During the Eucharistic Prayer

The gesture of the imposition of hands is a deeply significant gesture which in practice is frequently overlooked by many presiders. Yet in liturgical history and theology, it is considered so important that it has been reintroduced in most of the revised liturgical rites in the Roman rite of the Catholic Church. Some scholars such as Yves Congar suggest that the reintroduction of the imposition of hands may be one of the most important consequences of the Second Vatican Council, and other scholars such as Godfrey Diekmann suggest that the imposition of hands is actually the basic sacramental rite (pp. 22, 27). In liturgical history, the imposition of hands (seemingly derived from the simple gesture of touching) is the sign of transferring God's power, of transferring a special office, or of imparting the Holy Spirit. Many very early Christian liturgical texts mention with unusual prominence an action of touching or an "imposition of hands." The Gospels tell us time and time again that Jesus touched the sick to cure them, and the narratives of the Last Supper in the Christian Scriptures mention that Jesus "took" bread and then "took" the cup (cf. p. 26).

The gesture of the "imposition of hands" admits of some minor variants, but it basically consists of the presider extending his arms in front of him, almost parallel to each other, palms downward or toward the object or person(s) concerned. In some situations, the hands may be placed on the head of a person, such as at an ordination, or actually touch an object, such as is done by Episcopalians during the Eucharistic Prayer (cf. Appendix A). Such a practice finds a foundation in the Book of Leviticus regarding objects for sacrifice (e.g., Lev. 1:4; 3:2, 8, 18; 4:4; *et passim*). At other times, the hands may be extended over an object or a group of people without actually touching it (them). Such is the practice in the Roman Catholic Church during the invocation of the Spirit in the Eucharistic Prayer, and even seems to be the ancient method employed by "concelebrating" presbyters to indicate their union with the presiding bishop in offering the Eucharistic Prayer, as portrayed by Hippolytus (cf. Appendix A).

Some scholars suggest that the former neglect (and even present oversight) of Western Christians toward the importance of the gesture of the imposition of hands is connected to the lack of an adequate understanding of the role of the Holy Spirit in the sacred rites of Western Christianity. We tend to pay too much lip-service to the role of the Spirit in our rites and not enough practical changes are actually made. Besides being overlooked in the Eucharistic Prayer, the importance of the Spirit and the gesture of the imposition of hands is similarly being overlooked by many Catholic priests in the revised rites of Anointing the Sick and Reconciliation of Penitents as well, where the recent revisions have also tried to restore this gesture to its early importance.

Frequently, presiders using contemporary prayers will completely omit any gesture of imposition of hands. This may be due to the deficiencies of some contemporary prayers which exhibit a very poor pneumatology. But it is also due, at times, to the lack of understanding by those who preside of the full meaning of gesture in a ritual action. There is more and more of a tendency to become wordier and wordier in our rites of worship, and to see ritual gesture as less and less important (cf. Gusmer, p. 287). However, perhaps nowhere is a gesture more appropriate during the Eucharistic Prayer than when the Spirit is invoked, and then the gesture of imposition of hands upon both the gifts and the entire community present can remind us of and reinforce in us the importance of this gesture in all of our religious rites.

Chapter Thirteen
PASTORAL PRACTICALITIES

a. Choosing a Eucharistic Prayer

Many different facts and opinions have appeared in the preceding chapters. All this knowledge is ultimately geared for one major purpose—to enable individuals to intelligently evaluate Eucharistic Prayers. The one to whom this burden falls most frequently is the presider, especially when a decision must be made as to which Eucharistic Prayer should be used for a given Eucharist. Twenty years ago in most Churches, this decision was simple, since there was usually only one lawful Eucharistic Prayer permitted. However, today, decisions are not so easy. A Roman Catholic priest has nine official prayers to choose from, although not all choices are available for use in every situation. An Episcopal priest, by using the "outline" Eucharistic Prayers found in "Rite 3" of the *Book of Common Prayer* (cf. Appendix A) in effect has an unlimited number of options, and thus could use, for example, the first part of any Eucharistic Prayer included in any of the many collections of contemporary prayers published in the last ten years (e.g., Mossi, Dallen, Hoey). It is obvious that not every Eucharistic Prayer written, whether it be ancient or contemporary, authorized or unauthorized, is of equal value or usefulness for a given Eucharist. A presider in such a situation must make a choice, and must base the choice on some reasons, however informed or not-so-informed these reasons may be. It is especially in situations such as these that much of what is contained in this book may be helpful.

Certainly a prayer should *not* be chosen *solely* because it is long/short/old/new/official/unauthorized. The structural comments which occurred in previous chapters should be seriously taken to heart whenever a judgment must be made. Some preliminary questions should be asked—for example, Does a given prayer exhibit a good structure and flow? Does it contain all the major parts? There are also some literary considerations which will be mentioned in the next chapter and which should be taken into account as well.

Mere age does not tilt the balance in favor of one prayer or the other either. Not all prayer texts and euchological treasures that history has given us as patrimony can be considered true family heirlooms. Some texts are merely ancient refuse which pious individuals keep on unearthing and using instead of leaving them in museums along with other mummies of ages past. For example, many people would consider the Eucharistic Prayer of Basil the Great, which forms the basis of Roman Eucharistic Prayer IV, Episcopal Eucharistic Prayer D, and the "Common Eucharistic Prayer," as a true gem and heirloom. The same people would consider the Roman Canon (Roman Eucharistic Prayer I), which dates from around the same time, as an ancient disaster which should be removed from common use and stored in a liturgical museum.

Length is another consideration. Just because a prayer is short does not mean it is best. The presider may be depriving the assembly of beautiful (and helpful) theological expressions of prayer (found in other possible prayers) by consistent use of only the shortest of all possible prayers. On the other hand, certain long prayers may be too much for certain congregations (e.g., school children), but quite suitable for others (e.g., charismatic groups, cloistered nuns, retreat groups). Long prayers (especially some contemporary versions) have a tendency to include all of salvation history in their proclamation sections. As a result, in many cases, the congregation gets bored and their attention is lost. The proper length, then, seems to be one which is long enough to have a balanced proclamation section, but not so long that many in the congregation get distracted only part-way through the prayer.

Whether we are evaluating ancient prayers or contemporary prayers, whether we do this just as an academic exercise or for the purpose of deciding which prayer to use at a given Eucharist, we must base our decisions on some norms for judgment. In making our decision, we are, in effect, determining to the best of our abilities what is wheat and what is chaff, or, shall we say, separating rhinestones from diamonds, and iron pyrites from 24 karat true gold.

b. Singing the Eucharistic Prayer

It has been traditional in the Western Church to sing the preface of the Eucharistic Prayer and at least part of the doxology at solemn celebrations. In recent years, after the Roman Canon was permitted to be pronounced aloud, the Institution Narrative has on occasion also been sung. In the East, usually only part of the preface was sung, but in many rites the words of the Lord were almost always sung.

Several contemporary attempts have been made to compose Eucharistic Prayers which are in the form of verses to an antiphonal song. The presider sings the verses which form the Eucharistic Prayer, and the congregation makes its response and participates by singing the refrain. On occasion, a schola or choir may be given a section in addition to the congregational parts to embellish the prayer. An example of such a prayer may be found in the *Experimental Liturgy Book* (p. 54, #610). However, this example seems to have a fundamental flaw since it is addressed to the congregation and not to God the Father. The choice of the song to which the verses are written may also be faulted in this instance—"Sons of God."

When an existing prayer (or a new composition) is adapted and modified to fit the pattern of a metrical verse or even a free-length chant style verse, some minor liberties with sections of the Eucharistic Prayer may be tolerated. However, music should not become the excuse for omitting major parts of the prayer, or for changing the form from that of the Jewish berakah. It should be remembered that music should serve as an aid to the proclamation of the Eucharistic Prayer. Music should not so become the object of concentration that the idea of thankful praying in memory of Jesus is overlooked or lost.

c. **The Use of Unauthorized Eucharistic Prayers**

As was mentioned above, many liturgists today advocate the use of more Eucharistic Prayers. Unfortunately, Church authorities do not usually comply with these wishes. As a result many local communities do use contemporary prayers, even though they have not been approved by the communities' ecclesiastical authorities. This practice, in many cases, produces an obvious tension.

In the summer of 1973, the Vatican issued a letter to Roman Catholic bishops throughout the world concerning the use of Eucharistic Prayers in the Roman rite. In this letter, Rome also gives us its reasons why only approved prayers should be used. The following paragraphs are taken from that letter.

> The ecclesial dimension of the eucharistic celebration should be considered paramount. . . . In the eucharistic prayer . . . it is not just an individual person, nor even a local community but "the one and only Catholic Church, existing in the local churches" [II Vat. Coun., *Church* #23] that addresses itself to God.

Whenever eucharistic prayers are used without any approval of the Church's authority, unrest and even dissensions arise, not only among priests, but with the communities themselves, even though the Eucharist should be a "sign of unity, and the bond of charity" [Augustine, *In Joannis* 26:13, cf. *Liturgy* #47]. Many people complain about the overly subjective quality of such texts, and participants have a right to make such a complaint. Otherwise the eucharistic prayer, to which they give their assent in the "Amen" they proclaim, becomes disorderly, or is imbued with the personal feelings of the person who either composes or says it.

Hence it is necessary to demand that only those eucharistic prayers be used which have been approved by the lawful authority of the Church, for they clearly and fully manifest the sentiments of the Church.

With a similar concern about unauthorized Eucharistic Prayers, Fr. Frederick McManus, the former Director of the U.S. Bishops' Committee on the Liturgy and a long-time advocate of liturgical renewal in the U.S., makes these comments in an article published in 1974:

> . . . a large proportion of original presidential prayers are apparently untheological, unliturgical and out of context. There seem to be a good many priests who do not even know whether they are addressing God the Father or God the Son. Similar weaknesses are found in original eucharistic prayers which have been published or reported. One extreme example is supposed to consist of a lengthy exhortation to the people rather than a *confessio* addressed to God; it is a series of invitations to the assembled congregation, interrupted once, perhaps because of a minimalistic sacramental theology, by the Last Supper narrative. Priests who employ such texts or com-

pose them are unlikely to be concerned with the pastoral or moral problems that may be associated with liturgical law. (p. 352)

In a recent issue of the *National Bulletin on Liturgy* of the Canadian Conference of Catholic Bishops (Vol. 13, Nov.–Dec. 1980), we read a similar evaluation of some contemporary prayers.

A calm assessment of home-made eucharistic prayers shows their shortcomings: they are often much too localized in time and space to be true reflections of the prayer of the Church on earth and in heaven; too often they exhibit the hang-ups and problems of the persons or communities who compose them. (p. 223)

Fr. McManus, the Canadian Liturgy Bulletin, and Fr. Tegels (see below, Chapter 14, section B) object to the use of some of the newer Eucharistic Prayers because they are frequently liturgically and theologically unsound. Besides giving that reason, the Roman document gives us a reason which is more theological—the unity of the Church. Although the Roman document did mention the necessity to examine prayers for their "proper" content, the basic reason given for using only approved prayers is the unity of the Church.

Let me attempt to give a small explanation of what is involved in the objection given by the Roman document. The unity of the Church has traditionally been expressed by communion of the faithful with the local bishop and the communion of bishops with one another. (This was spoken of in slightly greater length in Chapter 4.) If a given priest or local Christian community celebrates the liturgy in a manner different from that approved by the local bishop, they act in violation of Church law, and in this way they do damage to the unity of the Church—a unity dearly prayed for by Christ himself on the night before he died (Jn. 17:21).

Communion with the bishops and obedience to their wishes need not mean total uniformity or restricted liturgies. Quite the contrary. In the very early Church, there were no regulations concerning the Eucharist—those who presided (probably) used the variants of Jewish meal prayers (cf. Chapter 2). The presider prayed as best he could, led by the Spirit and (we hope) sensitive to the community. Gradually (it seems) prayers became written down and repeated, and presiders began to feel less free in composing new prayers. In a third century manuscript, we do find St. Hippolytus mentioning that a bishop could extemporize the Eucharistic Prayer if he wished (see Appendix A). However, as Fr. Tegels mentions ([1], p. 502), we have no evidence that priests (presbyters) associated with the bishops were allowed the same freedom. In our contemporary world, considering the total number of Eastern Churches in union with the See of Rome, the number of officially authorized Eucharistic Prayers in use by Roman Catholics throughout the world numbers around 150. With the amount of liberty allowed by Eucharistic Prayers 1 and 2 approved by the Episcopal Church in the United States (see Appendix A), an enormous amount of freedom is allowed an individual priest. However, in both of these cases, the individual priests, and the communities they serve, celebrate the Eucharist according to norms approved by their respective bishops and so there is no affront to the unity of the Church.

The question of the use of unauthorized Eucharistic Prayers also raises the much bigger question of (educated) dissent in the Church. Granted that we may agree that violating Church laws in some way does damage to unity in the Church, is it still possible that the subject with which the law deals is in reality so minor that the disunity that a violation of the law regarding it causes may be considered almost nil?

Some may suggest that the use of a new prayer is, in certain situations, just an example of appropriate dissent against restrictive and relatively minor legislation. But are all the assumptions made in this statement actually true? Would the use of such a new prayer truly be "appropriate" dissent? In most Churches, there are legal means available to express constructive dissent, and these means may ultimately speak more eloquently than disobedient non-observance of certain laws. Is such a law restrictive or of minor importance? In some Churches, the centrality of the Eucharist in the life of the Church (and the centrality of the Eucharistic Prayer in the celebration of the Eucharist) may make certain legislation concerning the Eucharist (and the Eucharistic Prayer) of major importance. In this situation, the centrality of the Eucharist itself, rather than hierarchical authority, is what makes such laws expressive of true unity, rather than being restrictive of true liberty.

Dissent is nothing new in the Church. St. Paul disagreed with St. Peter (Gal. 2:11ff.) and convinced Peter to change his ways. In areas which do not deal with defined Church doctrine, it is possible that present theological speculation may eventually lead to further development and renewal in Christian life.

Such speculation may even include calls to change what may seem to some as being overly-restricting established practices. We noted above that due to requests from scholars and bishops alike, the Roman Catholic Church now theoretically allows new prayers to be composed, but insists that they be properly approved by legitimate authority before actual public use. However, critics may point out that, in spite of this recent legislation, very few new prayers have appeared for general use!

As can easily be seen from the points raised, the entire question is very advanced and complicated, and requires correspondingly sophisticated arguments, much more sophisticated than I have tried to propose here. What I have tried to do here is to raise the point that the use of unauthorized prayers is a bigger question than *just* violating a law of some authority (it has more implications than, for example, going through a red light).

One should also realize that there may be certain liturgical practices which, on the surface, may seem to be very minor adaptations, but in reality may even be more seriously harmful to good and lawful liturgy than the use of an unauthorized Eucharistic Prayer. For example, Keifer suggests that a communally recited Eucharistic Prayer is actually worse than an unauthorized Eucharistic Prayer (cf. [3], p. 140).

Such is the tension inherent in the Church. The need to express a given community's love of God must at times be tempered by the wishes of those who have been given charge over that community—the bishop of the diocese. Which is more important—the wishes of the local community, or the unity of the Church as expressed (in one relatively minor yet still significant way) by obedience to the liturgical norms of a given bishop? The implications of Christian unity are not always easy—it involves give and take, and at times pain and restriction. A certain hypothetical community may come to a point in the development of its spiritual life that it sees the use of unauthorized Eucharistic Prayers as a viable option in its daily liturgical life for numerous reasons and does not see this practice as severing or damaging Christian unity in any way (it is even possible that the unauthorized prayers may be more expressive of unity of the local community with the bishop and [in the case of Catholics] with the Pope than those prayers presently authorized).

In response, one can validly raise the question of how this particular community (and its presider[s]), views "unity." Is it some amorphous concept, free-floating, like smog, which is "out there," but which does not concern them in the concrete? Or, is it practical, like the concrete actions of love shown in the assigned chores done by members of a family? And, one may also raise the question of how this particular action by our hypothetical community might be viewed by members of the larger Church not part of this community. Would others see the use of an unauthorized prayer as an act of loving union or of defiant disobedience? Both the council of Jerusalem (Acts 15, Gal 2) and St. Paul (1 Cor

8) grappled with the subtleties of restrictions placed on some Christians for the sake of others who may have weaker faith. The gospels quote Jesus as even being more blunt about this matter (cf. Mt 18:6–7, "better for him if a millstone were tied around his neck"). Even if a given community does not share the same opinions about the importance of certain practices held by the larger Church with which they considered themselves united (e.g. using only certain prayer-texts as the central prayer in the celebration of the Eucharist—the central sacrament of Christian life), nevertheless, they should not ignore these opinions or arbitrarily hold themselves excused from those practices either. In the end, we must agree that no community which *totally* neglects all the many levels of the unity of the Church can be said to fully realize what they are doing when they celebrate the Eucharist, which is *the* sacrament of unity. Every group of Christians must always pray that they be kept open to the promptings of the Spirit and that their actions do aid the spreading of the Christian message.

Chapter Fourteen
SOME LITERARY CONSIDERATIONS

a. Stance of the Celebrant

Once in a while Eucharistic Prayers are written for occasions where the focus of the celebration is on certain individuals present in the congregation, such as a couple about to be married. If the source of the prayer is not well known, it should be examined with regard to the "stance of the speaker."

The person who proclaims the Eucharistic Prayer represents the entire praying community. The prayer is made in the name of the community. The "we" which is used in the prayer is the "we" which includes all present at the Eucharist being celebrated in union with the entire Church. When a prayer is composed for a wedding or similar occasion, the author of such a prayer must keep this in mind. Prayers have been written for such occasions which should have been said by the wedding couple (or others), and which were truly prayers of those individuals. However, because of the literary stance of the composer of the prayer, such prayers were inconsistent coming from the lips of the presider and praying in the name of the entire community. All references in such prayers were solely to the wedding couple (or other individuals) as if no one else (including the presider) were present at the celebration.

Although this problem has the possibility of occurring only very infrequently, nevertheless, when such situations do occur, such a prayer should be examined to see that it is a prayer of the entire assembled community, even though a married couple or other individuals may have a special reference made to them during the Intercessions of the prayer.[26]

b. Choice of Language and Terms

"De gustibus non est disputandum" (no one can argue about taste), yet in general a few basic principles should be observed about the language used in the Eucharistic Prayer. This is a solemn and sacred ritual action, even in the most casual and secular of settings. For this reason, the language employed should reflect the dignity of what is happening.

Many people are open to alternative Eucharistic Prayers, but because of the language employed in the ones they have heard in use, they frequently prefer the official prayers (although limited in number) to the many alternatives available. Frequently contemporary compositions are theologically unsound and grammatically incorrect. Often, well-worn clichés are used which detract from rather than aid the worship taking place. Fr. Aelred Tegels, O.S.B., the editor of *Worship,* made this comment recently:

> We have found unauthorized texts often rather wordy and repetitious, cliché-ridden, and subjective in expression; we would not regard most of them as superior, in any important respect, to the authorized texts. ([1], p. 502)

Oftentimes, the presider (or the planner) has not taken into account the congregation present, so that, instead of being the prayer of the assembled community, the Eucharistic Prayer becomes a series of statements proclaimed to a community for which it is ill-suited. I have heard one presider pray, "We thank you for pancakes and waffles, for donuts and dumplings." Rather than aiding the congregation, in this instance some of them left the Eucharist at that point, and many of those who stayed did so only because they felt that leaving would do more harm than good.

Some Eucharistic Prayers contain highly technical or hard-to-pronounce words. "Mechanistical" can be a tongue-twister in normal conversation, and much more so in a prayer. The Eucharistic Prayer then becomes an exercise for the presider to convey the meaning of something which only a scholar can understand. Some words, when pronounced, can sound so much like another word that a presider has to be very careful about his pronunciation so that he is not misunderstood. "Depth of your love" often sounds like "death of your love." Other examples may be given, but I think that the point has been made. As one scholar commented, a Eucharistic Prayer should be able to be used in almost any situation for almost any group with a minimum of change.

English-speaking people have a particular problem in trying to develop a suitable "liturgical English" since our language is in more of a state of flux than most people are willing to admit. Words, phrases and grammatical forms that we once considered appropriate for religious usage now seem hopelessly out-of-date and out-of-touch with our contemporary mentality (e.g., thee, thou, quicketh, etc., i.e., a "King James Version" religious English). Our written literature is also changing from a body of words meant to be spoken to one that is primarily meant to be read, and this holds for both novels and other works of prose as well as for poetry. Yet, at the same time, because of modern means of mass communication (radio, television, movies), some feel that we are entering a new age of illiteracy. Some critics also suggest that English-speakers may well be losing the ability to write English that is dignified and can be understood by a *listener* and not only by a reader.

In particular, among Roman Catholics, there has been much

criticism of the liturgical texts prepared by the official body of translators, the International Commission for English in the Liturgy, or ICEL (pronounced "eye-cell"). Critics have complained about mistranslations, misinterpretations, banal language, "street talk," etc. Yet, some of the alternatives proposed tend to use a style of English more suited to forty of fifty years ago, with long relative clauses and other grammatical constructions which nowadays are being used less and less often in common speech. There is no easy solution to the problems raised by these critics. The addition of a few picturesque words ("sky-blue waters," "wine-red mountains") does not necessarily or automatically make great poetry, yet, at the same time, authors and translators should not limit themselves to a vocabulary of the most common English words and to a style that resembles the daily newspaper. The language used should be biblically-based (using biblical images), dignified, "elevated," reminiscent of good poetry, meant to be *listened to* (and not only read). It should not embarrass a poorly educated person, nor be offensive to a person with two or three doctorates, yet it should inspire both toward a greater love of God and neighbor and lead them on to a deeper contemplation of the Christian mystery (cf. Toporoski).

c. **Theme Versus Event**

Quite often, the desire for a new Eucharistic Prayer stems from the desire to have all the variable elements of the liturgy reinforce a given theme. Such a theme may have been suggested by the readings of the lectionary, or the feast of the day, or the special circumstances that the worshiping community finds itself in (e.g., a retreat). Such a variation in the Eucharistic Prayer finds precedent in the Roman tradition of the variable preface. However, such thematic variations are generally foreign to most of the Eastern liturgical families.

The advisability of thematic liturgies still remains a debated question. Many writers favor them. However, other writers raise valid questions. Fr. Patrick Regan, O.S.B., former book review editor of *Worship*, comments as follows:

> Preoccupation with theme is as foreign to liturgy as it is to celebration in general. Celebration stems from events, not abstract concepts. Of course, thematic services do make use of evangelical events, but only insofar as they bear upon the chosen theme. By subordinating the gospel event to a previously agreed upon theme, the participants do not surrender to the event on its own terms, but grasp only that aspect of it which pertains to their purpose, thereby closing themselves to the possibility of receiving the event as it reveals and confers itself in its own freedom, and receiving instead more confirmation of their own thematic construct. This is neither celebration nor liturgy. It is self-gratification. (p. 600)

Even as recent as the summer of 1975, Dr. H. C. Schmidt-Lauber, at the biennial congress of Societas Liturgica in Germany, cast doubts on the usefulness of theme Eucharistic Prayers (Ryan [3], p. 562). It seems that the major reservation that some scholars have is that a person or congregation can easily get preoccupied with a theme and thereby overlook the fact that God is theme-less, or, rather, that thematizing God is putting huge constraints on all that God is. The Eucharist should broaden human horizons. Too often, theme liturgies inadvertently do the opposite.

d. Thanks Versus Praise

In his famous paper published in 1959, Fr. Jean-Paul Audet, O.P. examined the literary form and the words used in early Eucharistic Prayers and in biblical berakoth. His conclusion, which was also accepted by Lash and by Kavanaugh in subsequent publications, was that "thanksgiving" was much too narrow a classification for all that a Jew felt when praying a berakah.

He suggested that we would more profitably employ the word "praise" rather than "thanks" when discussing the berakoth and Eucharistic Prayers. In a paper published in 1967, Fr. Robert J. Ledogar generally accepts Fr. Audet's position and sees it as a great contribution toward a better understanding of the Eucharistic Prayer and its literary form. However, Ledogar suggests that tbe concept of "thanks" is still a valid way to express a major human emotion felt in the Eucharistic Prayer. He argues that Hebrew does not contain any word which we could directly translate as "thanksgiving." (However, the main verb in the second section of the *birkat ha-mazon, nodah,* is usually translated as "thanksgiving" even though it means "acknowledge" or "confess," derived from *yadah,* meaning "to point out"; cf. Chapter 2 above; Kadushin, p. 72; Talley [1], pp. 123, 128–30.) As a result, the Greek words used to translate Hebrew berakoth are not usually forms of the Greek word for giving thanks, *eucharistein* (Ledogar, p. 587). However, Ledogar suggests this does not mean that the emotion of gratitude was not present in a person praying a Hebrew berakah—Hebrew just had no (exclusive) word to express that emotion. Ledogar goes on to suggest that the Christian community had an authentic insight when the main verb which was used in its central prayer was *eucharistein,* "to give thanks" (cf. also above, Chapter 2). Thomas Talley agrees with Ledogar in seeing the change from "bless" or "praise" to "thanks" as distinctively Christian (cf. [1], esp. pp. 126–37). He suggests that the pre-eminence of thanksgiving is the reason why the two concepts have been inverted in the prayers found in the *Didache* (cf. above, Chapter 2), and also why, in many early prayers, "praise" is taken into "thanks," so that there are only two main motifs in the prayer, thanks and intercession, rather than three sections of praise, thanksgiving, and supplication as in the *birkat ha-mazon.*

As usual, both writers make very valid points. An over-emphasis on thanksgiving can obscure a wider praise of God the

Father. Similarly, concentration on praise can neglect specific items for which a community should give thanks.

Similarly, thanks and praise can also portray a tension between gift and gift-giver. When we thank someone, we usually are concerned with a gift which that person has given us. When we praise and honor someone, we are usually more concerned with the person as a whole, rather than any specific deed he has done.

Some contemporary Eucharistic Prayers contain whole litanies of objects for which the community gives thanks. However, such prayers seem, in some sense, to overlook the real depth of being that God has by concentrating on created objects alone. Similarly, once in a while a person finds a Eucharistic Prayer which praises and gives honor to God for all that he is in himself. But such prayers can overlook any relation of God to the human race. As usual, the ideal falls somewhere between the two extremes.

Chapter Fifteen
THE FUTURE

a. Other Literary Forms for the Eucharistic Prayer

Throughout this discussion on the Eucharistic Prayer, a basic presupposition has been that Christians must use some variation of the Jewish berakah. Is this necessarily the case? Could the form of the Eucharistic Prayer develop to a non-berakah style in the future? In a recent book by Fr. C. J. McNaspy, S.J., an example of a contemporary Eucharistic Liturgy was presented in which the "Eucharistic Prayer" consisted of the Institution Narrative alone, preceded by a very short consecratory epiclesis (pp. 78–81). Similarly, in some contemporary Protestant services, the Eucharistic Prayer seems to be reduced (for all practical purposes) to a recitation of an account of the Last Supper, sometimes preceded by a short preface and *Sanctus.* Examples of such liturgies can be found in the contemporary Lutheran service book entitled *Liturgies for Life* (cf. pp. 23–27—Mk. 14:22–25; pp. 75–78—1 Cor. 11:23b–26). The recently revised *Lutheran Book of Worship* (1978) provides three forms of a Eucharistic Prayer—a short form which is the Institution Narrative alone (following the preface and *Sanctus*), and two longer forms. The first longer form is a Eucharistic Prayer in classical style. The other longer form has a slightly modified form (after the *Sanctus,* there is a short proclamation, an epiclesis, and the Institution Narrative which concludes the entire prayer). All three forms are preceded by the preface and *Sanctus* (cf. # #31, 32, 33 on pp. 69–70; also pp. 88–91, 110–111). This is a change from older editions of the Lutheran service books. The previous edition had only one long form in addition to the Institution Narrative form, and in the earlier edition there was only one option for the Eucharistic Prayer—the preface, *Sanctus* and Institution Narrative.

We can see developments to non-berakah literary forms in prayers used to sanctify other sacramental objects. The old prayer for consecrating baptismal water consisted of an adapted form of a Eucharistic Prayer, including the introductory dialogue. The prayer was revised in 1970 for Roman Catholics to a prayer which does include a proclamation section and an epiclesis, but which lacks much of the references to thanks and praise that the older prayer possessed and also omits the introductory dialogue. However, in the revised Catholic rites for baptizing children and adults, alternate versions of prayers for blessing baptismal water are included in the ritual. These alternate versions consist of invocations of praise to the Father, the Son and the Spirit, each of which is followed by an acclamation by those present. One of the alternate prayers then continues with three petitions to the Father for the sanctification of the water, each of which is again followed by an acclamation (cf. Appendix A).

A similar alternate prayer of blessing is included in the revised ritual for Anointing the Sick. The alternative form consists of three invocations of praise to the Father, the Son, and the Spirit, followed by one concluding petition for sanctification of the oil. A second alternative form reduces the other long forms to a single sentence: "Lord, bless this oil and bless our sick brother whom we will anoint with it."

The theological question can be raised as to what other forms can be used by a community, which will "sanctify" bread and wine so that the community will be able to fulfill the command that is recorded in Scripture as spoken by Christ to repeat the Last Supper in his memory. The Roman Missal provides that if for some reason wine were not consecrated during the Eucharistic Prayer, the celebrant should repeat a shortened version of the prayer, omitting any reference to the bread (*IGMR* #286). The Episcopal Church has for many years provided a "short form" of a Eucharistic Prayer in the event that the previously consecrated bread or wine did not suffice for all the communicants. The prayer is as follows:

> Hear us, O heavenly Father, and with your Word and Holy Spirit bless and sanctify this bread [wine] that it, also, may be the Sacrament of the precious Body [Blood] of your Son, Jesus Christ our Lord, who took bread [the cup] and said, "This is my Body [Blood]." Amen.

Alternately, the Episcopal priest may use one of the Eucharistic Prayers, beginning after the *Sanctus* and ending with the Epiclesis (*Book of Common Prayer* p. 408). Such prayers are, of necessity, minimal due to the situation in which they are used. Yet they suffice for the sanctification of the Eucharistic bread and wine. What prayer forms will evolve for future Christians which will be truly Eucharistic Prayers, yet be totally different from those presently in use?

b. Suggestions for the Second Half of a Eucharistic Prayer

As the reader can see, after the beginning of the Institution Narrative, the Eucharistic Prayer leaves very little room for innovation or thematic expression. In addition, there are many theological subtleties that must be watched out for. Because of this, it seems that there should normally be very few differences introduced into the second half of any new prayer.

This is the procedure suggested by the Episcopal Church in its *Book of Common Prayer.* The two Eucharistic Prayers found in what is commonly called "Rite 3," pages 400–05, give a basic introduction, followed by a rubric which states that the presider should praise the Father for the work of creation. After an optional lead-in for the *Sanctus,* a rubric then states that the presider should praise the Father for salvation through Jesus. Then the text prints the Institution Narrative to the final doxology without any additional opportunity for any further extemporaneous prayers (in form 1) or with only a brief opportunity for including intercessions (form 2) (cf. Appendix A).

Chapter Sixteen
ONE AND MANY

a. Distribution of the Parts of the Eucharastic Prayer

It was the duty of the father of the Jewish family or a synagogue leader to pronounce the entire berakah when one was prescribed. The rest of the family (or assembly) participated by making responses. In the Christian Eucharist, this rule was also followed. The Eucharistic Prayer is, par excellence, the prayer of the presider, the president of the community which is gathered in prayer. In some usages, however, deacons or subdeacons have been allotted certain parts of the prayer to say, specifically the intercessions. This comes from a time when the presider would offer prayers for a general category of Christians, and the deacon (or other major liturgical assistant) would list the names of those in that category.

In the Byzantine rite, there still exists a remnant of this practice when, after the audible commemoration of the hierarchy is made by the priest, the deacon is directed to "mention the living" by the rubrics. However, the instruction *Inaestimabile Donum* (1980) forbids the practice of anyone other than a presbyter or bishop reciting sections of the Eucharistic Prayer for the Roman rite (section 4). When two or more priests or bishops are present, there is precedent for distributing the more "priestly" sections of the prayer. There is a reference in ancient texts to a bishop of one city pronouncing the section of the Eucharistic Prayer relating to the bread and inviting a visiting bishop to "speak over the cup" (Syrian *Didascalia Apostolorum* II, 58, 3, written ca. 250).

In general, it would be better if the prayer would be short enough so that one presider could easily pray the entire prayer without wanting to relegate sections of it to others present. In fact, a number of contemporary scholars seem to have misgivings about this practice of dividing the Eucharistic Prayer up among a number of concelebrating priests, and this concern will be explained below (cf. Walsh, p. 48). When, because of length or other circumstances, distributing sections does seem desirable, parts of the proclamation section may be given to concelebrating priests, and the intercessions might even be given to deacons or to other non-priests who are liturgical assistants. However, the central sections—introduction, Institution Narrative *along with* the anamnesis-offertory-epiclesis, and the doxology—should be prayed by the presider of the worshiping community.

The practice has also sprung up in some places of the congregation reciting major sections of the Eucharistic Prayer along with the presider. The "justification" for this practice is usually one of two types: the first type is due to a deficient (and somewhat outmoded) *sacramental* theology which says that all the priest has to say are the "words of consecration," and, therefore, anyone else can say the rest of the Eucharistic Prayer; the second usual justification is due to a deficient *liturgical* theology which says that since all Christians are priests by their baptism, they too can say the "priestly" Eucharistic Prayer with the ordained (ministerial) priest. Both of these "justifying" reasons are simplistic. The first overlooks the contemporary realization that the words of the Lord are only one part of the "form" of the sacrament and must be enshrined in a context of prayer, specifically a Eucharistic Prayer proclaimed by a leader of a community of worship. (Those

who advocate this practice, therefore, while trying to be liturgically avant-garde, are actually demonstrating a very outmoded
theology!) The second reason given above overlooks the fact that
we are really speaking about two different things when we use
the (English) word "priest," and overlooks the basic two thousand year tradition of the Eucharistic Prayer as a *presidential*
prayer, i.e., one said by the presider of the assembly. This second
reason may be worth more discussion.[27]

In the Christian Scriptures (e.g., Heb. 5:5) and in the writings of the Apostolic Fathers, there is only one priest (*hiereus* in
Greek), and he is Christ. Christ alone has offered and can offer
sacrifice to God his Father. In one sense, no one today can be a
priest (*hiereus*) and offer sacrifice to God, since that sacrifice
would be meaningless after the "once for all" sacrifice of Christ
on the cross (cf. Heb. 10:10–14). But since through Baptism we
are joined to Christ and together as a people form the Body of
Christ in the world today, we can rightfully be considered a
priestly people (cf. 1 Pet. 2:9), offering sacrifice to God through
our union with Christ, who is both our priest and Paschal Lamb
of sacrifice (cf. Rev. 5:6–14; Jn. 1:29, 19:31, 33, 36). The person
who presides at the Eucharist is frequently, in episcopally-struc-
tured churches, called (in English) a "priest." However, this
word, in this Christian liturgical context, is used to translate a
totally different word from Greek—*presbyteros*—a word meaning
elder or leader (frequently rendered into English as "presbyter").
A priest (*presbyteros*) can also be considered to be a priest (*hiereus*) only because, in the context of worship, he can be viewed as
symbolizing Christ our true priest (*hiereus*), who leads a re-
deemed humanity in a joyful sacrifice of praise and petition to
God our Father (cf. writings of Ignatius of Antioch, John Chrysostom).

In discussing and determining our rites of worship, we must
not confuse the rights and duties of a priest (*hiereus*) with those
of presbyters. In praying the Eucharistic Prayer, it is the role of

the presider, whether he be a presbyter or a bishop, to lead the assembled community in worship. It is not a usurpation of any rights of the assembly for the presider to pray the entire Eucharistic Prayer by himself, since it *properly* belongs to him *in his role as presider.* (This is what is really meant by saying that the Eucharistic Prayer is a presidential prayer.) To argue otherwise would be like arguing that the father of a Jewish household is usurping the rights of his children when he prays the *birkat hamazon* alone. It is not a question of usurpation of rights—it is a question of a *role* that our religious tradition has given one person within a group of people who together form a community of love ultimately bound together by God.

All baptized Christians exercise their priesthood by their very presence at a Eucharist and taking part in it according to their rank in the Christian community. Too often we forget that the Christian Eucharist is not for everyone. We forget that in the early centuries of Christianity, the non-baptized catechumens were dismissed at a given point of the liturgy at the end of the service of the Word of God, and that the doors were then barred. Only after their Baptism were the neophytes allowed to remain for the Eucharistic part of the liturgy. As baptized Christians, they could then exercise their priesthood and join in offering the sacrifice of praise to God by participating in the responses, hymns, and actions of the Eucharistic Liturgy. The presider was seen as the person who had a special role—that of giving voice to the sentiments of the assembled community by his solemn prayers to God—summing up and joining many voices into one, as he prayed on the community's behalf. His *one* voice was a symbol of the one voice of Christ, who, as head of his Body, continued to praise and pray to God his Father.

Some scholars still consider this view of the rights and role of the presider as important today. It is good for us to have *one* voice of leadership and presidency over a worshiping community. This does not mean that the presider must do everything by himself, but that the primary prayers including the *entire* Eucharistic Prayer should be recited by him alone. Even when there are some concelebrating priests (presbyters) or bishops, the role of a concelebrant is not really that of a co-presider, and so some scholars would suggest that it is preferable to have the presider (principal concelebrant) proclaim the Eucharistic Prayer by himself without relegating any sub-section to anyone else.

b. Additional Objects of Sanctification

In the Roman tradition, the oil used for the Sacrament of the Anointing of the Sick has traditionally been blessed by inserting a prayer into the Eucharistic Prayer before the final doxology. It seems plausible that other objects were also blessed during the Eucharistic Prayer at this point. The present text of the Roman Canon seems to hint at this in the small section which precedes the doxology: "Through Christ our Lord, you give us all these gifts. You fill them with life and goodness, you bless them and make them holy."

At certain solemn celebrations, it may seem appropriate to again insert a formula of blessing into the Eucharistic Prayer at this point, especially if some object were intimately connected with the reason for the celebration. This may occur at a marriage, for the blessing of rings, or during a religious profession, for the blessing of the signs of consecration (rings or crucifixes). Such an insertion and blessing should not be used indiscriminately, however. The objects blessed should be those which can convey the love of God the Father to those who will use these objects, a love which is easily seen in the Sacrament of the Eucharist or the Sacrament of the Sick.

In the revised Roman Catholic ceremony for the dedication of a church and altar, there is a special preface for the Eucharistic Prayer which is termed an "integral part of the rite" (Rite of Dedication, Chapter 2 [Provisional Text], number 75). The Introduction to this rite emphasizes that it is the celebration of the

Eucharist which is the most important part of the rite (# 15, 17), although an ancient tradition continued in the revised rites includes another "prayer of dedication" immediately before the altar is anointed and prepared for the Eucharistic liturgy. In effect, the preface may even be considered a "blessing" because of its wording. Since the church building and the altar are so closely related to the celebration of the Eucharist, it seemed appropriate to those who revised the ritual to include the essential "blessing" as part of the Eucharistic Prayer said by the bishop during the Mass of Dedication.

c. Additional Acclamations

All three of the Roman Catholic Eucharistic Prayers for Children contain acclamations in a number of different places, the second prayer containing a total of twelve acclamations instead of the usual three (*Sanctus,* memorial acclamation and Amen). These additional acclamations were introduced to encourage more participation by children in praying the Eucharistic Prayer and, in this way, in the hopes of avoiding boredom. In many of the Eastern Churches, there are also numerous places for acclamations by the people. But, in most cases, the acclamations follow the principle mentioned above (cf. Chapter 7, section B), that is, the people address Christ while the celebrant addresses God the Father. However, when the same acclamation is repeated a number of times, as in the new Catholic Eucharistic Prayers for Children, a different literary style has been introduced. These short acclamations are directed to God directly or are exclamations of praise proclaimed to no one in particular (e.g., "Glory to God in the highest," or "Blessed be God"). As mentioned before, these new acclamations should more properly be considered "refrains" rather than "memorial acclamations" in the classical sense.

Some authors have advocated dialogical Eucharistic Prayers for small congregations with both the presider and the congregation addressing the Father in prayer (cf. Episcopal *Book of Common Prayer*, Eucharistic Prayer C, pp. 369ff.). However, this necessitates both the presider and everyone in the congregation having copies of the Eucharistic Prayer, and in most cases it becomes an exercise in choral reading, rather than being a prayer of a community led by a leader of prayer. In general, then, more acclamations for the congregation can be very beneficial, but these new acclamations should be simple, and, with profit, repeated a number of times, such as singing a triple Alleluia at regular intervals throughout the Eucharistic Prayer (cf. Dallen [2]).

Section Six

CONCLUSION

Chapter Seventeen
GRATIAS AGAMUS
DOMINO DEO NOSTRO

In a paper written a few years ago, Fr. Kenneth Smits, O.F.M. Cap., presents his thoughts on the Eucharistic Prayer. He concludes with a wise admonition:

> We are talking about the central prayer of Christianity. We cannot afford to be careless or arbitrary in such a central expression of our faith. Not any gospel will do, not any creed will do, not any eucharistic prayer will do. (p. 20)

He then gives a beautifully concise definition of a Eucharistic Prayer:

> A eucharistic prayer is:
>   public praise of God
>   in which we recall in thanksgiving
>   the saving deeds of God,
>   above all the Paschal Mystery of Christ,
>   in relation to bread and wine,
>   so that these gifts of bread and wine,
>   signs of our own lives,

147

become the symbol/reality of Christ among us,
   in the power of the Holy Spirit,
renewing his covenant love among us
to the continued working out of his plan of salvation
all to the final praise of God.

Throughout this work, I have tried to examine all the many dimensions of the Eucharistic Prayer, dimensions quite concisely expressed in this definition by Smits. I have also tried to take the admonition of Smits seriously in evaluating the importance of each part of this prayer. I hope that my efforts have been successful.

    This work was written in the hopes that it would be of value to those Christians interested in expanding their knowledge about the Eucharist and the Eucharistic Prayer. I hope that I have done justice to the various authors I consulted and quoted in my attempt to compile their varied thoughts into one work. I myself have often wished that I could have had available a book which gave a more or less detailed and balanced explanation of the parts of the Eucharistic Prayer. I hope that others will find these efforts of mine useful and helpful.

    I was motivated to compile this work from the need I felt to have something available for those who wished to evaluate Eucharistic Prayers both old and new. Over the past ten to fifteen years, many people have tried to compose new Eucharistic Prayers, but, it seems to me, only a very few have really been successful. Most people, like myself, who try, end up with mediocre prayers—perhaps more of a reflection of our lives as Christians than we would like to admit.

    Christian communities will need men and women in touch with God and with other human beings to give expression to the Christian beliefs through the composition of Eucharistic Prayers for the contemporary Church. What should modern day authors do when they attempt to write such prayers? After reading a number of scholars and trying to digest their discoveries, one might be tempted to abandon all hope of success. Yet, if the Church sees new Eucharistic Prayers as a need, and if this impulse is truly a grace from God, then God will inspire men and women to be able to put words on paper and compose prayers suitable for Christian worship in this day and age. Any would-be author should first and foremost remember to pray. For pray*ers* cannot be written without first pray*ing*. Authors should not be afraid to submit their first attempts to friends for critiques and suggestions, for each of us tends to be blind to some of our most obvious errors or oversights. Newly-composed prayers should also be critiqued in the light of the recent findings of liturgical scholars as found in this work and elsewhere. And when all is said and done, and authors think that they have composed truly outstanding prayers for worship, they should try to pray them again—try to use them to express their sentiments, their longings, their sighings of love for the Lord—and see if the prayers do in fact do what they were meant to do.

As I mentioned at the very beginning, the composition of a prayer is not as simple as the composition of a college English paper. A prayer is a message of love from a person to the Beloved One. Because of this, in some sense it can never be evaluated or graded. It is also an expression of faith, of hope, and of the composer's understanding of the paschal mystery effected by Christ our Lord.

And yet a prayer is also a piece of literature. Moreover, it is also a work of art. Not everyone is gifted with the ability to be a poet or an artist, and so it seems that not everyone should attempt to compose new Eucharistic Prayers. Nevertheless, prayers already existing must be examined and evaluated. They should be prayed over in private and in public. They should be improved if needed, abandoned if necessary, and accepted if they are truly expressive of the Christian community's living faith. Only by actively reflecting upon and evaluating past deeds and actions will today's Christians be able to grow into the living body of Christ in the world, ever praising the Father who gives us everything that we need and possess.

NOTES

1. The English word "Eucharist" is derived from the Greek root word *"eukharistein"* which means "to give thanks." When speaking about "the Eucharist," contemporary (and ancient) writers usually refer to the entire celebration of the Mass, or the Holy Communion Service of Christian Churches (i.e., the entire celebration of giving thanks), or, sometimes, to the elements of bread and wine after the Eucharistic Prayer (or "Prayer of Thanksgiving") has been prayed over them (and so have become "eucharistized" or "items for which God has been thanked").

2. ICEL, the International Commission on English in the Liturgy, the body entrusted with providing translations into English of the revised Roman Catholic liturgical rites issued by the Holy See, in May 1980 established a subcommittee to deal with Eucharistic Prayers. This subcommittee will concern itself with three areas: (a) composition of completely new texts in English, (b) translation of ancient texts not presently in use in the Roman liturgy, and (c) composition of interpolations for special occasions for use in the present Eucharistic Prayers. The agenda for 1981 for this subcommittee included examining two newly composed prayers and the translations of two ancient prayers. After drafts have been submitted, critiqued, and reworked by the subcommittee, they will be submitted to English-speaking episcopal conferences for their perusal and possible approval, and then the various national episcopal conferences can individually and independently submit them to the Holy See for confirmation for use in their respective English-speaking countries.

3. The Roman Catholic Order of Mass of 1969, in the accompanying General Instructions (*IGMR*), lists the following as the eight parts of the Eucharistic Prayer (section 55): (a) Thanksgiving (i.e., preface and proclamation), (b) Acclamation (i.e., *Sanctus*), (c) Epiclesis, (d) Narrative of the Institution and Consecration, (e) Anamnesis, (f) Offering, (g) Intercessions, (h) Final Doxology.

4. It is interesting to examine the variations of this introduction to prayer. The short Jewish form is "Let us bless" (or, perhaps a better English translation would be "Let us say the blessing," or "Let us say the 'berakah' "). Old rabbinical regulations prescribed that when ten males were present, the invitation should be "Let us bless *the LORD*," and in large gatherings, when at least one hundred were present, the invitation should be "Let us bless the LORD, *our God.*" The Byzantine rite today employs the invitation, "Let us give thanks to the Lord," based on the old Jewish form for between ten and one hundred people, and the Western liturgies normally use the form "Let us give thanks to the Lord, our God," based on the old Jewish form for over one hundred people. This may well indicate the typical sizes for Eucharists celebrated in the East and West in the early centuries (cf. Mishnah Tractate, *Berakoth,* vii, 4, 5; viii, 3; Dix, p. 127; Kucharek, p. 566; Martimort, p. 141, n. 36). There is still some variation to be found in contemporary Jewish prayer books. The invitation to the *birkat ha-mazon* is omitted completely if less than three males have eaten together, and some of the responses have "our God" added, if ten or more males have eaten (cf. Hertz, pp. 965–67).

5. This is the nature of the tradition of "faculties for preaching and hearing confessions" in the Roman Catholic Church.

6. For the meaning of *bebaia,* cf. Kittel, Vol. 1, p. 603, or Moulton & Milligan, p. 107. We must be careful of either reading modern understandings into ancient texts or totally dismissing any relation between the two either. In this particular case, perhaps we should grant some *legal* status to the use of *bebaios* in

Ignatius, although what he is probably intending to say is something like this: "There is *something significantly lacking* in a Eucharist which is celebrated neither by the bishop nor by his delegate." The same word is used in IgMag. 4 in a similar context.

7. However, some suggest that when we view the Eucharist as a sign of unity, we should rather understand this as a "unity to be fostered." With this understanding the Eucharist becomes a means for achieving juridical unity, and thus all should be permitted to receive it who desire such unity.

8. Let me, however, preface this present discussion by saying that among contemporary theologians, such a discussion is undesirable theologizing, for this tends to split into subsections a reality (i.e., the entire Eucharistic Prayer) which should properly be considered as a whole.

9. Although the Roman Missal is generally consistent about prayers being addressed to the Father, popular piety has had its effects on non-Eucharistic presidential prayers found therein. There still exist some prayers (e.g., Opening Prayer for the Solemnity of Corpus Christi) addressed to Christ, although some liturgists are hopeful that the next revision of liturgical texts will eliminate these, so that the old custom of publicly praying only to the Father may be kept unchanged.

10. Because of the extremely long history of this part of the Eucharistic Prayer (and it should be considered a part of the prayer and not just an added prelude), the introductory dialogue should be continued in use with contemporary prayers with little or no modifications.

11. When the beginning of the Eucharistic Prayer varies too much in content (or in some cases even in form) from a familiar stylized introduction, not only is the connection between the people's response and the "Eucharistic" nature of the prayer lost, but, at times, one can seriously wonder if the prayer being prayed is actually "Eucharistic" at all, since thanksgiving or praise is rarely, if ever, mentioned later on in the prayer.

12. Thus, in general, it would seem better for future prayers to concentrate on the wonders worked by the Father and narrated

in the Hebrew Scriptures, concluding this section by mentioning the greatest gift of the Father to humanity—Jesus Christ our Lord. A comment should also be made concerning the choice of items to mention in a Eucharistic Prayer. The *magnalia Dei* are many and varied, and for any imaginable theme, many Scripture references can be found to which a reference could be made in the Eucharistic Prayer. However, just as in a given homily not every possible Scripture citation should be mentioned, so also, in a given prayer, not every possible reference to a given theme or biblical event should be mentioned. If this should occur, the Eucharistic Prayer then becomes more a show of how well the author did his homework, or how well he could pack scriptural references into a prayer he wrote, rather than being an actual living prayer of a given Christian community. In these cases, the Eucharistic Prayer can become a source of distraction and boredom, and thus has the same faults it tries to eliminate in existing prayers.

13. I do not mean to imply that Eucharistic Prayers should not mention any objects of creation. As we saw above, the *birkat ha-mazon* in one of its sections gave praise to God as Creator of the material universe, and we must regain an attitude toward material reality that views created things as filled with the presence of God and as salvific in themselves. However, when contemporary prayers juxtapose material objects with prophetic persons and salvific events, then they open themselves up to being drastically misunderstood by the majority of Christians, for, frequently, this juxtaposition has the effect of making people and events seem as insignificant as most elements of creation seem to the majority of humanity today. The language employed must be such as to emphasize on the one hand the reality of God's communication to us through created elements, yet, on the other hand, emphasize that this communication is intensified even more through salvific events and grace-filled individuals.

14. Some contemporary prayers, seemingly due to the composer's feelings about the existence (or lack thereof) of angels, use very awkward transition statements leading to the *Sanctus.*

This leads to a problem for some hearers of such prayers—a person is left with the thought, "Why use this hymn rather than any other?" Traditionally, the introduction to the *Sanctus* has referred to angels in heaven, since such is the context in which the *Sanctus* is presented in both Isaiah and Revelation. Although we may be less likely today to employ angelic imagery in new prayer compositions, nevertheless it seems that any transitional introduction to the *Sanctus* should respect its scriptural context and try to situate it in a similar setting, in order to emphasize that we join God's praise by joining in singing a hymn constantly sung in heaven.

15. It is unfortunate that "preface" is usually taken to mean a (relatively unimportant) section which precedes what many feel is the "Eucharistic Prayer" properly (and incorrectly) speaking. One frequently hears priests say, in referring to such "Sanctus-less" prayers (e.g., Mossi, pp. 28, 40, 44), "This prayer doesn't have a preface," when the reality is that the prayer in question, like the Hippolytus Canon, is just missing the *Sanctus*.

16. There seems to be little advantage in varying the Institution Narrative in a typical Eucharistic Prayer. This section is a narration which gives those present the ultimate reason why they are celebrating the Eucharist—the Lord Jesus did the same thing before his death and commanded us to repeat what he did. It also is difficult to try to include themes in this section. Therefore, in most instances, it would seem best for new compositions to use the format which is most common to the community at prayer, probably duplicating the Institution Narrative of one of the existing official Eucharistic Prayers with only minor changes.

17. It seems that placing the acclamation during the next major section, while it has the advantage of allowing the presider to first mention the Lord's death and resurrection prior to the congregation's mention of them in the acclamation, breaks up the literary unity of the Eucharistic Prayer in this section. However, after the words of the Lord in the Institution Narrative, there is a change of pace as well as emphasis in the prayer, and so the placement of the acclamation at this point does not seem to do as

much damage to the text. In addition, the memorial acclamation is in this position in the majority of Eastern liturgies. Since it is usually addressed to Christ rather than the Father, it comes as a natural response to the words just narrated by the presider, "Do this in memory of me." However, there are good reasons for postponing the acclamation as well. These reasons will be mentioned below in Chapter 8, section D.

18. Unfortunately, too often this importance is not realized, and so this section is overlooked, misinterpreted, relegated to a minor minister, or in some contemporary prayers omitted altogether.

19. Too often, in contemporary Eucharistic Prayers, these three sub-sections (if all of them occur) are very hyphenated, and also disconnected, as if the author of the prayer knew that each of the sub-sections should be in the prayer, but knew nothing about their inter-relationship.

20. There has been a long tradition of considering the Institution Narrative as *the* high point of the Eucharistic Prayer, and this over-emphasis has, among other things, led to the illicit practice among Roman Catholic priests of concelebrating by reciting only the first epiclesis and the Institution Narrative or even by reciting only the Institution Narrative or only the words of Christ. After the memorial acclamation, as it appears in the Roman Missal, the next sections of the Eucharistic Prayer (i.e., the anamnesis-offertory-epiclesis) are seemingly (and in practice) considered unimportant and are even sometimes relegated to only one of the concelebrants, even though technically the rubrics direct that *all* concelebrants should continue to recite the Eucharistic Prayer together until the (second) epiclesis.

21. Therefore, in most cases, it would be preferable to have one invocation of the Spirit, occurring after the memorial-offertory, which asks that the Spirit both come upon the community and the gifts, and sanctify the bread and wine, so that all who share them may be united into the one body of Christ (cf. McKenna [1], pp. 281–83; Albertine, esp. p. 202).

22. However, in general, it seems best to limit this section to

a minimum and include the majority of intercessory prayers at the General Intercessions which (usually) occur after the homily. Oftentimes little can be done practically here to reinforce a given theme, except for a small petition asking for a given particular virtue (e.g., "Father, we pray that as a community we may always show your love to everyone we meet"). But, theoretically, much is still possible, as recent thematic prayers written by James Dallen have shown (cf. Bibliography). Much said during this section is oftentimes anticlimactic to many people, and so even though it may be "heard," it is often not "listened to" by those present.

23. An example of such a transition is the following: "Father, we make this prayer through him who loves us and gave us an example of love, your Son, Jesus Christ our Lord. For, through him, with him. . . . "

24. Pastorally, however, the congregationally recited doxology may be the best solution to a difficult dilemma, especially at (weekday) liturgies at which nothing is sung. This, however, still continues the linguistic oddity of the congregation responding "Amen" to their own acclamation!

25. Actually, most moralists and canonists would consider such a baptismal formula as doubtfully valid or probably valid. In practice, this would require conditional rebaptism, using a formula such as, "If you are not already baptized, I baptize you in the name of the Father, and of the Son, and of the Holy Spirit."

26. The problem of an individual leading public prayer as a "we" may be a bigger problem than most Christians would consider at first. Christian communities have had a problem for years of finding presiders who really know how to *preside* over a communal worship situation. Perhaps, the problem has become more recognizable in those traditions where the presider has changed from facing a wall fifteen or so years ago, to facing the assembly at the altar (such as in the Roman Catholic and Episcopal traditions), and realized that he really does not know how to lead a group in prayer. There may properly be a real concern for the future to locate and instruct presiders in the art of public

praying so that they can lead an assembly in prayer in such a way
that *everyone* is included in the act of praying. One example of a
problem area is with regard to eye contact. Too often the "eye
contact" during formal prayers is more of a "teaching" posture—
looking at the congreagation as during a speech or class lecture.
There is a way of keeping eye contact with the congregation that
is appropriate during prayer, yet that is different from a lecturing
eye contact. A person can look at a congregation and still convey
an attitude of prayer to God. This entire area of body posture is
one which needs more thought and examination in the future.
There is a difficulty of trying to keep contact with those who are
being led in prayer. There is a difficulty of a presider being
comfortable with his body movements, especially in front of an
assembly, and particularly when the presider is an American male
who has had no such previous experience of using his body in
such a manner publicly before (cf. Walsh, p. 45).

27. As mentioned in Chapter 13, section C, Keifer suggests
that a communally recited Eucharistic Prayer is worse than using
an unauthorized Eucharistic Prayer (cf. [3], p. 140).

Appendices

Appendix A
SAMPLE PRAYERS

Eucharistic Prayers from the Episcopal *Book of Common Prayer* (pp. 402–05):

Form 1

Celebrant	The Lord be with you.
People	And also with you.
Celebrant	Lift up your hearts.
People	We lift them to the Lord.
Celebrant	Let us give thanks to the Lord our God.
People	It is right to give him thanks and praise.

The Celebrant gives thanks to God the Father for his work in creation and his revelation of himself to his people;

Recalls before God, when appropriate, the particular occasion being celebrated;

Incorporates or adapts the Proper Preface of the day, if desired.

If the Sanctus is to be included, it is introduced with these or similar words
And so we join the saints and angels in proclaiming your glory, as we sing (say),

Celebrant and People

Holy, holy, holy Lord, God of power and might,
heaven and earth are full of your glory.
    Hosanna in the highest.
Blessed is he who comes in the name of the Lord.
    Hosanna in the highest.

*The Celebrant now praises God for the salvation of the world
through Jesus Christ our Lord.*

The Prayer continues with these words

And so, Father, we bring you these gifts. Sanctify them by your
Holy Spirit to be for your people the Body and Blood of Jesus
Christ our Lord.

*At the following words concerning the bread, the Celebrant is to
hold it, or lay a hand upon it; and at the words concerning the
cup, to hold or place a hand upon the cup and any other vessel
containing wine to be consecrated.*

On the night he was betrayed he took bread, said the blessing,
broke the bread, and gave it to his friends, and said, "Take, eat:
This is my Body, which is given for you. Do this for the remembrance of me."

After supper, he took the cup of wine, gave thanks, and said,
"Drink this, all of you. This is my Blood of the new Covenant,
which is shed for you and for many for the forgiveness of sins.
Whenever you drink it, do this for the remembrance of me."

Father, we now celebrate the memorial of your Son. By means of
this holy bread and cup, we show forth the sacrifice of his death,
and proclaim his resurrection, until he comes again.

Gather us by this Holy Communion into one body in your Son Jesus Christ. Make us a living sacrifice of praise.

By him, and with him, and in him, in the unity of the Holy Spirit all honor and glory is yours, Almighty Father, now and for ever. *AMEN.*

Form 2

Celebrant	The grace of our Lord Jesus Christ and the love of God and the fellowship of the Holy Spirit be with you all.
People	And also with you.
Celebrant	Lift up your hearts.
People	We lift them to the Lord.
Celebrant	Let us give thanks to the Lord our God.
People	It is right to give him thanks and praise.

The Celebrant gives thanks to God the Father for his work in creation and his revelation of himself to his people;

Recalls before God, when appropriate, the particular occasion being celebrated;

Incorporates or adapts the Proper Preface of the day, if desired.

If the Sanctus is to be included, it is introduced with these or similar words

And so we join the saints and angels in proclaiming your glory, and we sing (say),

Celebrant and People

Holy, holy, holy Lord, God of power and might, heaven and earth are full of your glory.

Hosanna in the highest.
Blessed is he who comes in the name of the Lord.
Hosanna in the highest.

The Celebrant now praises God for the salvation of the world through Jesus Christ our Lord.

At the following words concerning the bread, the Celebrant is to hold it, or lay a hand upon it; and at the words concerning the cup, to hold or place a hand upon the cup and any other vessel containing wine to be consecrated.

On the night he was handed over to suffering and death, our Lord Jesus Christ took bread; and when he had given thanks to you, he broke it, and gave it to his disciples, and said, "Take, eat: This is my Body, which is given for you. Do this for the remembrance of me."

After supper he took the cup of wine; and when he had given thanks, he gave it to them, and said, "Drink this, all of you: This is my Blood of the new Covenant, which is shed for you and for many for the forgiveness of sins. Whenever you drink it, do this for the remembrance of me."

Recalling now his suffering and death, and celebrating his resurrection and ascension, we await his coming in glory.

Accept, O Lord, our sacrifice of praise, this memorial of our redemption.

Send your Holy Spirit upon these gifts. Let them be for us the Body and Blood of your Son. And grant that we who eat this bread and drink this cup may be filled with your life and goodness.

The Celebrant then prays that all may receive the benefits of Christ's work, and the renewal of the Holy Spirit.

The Prayer concludes with these or similar words

All this we ask through your Son Jesus Christ. By him, and with him, and in him in the unity of the Holy Spirit all honor and glory is yours, Almighty Father, now and for ever. *AMEN.*

The Eucharistic Prayer of Hippolytus

(This prayer is taken from the *Apostolic Tradition* of Hippolytus, probably written around 215–217 A.D.)

> It is not absolutely necessary that the bishop should use the same words as we have given, as if he were saying them from memory while offering the thanksgiving to God. Rather, let each one pray according to his ability. If he is able to pronounce a lengthy and solemn prayer, it is in order. If, on the contrary, he limits the length and prays according to a set form, no one may hinder him. But every prayer must be correct and orthodox [conform to the faith]. (Chapter 9—Botte's numeration)

(Chapter 4:2–13)

> Then the deacons are to bring him [the bishop] the offerings. Together with all the presbyters, he lays his hands on the oblation, and gives thanks in this way:
> The Lord be with you.
> And all shall reply: And with your spirit.
> Lift up your hearts. We have them with the Lord.
> Let us give thanks to the Lord.
> It is right and proper.

And then he shall continue thus:

Stylized Introduction

> God our Father,
> we give you thanks
> through your beloved Son, Jesus Christ.

Proclamation—motive

> For, in these final days,
> you have sent him to us
> to be our savior, our redeemer,
> and the messenger of your will.
>
> He is your Word,
> inseparable from you,
> and through him you made the universe.

(Sanctus omitted)

> You sent him, with whom you were well-pleased,
> to become a virgin's child.
> Conceived by the power of the Holy Spirit,
> he took flesh, was born of that virgin,
> and was revealed as your Son.
>
> For our sake he opened his arms on the cross
> to free from suffering
> all who believed in you.
> In this he fulfilled your will
> and won for you a holy people.
>
> He freely accepted that death
> so that he might conquer death
> and break the bonds of Evil
> by crushing hell itself.
>
> By doing this, he would lead the just to the light,
> make a new covenant with them,
> and show them the resurrection.

Institution Narrative

> Before he was given up to his death,
> he took bread,
> and, giving thanks, he said
> > Take, eat:
> > this is my body, which is broken for you.

> In the same way he took the cup and said:
> > This is my blood, which is shed for you.

> > As often as you do this,
> > do it in memory of me.

(Acclamation Omitted) Anamnesis—Offertory

> In memory of his death and resurrection,
> we offer you this bread and this cup.
> We thank you for counting us worthy
> to stand in your presence and serve you as priests.

Epiclesis

> We ask you to send your Holy Spirit
> upon the offerings of your Holy Church.
> Gather together into one
> all who receive from these Holy Mysteries,
> so that they may be filled with the Holy Spirit
> and their faith may be strengthened in your truth.

(Intercessions omitted) Doxological transition

> Thus we may praise you and glorify you,
> through your Son, Jesus Christ.

Doxology

> For through him,
> glory and honor is yours,
> Father and Son, with the Holy Spirit,
> in the Holy Church,
> now and for ever.

> Amen.

1980 Methodist Eucharistic Prayer

(This alternate Eucharistic Prayer was prepared by the Commission on Worship of The United Methodist Church in the United States in 1972 and revised in 1980. In 1981, The United Methodist Church published *At the Lord's Table: Supplemental Worship Resources 9,* a collection of about 20 thematic and seasonal Eucharistic Prayers for official use.)

Stylized Introduction

> Father, it is right that we should always
> and everywhere give you thanks and praise.

Proclamation—motive

> Only you are God.
> You created all things and called them good.
> You made us in your own image.
> Even though we rebelled against your love,
> you did not desert us.
> You delivered us from captivity,
> made covenant to be our Sovereign God,
> and spoke to us through your prophets.

Sanctus

Therefore, we join the entire company of heaven
and all your people now on earth
in worshiping and glorifying you:

Holy, holy, holy Lord, God of power and might,
heaven and earth are full of your glory.
Hosanna in the highest.
Blessed is he who comes in the name of the Lord.
Hosanna in the highest.

Proclamation cont'd.

We thank you, holy Lord God,
that you loved the world so much
you sent your only Son to be our Savior.
The Lord of all life came to live among us.

He healed and taught,
ate with sinners,
and won for you a new people
by water and the Spirit.
We saw his glory.
Yet he humbled himself in obedience to your will,
freely accepting death on a cross.
By dying, he freed us from unending death;
by rising from the dead, he gave us everlasting life.

Institution Narrative

On the night in which he gave himself up for us,
the Lord Jesus took bread.
After giving you thanks,
he broke the bread,
gave it to his disciples, and said:

Take, eat; this is my body which is given for you.
When the supper was over,
he took the cup.
Again he returned thanks to you,
gave the cup to his disciples, and said:
Drink from this, all of you,
this is the cup of the new covenant in my blood,
poured out for you and many,
for the forgiveness of sins.
When we eat this bread and drink this cup,
we experience anew
the presence of the Lord Jesus Christ
and look forward to his coming in final victory.

Acclamation

Christ has died,
Christ is risen,
Christ will come again.

Anamnesis—Offertory

We experience anew, most merciful God,
the suffering and death,
the resurrection and ascension of your Son,
asking you to accept
this our sacrifice of praise and thanksgiving,
which we offer
in union with Christ's offering for us,
as a living and holy surrender of ourselves.

Epiclesis (Intercessions omitted)

Send the power of your Holy Spirit on us,
gathered here out of love for you,
and on these gifts.

May the Spirit help us know
in the breaking of this bread
and the drinking of this wine
the presence of Christ
who gave his body and blood for all.
And may the Spirit make us one with Christ,
one with each other,
and one in service to all the world.

(*Last sentence of epiclesis is a Doxological transition.*)

Doxology

Through your Son Jesus Christ
with the Holy Spirit in your holy Church,
all glory and honor is yours, Almighty Father,
now and for ever.
Amen.

Roman Catholic Prayer for Blessing Baptismal Water

Celebrant:
Praise to you, almighty God and Father, for you have created water to cleanse and give life.
All: Blessed be God *(or some other suitable acclamation by the people).*

Celebrant:
Praise to you, Lord Jesus Christ, the Father's only Son, for you offered yourself on the cross, that in the blood and water flowing from your side, and through your death and resurrection, the Church might be born.
All: Blessed be God.

Celebrant:
Come to us, Lord, Father of all, and make holy this water which you have created, so that all who are baptized in it may be washed clean of sin, and be born again to live as your children.
All: Hear us, Lord *(or some other suitable invocation).*

Celebrant:
Make this water holy, Lord, so that all who are baptized into Christ's death and resurrection by this water may become more perfectly like your Son.
All: Hear us, Lord.

The celebrant touches the water with his right hand and continues:

Lord, make holy this water which you have created, so that all those whom you have chosen may be born again by the power of the Holy Spirit, and may take their place among your holy people.
All: Hear us, Lord.

Appendix B
DOCUMENTATION: ROMAN CATHOLIC ARCHDIOCESE OF LIVERPOOL, ENGLAND, DECEMBER 1974

Guide Lines for the Composition of Children's Eucharistic Prayers

I. Essential Elements
To be satisfactory liturgically and doctrinally, children's Eucharistic Prayers should contain:

Praise of God (including the mention of what God has done in Christ for us).

Prayer for the transformation of the gifts of bread and wine.

The Institution Narrative.

An anamnesis prayer, expressing our celebration of the memorial of Christ and the offering of Christ in his Paschal Mystery, and expressing the offering of ourselves with him as a Church.

A prayer for fruitful communion (asking for the gift of the Holy Spirit, at least as a rule, cf. Note 1 below).

Intercessions (cf. Note 2 below).
Doxology.

Note 1
It is felt that mention can and should be made of the Holy
Spirit in the prayers for the transformation of the gifts and for a
fruitful communion, except for the youngest age group, 6–8
years.

Note 2
Historically, intercessions have not always been featured in
the Eucharistic Prayer and some feel that they duplicate the
Bidding Prayers. However, it is felt that, as a general rule, they
should be kept for two reasons:
(a) they offer an opportunity for the children's participation;
(b) they stress the sacrificial nature of the Mass, and can include
    reference to our eschatological communion with Mary and
    the saints.

II. Adaptation to Age Groups

Guide Lines for the Composition of Eucharistic Prayers, 6–8

1. Preface to be realistic—praising God for what is most real and
   important in children's own life experience (homes, friends,
   shared pleasures, wonders of the natural world, etc.).
2. Canon to be kept short and be based on one aspect of relationship with Jesus explored in the Infant Syllabus (e.g., Friendship: or Sharing in the new life of Jesus).
3. Desirable use of simple song-verse at Sanctus, Acclamation
   and Anamnesis to break up the narrative and provide participation.
4. Essential elements to be retained with possible exceptions of:
   (a) Intercessions. (Bidding Prayers should suffice.)
   (b) Prayer to Holy Spirit before Communion. The theology
       here is too involved for infants.

Guide Lines for the Composition of Eucharistic Prayers for 10+

1. All essential elements to be retained.
2. The Eucharistic Prayer to be based on theme already explored from Junior Syllabus (e.g., Responding to God's call; Light; Water; Living in Jesus' Way). In this way the class teaching is reinforced and the pupils see Liturgy as belonging to—and not remote from—their real lives.
3. Consecration as in Canon 2.
4. The offering of ourselves could be made with the Priest or repeated after him.
5. Remembrance of the Saints could consist of individual contributions. So could the prayer for the living and dead.
6. The Sanctus and Acclamation should be sung: also the great Amen.

Guide Lines for the Composition of Eucharistic Prayers for 1st and 2nd Year Secondary Pupils

1. Preface
   (a) Offering meaningful themes for praise of God through awareness of His wonderful works around them.
   (b) Opportunity for silent or acclaimed participation.

2. Canon
   A. *Praise of God leading to Consecration Narrative* to continue the themes of the Preface, including some or all of the following aspects of their own development and learning:
   1. God who created THEM and their world.
   2. God who sent Christ to bring message of Salvation and Joy.
   3. God who makes family, friends and all other people.
   4. God who allows them to be His own Family, including aspects of belonging, such as pride in special members of this family, concern for those near and far, and sorrow when relationships are bruised.

B. *Expression of Remembering and Offering,* including self-offering to contain such aspects as:
   1. The uniting of their own gifts, talents and ambitions with those of Christ.
   2. The offering of themselves as members of their own peer groups.
   3. The offering of their discontent and restlessness along with the sufferings of Christ.
C. *Prayer for Communion and Power of the Spirit*—to make use of group mentality which is developed by Sacramental experience given at this stage in most syllabi—awareness of Baptismal Commitments, realization of personal failures within the context of this family of God; the experience of the Holy Spirit in Confirmation.
D. *Intercessions*—for themselves, the Church, own family and friends.

3. Doxology
   To contain more direct reference to the Person of Jesus (as illustrated in the Eucharistic Prayer for 1st and 2nd Year Secondary Pupils (see text below).

Guide Lines for the Composition of Eucharistic Prayers for 3rd and 4th Year Secondary Pupils

1. Preface
   (a) Offering meaningful themes for praise of God through awareness of His Wonderful Works in and for them.
   (b) Opportunity for silent or acclaimed response.

2. Canon
   A. *Praise of God leading to Consecration Narrative* to continue and extend the themes of the Preface to include some or all of the following: Praise of God as the *Creator* who took upon Himself our Human Nature to become our *brother,*

our *rescuer*—as the Spirit of love whose power fulfills the needs and longings of the world. This prayer to include their identification and recognition of:

(a) God who places before them *group experiences* and *group security* (family, friends, cliques).

(b) God who enables them to relate to others.

(c) God who gives them awareness of the needs of others.

(d) God who gives them a purpose to fulfill in community.

(e) God who places before them a living organization with which to *identify and emulate.*

(f) God who strengthens their purpose through the merits of Christ sacrificed.

B. *Expression of Remembering and Offering, including Self-Offering* to contain such aspects as: Their Offering of their own frustrations, anxieties and inadequacies with the suffering, rejected Christ who triumphed. A reminder to God the Father of His promises to Abraham who placed His trust in the Lord, and whose faith was his overriding feature. A reminder to God of His dealings with Mary, who was justified because of her *trust* in God. A final remembrance of God's promise to so love the world as to send His only *Son to suffer,* die and redeem us. A reminder of the Promise of the Spirit, to sanctify and transform their efforts: "I will not leave you lonely, I will send the Comforter."

C. *Prayer for Communion and Power of the Spirit* to make use of group experiences synthesized in the following:

(a) The work of youth groups in our country—united to the agency of the Church in the World.

(b) Acknowledgment of our communion with friends, family, houses, personalities in the Church whom we can imitate.

(c) Identification with the work of the Spirit who unifies our purpose.

D. *Intercessions for themselves:* generosity, perseverance, sen-

sitivity for their country—the lonely, under-privileged: the aged, the neglected.
National Emergencies: political, social, religious.
Global problems: famine, deprivation, ignorance, injustice.

3. Doxology
    As for 1st and 2nd Year Secondary Pupils, to contain more direct reference to the Person of Jesus.

Finally, with regard to the 16–18 age group, it is felt that these should be becoming familiar with adult Eucharistic Prayers, provided adequate catechesis has been given. Consequently, we do not favour the composition of special Eucharistic Prayers for persons of this age. However, we would favour their being able to insert motives for praise before or during the Preface, and intentions for intercession during the relevant part of the Eucharistic Prayer. What is said elsewhere about participation in the Eucharistic Prayer would also apply here. Moreover it is to be hoped
(1) that the number of Eucharistic Prayers available for use with adults will increase, and
(2) that the opportunities for adults to participate actively in the Eucharistic Prayer will develop along the lines indicated below (under *Participation and Expression).*

III. Language

Any Eucharistic Prayer must be able to stand up to frequent use. Hence simplicity and brevity are not the only criteria for children's Eucharistic Prayers. A good Eucharistic Prayer will not yield up its full meaning at first, but will be capable of indefinite use. In other words it will combine simplicity with depth. Two sorts of language seem likely to be helpful here, in combination, poetic and scriptural. By poetic is meant language with a strong rhythm and which uses imagery. By scriptural is meant not necessarily biblical quotation, but rather allusion to scripture. Such language will not communicate a precise meaning once and for all; it will communicate a meaning, but in doing so will set off resonances in the minds of those present, so that in practice the prayers will be open to indefinite exploration and explanation.

IV. Participation and Expression

It is recognized by psychologists, and increasingly by liturgists, that if an emotion, sentiment or idea is to become truly part of a person, then that person needs to express it. This is why participation, and active participation at that, is necessary in the liturgy. At present active participation in the Eucharistic Prayer is confined to the dialogue before the Preface, the Sanctus, the acclamation after the consecration and the final Amen.

Some have sought to solve this problem by having everyone recite the Canon together. This seems to swing to the opposite extreme. It would seem better to provide further opportunities for congregational involvement as the eastern liturgies do or did, while still respecting the presidential nature of the Eucharistic Prayer.

One way of doing this would be to keep the beginning and end of the Preface, but to allow those present to pronounce their own motives for praising God in the middle of the Preface. Similarly, they could pronounce their intentions for petitionary prayer in a pause during this part of the Eucharistic Prayer.

Another way, as well as or instead of the first, would be to increase and vary the acclamations at various points in the Eucharistic Prayer: hence there could be acclamations:

at the end of the Preface (Sanctus, etc.)
after the prayer invoking the Spirit on the gifts
after the Institution Narrative
after the anamnesis (expression of offering)
after the invocation of the Spirit on the communicants
by joining in the final doxology (not merely the Amen).

V. Variety and Choice

It seems desirable that a fair number of Eucharistic Prayers should be commissioned and produced, firstly to suit the different age groups and secondly to provide a choice of prayers for each age group. In the Appendix we give examples of newly composed prayers for study and criticism. The age groups are:

(1) 6–8 years (first communicants)
(2) 9–11 (top juniors)
(3) 12–14 (years 1 and 2 seniors)
(4) 14–16 (top seniors)

After this they should be introduced to the adult prayers, but attention is drawn to what has been said previously about the need for more prayers for adults and greater scope for their participation in the Eucharistic Prayer.

Liverpool Archdiocesan Liturgical Commission
December 1974

APPENDIX TO GUIDELINES

Eucharistic Prayer for Children 6–8

We are very glad to come together to praise and thank you, God our Father, because you are so good to us. Everything we have is your gift—our homes and families, our friends and fun and all the wonderful things in your world.

Sing:
Holy, holy, holy.
Holy is the Lord.
Heaven and earth are praising you,
Lord most high.

(Infant Praise No. 33)

Your best gift of all is Jesus, your Son and our Brother. He lived and died for us and when he rose again he shared with us his Holy Spirit so that we could grow up good and loving like him.

Father, may our offerings of bread and wine be changed now by the Holy Spirit into Jesus himself.

On the night before he died, Jesus was having supper with his friends. He took some bread and thanked you, God our Father, for it. He broke the bread and gave it to his friends saying, "Take and eat this, all of you. This is my body."

Then he took a cup of wine, and when he had thanked you for it he gave it to his friends saying, "Take this, all of you, and drink. This is my blood; a sign of our friendship."

Sing:
Jesus is our friend.
He is with us now and always.

God our Father, we remind you that Jesus offered his life to you to help us. We join in his offering and we offer you our own lives too that we may all be friends with you and with each other.

Sing:
With Jesus
We offer ourselves to you.

We are glad to belong to your big family here on earth. We remember, too, Mary and all your friends in heaven and we ask them to help us to be good children of yours.

All of us, joined with Jesus, by the Holy Spirit, praise and thank you, God our Father, now and for ever. Amen.

Eucharistic Prayer for Top Juniors
Yes, it is right and fitting that we should come together to praise you, God our Father.

For you have called us into your family and you ask us to carry on the work of Jesus in our world, sharing with others the good news of your great love for us.

Sing:
Holy, holy, holy.

All through history you have been calling men and women to work with you, so that people might come to know you better and learn to live in your way. Abraham and Moses heard your call and trusted you to be with them in the unknown. Mary, too, welcomed you into her life and so gave your Son a home on this earth. Now you ask us also to live our lives in a way that shows everybody that we belong to you. This we can do, in the power of the Holy Spirit.

This same Holy Spirit is with us now so that our offerings of bread and wine may become Jesus Christ in our midst.

Consecration: Canon 2
Let us proclaim what we believe: SUNG Acclamation.

And so, Father:
   (with Priest) With these gifts, we offer ourselves, our lives, our senses, our talents, all that we can use in your service.

Accept us as you accept Jesus your Son whose life, death and resurrection we lovingly recall in this Mass.

May your Holy Spirit help us to find in this Communion strength and courage to follow in the footsteps of all the great men and women who have done your work throughout the ages. We remember especially . . . (individual contribution here).

Bless your Church everywhere, our leaders and all your people, those who are alive and those who have died (individual contributions).

May we all be one with Jesus, our Lord and Master. It is in him, and with the help of his Spirit, that we praise and thank you, God our Father, now and always. Amen.

Eucharistic Prayer for 1st and 2nd Year Secondary Pupils

Priest: Preface

It is right and fitting that we should meet as a family to praise and thank you, God our Father, for your great goodness to us—Pause—(Holy are You God our Creator and Father who makes all things for our good.) Acclamation I.

All: Holy are You, etc.—as Acclamation I.

Priest: We recognize your greatness in the beautiful things we see around us. (Pause for silent thought, spontaneous enumerations—and/or Acclamation I recited by All.)

We recognize your power in the great and small wonders of this world. (Pause—and/or Acclamation I recited by All.)

We recognize your wisdom in the knowledge and discoveries of people of our day. (Pause—and/or Acclamation I recited by All.)

We see your love in the day-by-day loving and living of people around us—in our parish (. . . . .) in our town (. . . . .) in our diocese (. . . . .) and in the whole world. (Pause—and/or Acclamation I recited by All.)

And so we join with these and all your family in Heaven and on earth as we say:

Holy, holy, holy, etc.

Priest: We learn more of your care and concern for us, through the life, death and ressurection of Jesus Your Son, whom you sent to be Your messenger of the Good News of your love.

All: Holy are You, etc.

Priest: We are proud to be your sons and daughters, and thank you for the countless times you welcome us back to your Family.

All: Holy are You, etc.

Priest: We rejoice to claim Mary as our Mother, and the saints as our family, especially (Pause for naming of Patron Saint of Church or area, or the Saint of the day).

All: Holy are You, etc.

Priest: We praise and thank You for all who have helped us to draw near to You—our parents, teachers, special friends, etc. (Pause).

All: Holy are You, etc.

Priest: We would like to join with all these and your whole family as we re-live the night before Christ died—when at table with His friends, Jesus took bread, gave you thanks and praise, broke the bread, gave it to them and said,
   "Take this all of you and eat it.
   This is my Body which will be given up for you."
And when the supper was nearly ended, He took the cup filled with wine, and again giving thanks and praise He handed it to His friends and said,
   "Take this all of you and drink from it. This is the cup of my blood, the blood which will seal the new pact between God and Man, and which will be shed for you and for all men, so that sins may be forgiven. Do this yourselves in memory of me."
Let us proclaim that we believe this great act of love.

All: (One of the four current Acclamations.)

Priest: And now Father, while we re-live this great act of love, we gladly remember how Christ Your Son offered Himself to You: we recall with thankfulness, His Death on the Cross, His triumphant Resurrection and His Ascension, and while we offer to you this holy and worthy sacrifice, we join with Christ to offer ourselves.

Loving Spirit of Christ, make this offering worthy and holy. (Acclamation II.)

All: (Repeat. . . . . .as Acclamation II.)

Priest: We offer with Christ all we are and all we do, all we would like to be and all we would like to do.

All: Loving Spirit of Christ, make this offering worthy and holy.

Priest: We offer with Christ our worries and fears.

All: Loving Spirit of Christ . . .

Priest We offer with Christ the joys of our friendships—the groups to which we are proud to belong, the people we are proud to know, the loves we find it hard to talk about.

All: Loving Spirit of Christ . . .

Priest: We offer with Christ the sorrow and pains of each day.

All: Loving Spirit of Christ . . .

Priest: We pray for all God's family—and especially for Paul our Pope, our Bishops, and all those who bear special responsibilities in this family; we pray for ourselves that our Communion with Christ may bring us to a fuller love and Union with each other; and we pray for all in great need today, those we know (Pause for individual intercession) and those we do not know so well who may be in need of our prayers. (Pause)

Lastly, we remember our relatives and friends who have died. (Pause for individual intercessions) and we join our prayers of praise with all God's family—

Through the Saving Power of Jesus
With the love of Jesus
Working with Jesus, in the Unity of His Spirit to give glory to God, our Father now and always.

All: Amen.

Eucharistic Prayer for 3rd and 4th Year Secondary Pupils

1st Response: "Father, we glory in your greatness and your love . . . it is right and fitting."
Father, it is indeed right that we should thank you. You made us out of love, and you know us all by name. (Response I.) You have set us amongst family and friends so that we might both give and share love. (Response I.)
Father, you have made it possible for us to speak our feelings to others, and find comfort in their company. (Response I.)
You have made us in your likeness so that we may return love for love. You have set us in a living family—the Church—through which we may know you and serve you. (Response I.)
Father, you strengthen our weaknesses and calm our fears through the saving strength of Jesus Christ, your Son. (Response I.) We want to thank you for Jesus Christ, who is your Son and our

brother. He fills the needs and longings of this world, and so we say to you with everyone on earth and in Heaven—

"Holy, holy, holy Lord . . ."

2nd Response: "Father, we glory in Jesus—Our Saviour and Our Friend".
Lord God, you sent your Son to us, to show us how to live. (Response II.)
It was He who helped the sick, who comforted the sad, and who cared for the poor. (Response II.)
He lived amongst us and now His Spirit remains, to help us to love each other as true brothers and sisters. (Response II.)
But when Jesus took our human nature, and brought the gift of His spirit—a spirit of love, wisdom and truth, a handful of men refused this gift of love and put Jesus to death. (Response II.)
But the living Spirit of Jesus was accepted by those who were His true disciples, and who then shared the gift of becoming your Sons, and co-heirs with Jesus, to your heavenly kingdom.
Jesus loved them so much that on the night before He died, in order that death might never separate them from Him—

"He took bread . . ."
(Eucharistic Prayer II)

Let us declare our faith in the Risen Christ (Acclamations).
This was the perfect offering—an offering of true love and obedience which is totally acceptable to you, Father, and so, gathered around your Holy Altar, we offer this bread of life and this saving

cup. Be pleased to accept our offering which we
make in union with Christ obedient on the Cross,
and in His Resurrection.

Be mindful of the redeeming actions of your Son,
Jesus Christ and grant us a share in His glory, and
a closer unity with each other through the Holy
Spirit.

3rd Response: "Father, keep us in your Spirit of truth."
Lord, remember the family of Your Church on
earth, and give us your Spirit to be our guide.
(Response III.)
Remember those who are building a world, worthy
of being united to its God (mention of youth/so-
cial action groups). (Response III.)
Father, look with love and pity on the less fortu-
nate—the hungry, the lonely, the homeless, and
give us the privilege of leading them into a better
world full of peace, love and joy. (Response III.)
Remember Lord, our parents, relatives, friends and
fellow students. (Response III.)
Father, send your Spirit of love upon us who are
about to receive the Body and Blood of Your Son,
Jesus Christ, our Saviour and our Brother. Keep us
true to your name and give us a share in the life of
heavenly joy with our Mother Mary, and those
saints who spent their lives in your service. Let us
try to be at peace with everyone—through the
saving power of Jesus,
With the love of Jesus.
Working with Jesus in the Unity of His Spirit. We
give glory to God our Father, now and forever.

Amen.

[*Note:* The Liverpool Archdiocese did not seek any official approval for its newly-composed Eucharistic Prayers since the Vati-

can issued its own Prayers for Children soon after the Liverpool Document appeared. Throughout the report, the British classification of younger children has been used. The report divides these children into four groups: (1) Children, Age 6–8; (2) "Top Juniors"—Children, age 9–11; (3) 1st & 2nd "Seniors" or "Secondary Students," age 12–14; and (4) "Top Seniors" or "3rd & 4th Secondary Students," age 14–16.]

Appendix C
DOCUMENTATION: ROMAN CATHOLIC EUCHARISTIC PRAYERS FOR USE IN INDIA

Of all the countries which have attempted to adapt the Roman Liturgy, India probably has had the most success. The native Indian culture and religious background gave liturgists something with which they could work and some background to use in the delicate work of adaptation.

The Roman Catholic India liturgists composed a number of Eucharistic Prayers in an attempt to exhibit prayers which were truly "Indian" in expression, culture, and religious outlook. Some of these prayers have received Vatican approval for public liturgical use. This appendix gives the short version of the adult Eucharistic Prayer, and also Eucharistic Prayer I for young people. Immediately below is an excerpt from an Indian publication which gives a brief summary of the Indian Liturgical Commission's understanding of the Eucharistic Prayer. (Cf. D. S. Amalorpavadass, *Towards Indigenisation in the Liturgy*, Bangalore, India [1974], pp. 62–63.)

Introduction

The nature of the Eucharistic Prayer as a proclamation made in a spirit of praise and thanksgiving gives the key to a proper understanding of its structure. The nucleus of the Eucharistic Prayer is the institution-anamnesis, two elements always bound together in the early liturgies. The institution-narrative retells and thereby celebrates in memorial what Christ said and did at the Last Supper. In the Anamnesis the Church explains to herself the meaning of this reiteration of Christ's words and actions: it is the memorial of the Christ-event and the sacramental offering of his sacrifice. This nucleus is enshrined in a double framework: at the beginning comes the proclamation of God's wonderful deeds in the history of salvation, culminating in the Christ-event, and at the end the doxology which is the climax of the entire anaphora. Two more elements are found, the structure and position of which vary: they are the epiclesis and the intercessions-commemorations. Originally, the intercessions-commemorations seem to have been grouped into one unit after the institution-anamnesis, either before or after the epiclesis. In view of their nature, and so that they may not distract the attention from the main action, it seems more appropriate to place them after the (post-institutional) epiclesis. The case of the epiclesis is more complex. God is called upon to send the Holy Spirit for a threefold end: the change of the Eucharistic gifts into the body and blood of Christ, the acceptance of the sacrifice and the graces of unity and life to be derived by the Church from its partaking in the Eucharistic banquet. All the historical evidence being considered, it would seem that originally the first epicletic motif was found in a pre-institutional epiclesis, the second and third belonging to a post-institutional epiclesis. The unification of all three motifs into one post-institutional epiclesis appears to be a later development proper to the Eastern liturgies.

The whole Eucharistic Prayer must be experienced as one continuous movement, but with a definite structure. The structure adopted by the new Eucharistic Prayers of the Roman rite

does justice to that movement and has solid foundations in the
liturgical tradition. It is composed of the following elements:

1. Introductory dialogue.
2. Proclamation of God's deeds in creation and in the history
   of salvation.
3. Pre-institutional epiclesis (first epicletic motif).
4. Institution-narrative and anamnesis.
5. Post-institutional epiclesis (second and third epicletic motifs).
6. Intercessions and commemorations.
7. Doxology.

Short Version

Introductory Dialogue (Mangalacaranam)

Cel. *   May your Holy Spirit, O God, enlighten
                      our minds and open our lips,
                      that we may sing the wonders of your
                      love!

Cong.   Help us, Spirit Divine,
                      to proclaim God's mercy!

Cel.   Let us praise and thank the Lord, our
                      God,
                      whose majesty pervades the universe!

Cong.   Great is his name and worthy of praise!

Cel.   Let us celebrate the glory of the Lord
                      whose splendour shines in the depths of
                      our hearts.

---

*Cel.—Principal celebrant; c.—one concelebrant; cc.—all concelebrants.

Cong.	Glory to Him in whom we have our being!

Proclamation
I. Cel.

O Supreme Lord of the Universe,
You fill and sustain everything around
    us.
You are the Ancient of Days
You turned, with the touch of your hand,
chaos into order, darkness into light.
Deep and wonderful, the mysteries of
    your creation.
You formed men in your own image,
entrusted the earth to their care,
and called them to share
in your own being,
your own knowledge.

Cong.

Om sacidananda svarupaya namah
Om mitya vastune namah
Om subhalakshana sampurnaya namah
Hail to the one
Who is being, knowledge, bliss
Hail to the fullness of all perfections

Or

Hail to the supreme reality
Being, knowledge, bliss
Hail to the eternal being,
The fullness of all perfections.

II. c.

Father most kind and merciful,
you want all men to reach the shores of
    salvation.

You reveal yourself to all
who search for you with a sincere heart.
You are the Power almighty
adored as Presence hidden in nature
the Light that shines bright
in the hearts of all who seek you
through knowledge and love, sacrifice
    and detachment.
You chose for yourself a people
and made with them a lasting covenant
Despite their infidelity,
you were true to your promise,
and taught them to long for the day of
    the Saviour
the day of peace and salvation for all
    men.

Cong.

Hail to the expectation of the nations,
Hail to the promised one of Israel,
Hail to him who comes in the name of
    the Lord.

III. c.

O God invisible,
at the favourable time
you were pleased to become visible to us.
Your Word, your only-begotten Son,
took on our human condition
and was born of the Virgin Mary.
As Supreme Teacher and Master,
he imparted the words of eternal life
to the poor and humble of heart.
He went about doing good.
When his hour had come,
of his own accord he laid down his life
as a sacrifice for our sin.
Raised from the dead by you, Father,

he became for us the source of life
and sent the Holy Spirit
to fill the world with joy and peace.

First Epiclesis
IV. cc.

Now we pray you, Father,
send this same Spirit
to fill these gifts of bread and wine
with his divine power,
and to make present among us
the great mystery of our salvation.

Cong.

Come, O Spirit Supreme,
Come, O Spirit All-Holy,
Come, O Spirit who fill the whole world.

Institution-Narrative
V. cc.

At the Supper
which he shared with his disciples,
your Son, Jesus Christ,
took bread in his sacred hands,
gave you praise and thanks,
broke the bread and gave it to his
disciples, saying:
TAKE THIS, ALL OF YOU, AND EAT
IT:
THIS IS MY BODY
WHICH WILL BE GIVEN UP FOR YOU.
DO THIS TO CELEBRATE THE
MEMORIAL OF ME.

Cong.

Amen.

cc.

In the same way after supper,
he took the cup.

Again he gave you praise and thanks,
gave the cup to his disciples, saying:
TAKE THIS, ALL OF YOU, AND DRINK
    FROM IT:
THIS IS THE CUP OF MY BLOOD,
THE BLOOD OF THE NEW AND
    EVERLASTING COVENANT.
IT WILL BE SHED FOR YOU AND FOR
    ALL MEN SO THAT SINS MAY BE
    FORGIVEN.
DO THIS TO CELEBRATE THE
    MEMORIAL OF ME.

Cong.

Amen.

Anamnesis
VI. cc.

And so, Father,
in gratitude we celebrate the memorial
of the obedient death of your Son,
of his glorious resurrection from the
    dead,
his triumphant ascension into heaven
and his outpouring of the Spirit in whom
    the Church is born
while we offer you
his unique and holy sacrifice
we await his return in glory
when he comes he will gather up the
    fruits of redemption
and hold them together in his fullness
and place them at your feet.

Acclamations
Cong.

1. We announce your death
    and proclaim your resurrection,
    Lord Jesus;

gather all your people into your
  kingdom
when you come in glory.

Or

2. We proclaim your death, Lord Jesus,
   until you come in glory.

Or

3. Your resurrection is
   the hope of our salvation.

Second Epiclesis
VII. cc.
Loving Father,
Send down your Spirit,
The fullness of your bliss,
To fill with joy and peace
All of us who share in the Body and
  Blood of Christ,
That we may be one in Him,
And manifest our unity in loving service.
May He be the pledge of our resurrection
And lead us in hope to the shore of
  eternal life
With the just in the Kingdom of Heaven.

Intercessions and Commemorations
VIII. c.
Merciful Father,
bring together all your people in the Holy
  Spirit;
help them live in unity and fellowship
with Paul, our Pope,
N., our Bishop,
the patriarchs, bishops and pastors of all
  the Churches.
Bless all our brethren
who are not present at this Eucharist.

c.   Bless also the efforts of all those who
                   labour
              to build our country into a nation,
              where the poor and the hungry will have
                   their fill,
              where all peoples will live in harmony,
              where justice and peace, unity and love
                   will reign.

c.   Grant to all the departed
              a share in your bliss.
              Welcome them into your Kingdom,
              where, Mary the Virgin Mother of God,
              the Apostles and Martyrs,
              the Saints of all lands and ages,
              St. Thomas, St. Francis Xavier and
                   St. N . . .
              Unceasingly pray for us
              and help us share in the riches
              of your Son, our Lord Jesus Christ.

Doxology
     The arati is made during the doxology.
     The consecrated gifts are lifted by the celebrant while repre-
sentatives of the congregation do the arati with flower, incense
and camphor. Bell is also rung.

IX. Cel.   In the Oneness of the Supreme Spirit,
              through Christ who unites all things in
                   his fullness,
              we and the whole creation
              give to you,
              God of all, Father of all,
              honour and glory
              thanks and praise,
              worship and adoration,

now and in every age,
for ever and ever.

Cong. Amen. You are the Fullness of Reality,
One without a second,
Being, Knowledge, Bliss!
Om Tat Sat!

After the doxology all make a panchanga pranam or prostrate.

Eucharistic Prayer Particularly for the Young People I

Father in heaven, it is right that we should give you thanks and
glory;
You are the Father of all men and women,
Source of all life, all light and all goodness
You created us with the ability to understand and to be understood,
to give and to receive,
to love and be loved,
So that one day we may be one with you, who are a God of
love,
We thank you for your Son, Jesus Christ, who out of love died
for us,
Who by dying out of love taught us how to live for and with
one another.
Who gave Himself as our food and drink,
When He celebrated the Last Supper with His friends.
We wish to join Him and all the angels and saints, saying:

Holy, Holy, Holy . . . .

God, you are really good,
We will never fully understand your goodness;
Your Son, Jesus, showed how good you are

When he became one of us,
   The Son of Mary, a young woman, full of life and with a
     great capacity for love, like all of us.
Father, we thank you for your Son, Jesus Christ,
   Who cured the sick,
   Who fed the hungry,
   Who really cared for those rejected by society,
     for those oppressed by the powerful
       for those who did not find anyone to understand them,
       for those who had no true friend;
Truly he was more concerned about his fellow men than about
   himself.
This why he sacrificed himself out of love for all of us,
     obeying your Holy Will,
       though it was very hard and difficult
     for—who likes to die, when he is in his thirties?
He shows how much he loves us
     by giving Himself as food and drink.

When he gathered his friends around the table for supper,
He took bread, blessed it, broke it,
And shared it with them, saying:

Take this, all of you, and eat it:
This is my body, which will be given up for you.

At the end of the same supper,
He took the cup with wine,
He thanked you, blessed the cup and shared it with His friends,
   saying:
Take this, all of you, and drink from it:
This is the cup of my blood
The blood of the New and Everlasting Covenant,
It will be shed for you and for all men,
So that sins may be forgiven. Do this in memory of me.

Let us proclaim the mystery of our faith:

Christ has died,
Christ is risen,
Christ will come again.

In gratitude, heavenly Father, we recall
That Your Son suffered and died for us,
That He overcame death by His resurrection,
That He is now with You in heaven.
Full of hope we are looking forward to the day,
When he will come to take away all our sorrows and sufferings
And make all mankind share in the immeasurable Joys of love.

Lord, send Your Spirit among us,
To fill us with His light and life,
So that we who are gathered around this altar,
May grow into your family united in love.
Lord, You have made us responsible for our world.
It depends on us whether it will be a valley of tears
Or a family united in love, of which you are the Father.
Please, send Your Holy Spirit,
To help us in that great task.
May we see with your eyes,
        hear with your ears,
        understand with your mind,
        speak, respond and inspire with your mouth,
        love with your heart,
        act with your strength,
        be your loving hands in this our world.
In union with the whole Church and all people of good will,
        with our Holy Father, Pope Paul and our bishop . . .,
We pray for the young people all over the world,
    particularly for those who have to suffer or are persecuted for
    their convictions,

and for those who have no hope or conviction left,
because all their dreams have been shattered.
We pray for the young people of our country,
that they may have ideals worth living for,
and for which they may even be prepared to die.

Finally Lord, we pray for all those who are very close and dear
to us. . . . . .
(other intentions are added)
All glory to the Father,
To the Son, and to the Holy Spirit
Who are true life and true love, one God, forever and ever.
Amen.

BIBLIOGRAPHY AND REFERENCES

"Aberrazioni." *Notitiae.* 11 (1975), p. 169.

Albertine, Richard, M.M. "Problem of the (Double) Epiclesis in the New Roman Eucharistic Prayers." *Ephemerides Liturgicae.* v. 91 (May–June 1977), n. 3, pp. 193–202.

Amalorpavadass, D. S. *Towards Indigenisation in the Liturgy.* Bangalore, India: National Biblical, Catechetical & Liturgical Centre, no date [1974].

At the Lord's Table (Supplemental Worship Resources #9) Nashville, TN: Abingdon Press, 1981. (A collection of about 20 new seasonal and thematic Eucharistic Prayers for use in the United Methodist Church.)

Audet, Jean-Paul, O.P. "Literary Forms and Contents of a Normal *Eucharistia* in the First Century." *Studia Evangelica* (published as vol. 73 of *Texte und Untersuchungen zur Geschichte der Altchristliches Literatur*). Berlin, 1959, pp. 623–62.

The Book of Common Prayer. New York: The Church Hymnal Corporation, 1979. [Protestant Episcopal Church]

Bouley, Allan. *From Freedom to Formula: The Evolution of the Eucharistic Prayer from Oral Improvisation to Written Texts* (Studies in Christian Antiquity, v. 21). Washington, D.C.: Catholic University Press, 1981.

Bouyer, Louis. *Eucharist: Theology and Spirituality of the Eucharistic Prayer.* Notre Dame: University of Notre Dame Press, 1968.

Brown, Raymond E., S.S. *Priest and Bishop: Biblical Reflections.* Paramus, N.J.: Paulist Press, 1970.

Buxton, Richard. *Eucharist and Institution Narrative.* Great Wakering, England: Mayhew-McCrimmon, Ltd., 1976 (published for—London: Alcuin Club, Alcuin Club collections number 57).

[Chambésy Meeting, Dec. 1977, Documents] "Reflections by Orthodox and Catholic Theologians on Ministries." *The Clergy Review.* v. LXIII, n. 6 (June 1978), pp. 232–36.

Cotone, Michael, O.S.C. "The *Apostolic Tradition* of Hippolytus of Rome." *American Benedictine Review.* (1968) pp. 492–514.

Crehan, Joseph H., S.J. "Eucharistic Epiklesis: New Evidence and a New Theory." *Theological Studies.* v. 41, n. 4 (Dec 1980), pp. 698–712.

Cutrone. "Anaphora of the Apostles." *Theological Studies.* v. 34, n. 4 (Dec. 1973), pp. 624–42.

Dallen, James [1]. *Possible Patterns.* Cincinnati: North American Liturgy Resources, 1970 et al. (4 vol.).

————[2]. "The Congregation's Share in the Eucharistic Prayer." *Worship.* v. 54, n. 4 (July 1978), pp. 329–41.

Daly, Robert J. *The Origins of the Christian Doctrine of Sacrifice.* Philadelphia: Fortress Press, 1978.

Daniélou, Jean. *The Theology of Jewish Christianity.* Chicago: The Henry Regnery Co., 1964. (The Development of Christian Doctrine before tbe Council of Nicaea. Vol. 1.)

Davies, J. G. (ed.) *A Dictionary of Liturgy and Worship.* New York: The Macmillan Company, 1972.

Deiss, Lucien. *Early Sources of the Liturgy.* Staten Island, N.Y.: Alba House, 1967.

Diekmann, L. Godfrey, O.S.B. "The Laying On of Hands: The Basic Sacramental Rite." *Liturgy.* v. 21, n. 1 (Jan 1976), pp. 22–27. [Also found in *Proceedings of the Catholic Theological Society of America* v. 29 (1974), pp. 339–51, with comments by J. Powers and E. Kilmartin on pp. 353–6, 357–66.]

Dix, Gregory. *The Shape of the Liturgy.* Westminster: Dacre Press, 1964.

[On the Doxology] *Notitiae.* 14 (1978), # #143–44 (June–July), pp. 304–05.

Elert, Werner. *Eucharist and Church Fellowship in the First Four Centuries.* St. Louis, MO: Concordia Publishing House, 1966.

Empereur, James. "Rite On." *Modern Liturgy.* 5 (1978), #2 [March—Holy Thursday Issue], p. 15.

Eucharistiae Participationem. Sacred Congregation for Divine Worship. April 27, 1973. [Letter regarding Eucharistic Prayers]

[Eucharistic Prayers] *Studia Liturgica.* v. 11 (1976–1977).

[Eucharistic Prayers and Eucharistic Piety] *Resonance.* v. 6 (1971), #1.

Fulco, William, S.J. "Jewish Storytelling and Anamnesis." *Modern Liturgy.* v. 3, n. 8 (Nov./Dec. 1976), pp. 8–9.

Gusmer, Charles W. "A Bill of Rites: Liturgical Adaptation in America." *Worship.* v. 51, n. 4 (July, 1977), pp. 283–9.

Guzie, Tad W. *Jesus and the Eucharist.* New York: Paulist Press, 1974.

Henderson, J. Frank. " . . . In Memory of Me." *Liturgy.* 23 (March 1978), #2, pp. 23–25.

Hertz, Joseph H. *The Authorized Daily Prayer Book.* New York: Bloch Publishing Co., 1948.

Hippolytus of Rome. *Apostolic Tradition.* For English translations, see Cotone, Deiss.

Hoey, Robert F., S.J. *The Experimental Liturgy Book.* New York: Herder & Herder, 1969.

Hovda, Robert W. "The Eucharistic Prayer Is More Than Words." *Living Worship.* v. 11, n. 4 (April 1975).

Hussey, M. Edmund. "Nicholas Afanassiev's Eucharistic Ecclesiology: A Roman Catholic Viewpoint." *Journal of Ecumenical Studies.* 12 (1975), pp. 235–52.

Inaestimabile Donum. Instruction (on Liturgical Practices). Sacred Congregation for the Sacraments and Divine Worship. April 3, 1980.

Jasper, R.C.D. and Cuming, G.J. *Prayers of the Eucharist: Early and Reformed.* London: Collins, 1975.

Jeremias, Joachim [1]. *The Eucharistic Words of Jesus.* London: S.C.M. Press, 1966.

———[2]. *The Lord's Prayer.* Philadelphia: Fortress Press, 1964. (Facet Book. Biblical Series #8.)

Jones, Cheslyn; Wainwright, Geoffrey; Yarnold, Edward, S.J. (eds.) *The Study of Liturgy.* New York: Oxford Univ. Press, 1978.

Jungman, Josef A. [1]. *The Mass of the Roman Rite.* 2 vols. New York: Benziger, 1951.

———[2]. *The Eucharistic Prayer.* (Robert L. Batley, trans.) Chicago: Fides, 1956.

Kadushin, Max. *Worship and Ethics: A Study in Rabbinic Judaism.* Northwestern University Press, 1964.

Kavanagh, Aidan, O.S.B. [1]. "Thoughts on the Roman Anaphora" [Part 1]. *Worship.* v. 39, n. 9 (Nov. 1965), pp. 515–29.

———[2]. "Thoughts on the Roman Anaphora" [Part 2]. *Worship.* v. 40, n. 1 (Jan. 1966), pp. 2–16.

———[3]. "Thoughts on the New Eucharistic Prayers." *Worship.* v. 43, n. 1 (Jan. 1969), pp. 2–12.

———[4]. "How Rite Develops: Some Laws Intrinsic to Liturgical Evolution." *Worship.* v. 41 (1967), pp. 337ff.

Keifer, Ralph A. [1]. "Preparation of the Altar and the Gifts or Offertory?" *Worship.* v. 48, n. 10 (Dec. 1974), pp. 595–600.

———[2]. "Liturgical Text as Primary Source for Eucharistic Theology." *Worship.* v. 51, n. 3 (May 1977), pp. 186–96.

———[3]. *To Give Thanks and Praise.* Washington, D.C.: National Association of Pastoral Musicians, 1980.

———[4]. "The Eucharistic Prayer, Part I: Thoughts on Its History." *Pastoral Music.* v. 6, n. 1 (Oct.–Nov. 1981), pp. 15–17.

———[5]. "The Eucharistic Prayer, Part II: Restoring the Assembly's Role." *Pastoral Music.* v. 6, n. 2 (Dec.–Jan. 1982), pp. 12–15.

Kilmartin, Edward J., S.J. "Sacrificium Laudis: Content and Function of Early Eucharistic Prayers." *Theological Studies.* v. 35, n. 2 (June 1974), pp. 268–87.

Kittel, Gerhard (ed.). *Theological Dictionary of the New Testament.* Grand Rapids, Mich.: Wm. B. Eerdmans Publ. Co., 1964.

Krouse, Dennis W. "The Historical Experience: A Review of the Great *Amen* in Christian Tradition." *Chicago Studies.* 16 (1977), 1 (Spring), pp. 135–56.

Kucharek, Casimir. *The Byzantine-Slav Liturgy of St. John Chrysostom.* Allendale, N.J.: Alleluia Press, 1971.

[Language and the Liturgy—Subject of entire issue] *Worship.* v. 52, n. 6 (Nov. 1978).

Lash, Nicholas. *His Presence in the World.* Dayton: Pflaum Press (London: Sheed and Ward), 1968.

Ledogar, Robert J. [1]. "The Eucharistic Prayer and the Gifts Over Which It Is Spoken." *Worship.* v. 41, n. 10 (Dec. 1967), pp. 578–96.

———[2]. *Acknowledgement: Praise Verbs in the Early Greek Anaphoras.* Rome, 1968.

Lengeling, Emil J. "Le probleme des nouvelles prieres eucharistiques dans la liturgie romaine." *Questions Liturgiques.* v. 53 (1972), p. 251.

Life and Worship. (n. 172), v. XLI, n. 4 (Oct. 1972), p. 8, n. 17.

Ligier, Louis. "The Origins of the Eucharistic Prayer: From the Last Supper to the Eucharist." *Studia Liturgica.* 9 (1973), pp. 176–85.

Liturgie et vie chrétienne [French Canadian]. July–Sept., 1974. [This entire issue was devoted to the composition of new Eucharistic Prayers and includes articles concerning guidelines for language and criteria for evaluation.]

Liverpool, England, Roman Catholic Archdiocese of. "Eucharistic Prayers for Children—Guidelines for Composition." Dec. 1974 (among other places, it may be found in *The Clergy Review.* v. LX, n. 8 [August 1975], pp. 535–41, and v. LX, n. 10 [October 1975], pp. 664–71.)

Lundin, Jack W. *Liturgies for Life.* Downers Grove, Ill.: C.C.S. Publishing House, 1971.

Lutheran Book of Worship. Minneapolis: Augsburg Publishing House, 1978.

Martimort, A. G. *The Church at Prayer: The Eucharist.* New York: Herder and Herder, 1973.

McKenna, John H., C.M. [1]. "Eucharistic Epiclesis: Myopia or

Microcosm?" *Theological Studies.* v. 36, n. 2 (June 1975), pp. 265–84.

————[2]. *Eucharist and Holy Spirit: The Eucharistic Epiclesis in 20th Century Theology.* Great Wakering, England: Mayhew-McCrimmon, Ltd., 1975 (published for—London: Alcuin Club, Alcuin Club collections no. 57).

McManus, Frederick R. "Liturgical Law and Difficult Cases." *Worship.* v. 48, n. 6 (June–July 1974), pp. 347–66.

McNaspy, C. J., S.J. *What a Modern Catholic Believes About Worship.* Chicago: Thomas More Press, 1973.

Meyendorff, John. "Notes on the Orthodox Understanding of the Eucharist." *Concilium.* v. 24. New York: Paulist Press, 1967, pp. 51–58.

Mitchell, Nathan, O.S.B. "Christian Initiation: Decline and Dismemberment." *Worship.* v. 48, n. 8 (Oct. 1974), pp. 458–79.

Mossi, John P., S.J. *Bread Blessed and Broken.* New York: Paulist Press, 1974.

Moulton, James Hope, and Milligan, George. *The Vocabulary of the Greek Testament.* London: Hodder and Stoughton, Ltd., 1957.

Music in Catholic Worship. Bishops' Committee on the Liturgy. Washington, D.C.: United States Catholic Conference Publications Office, 1972.

National Bulletin on Liturgy. Canadian Conference of Catholic Bishops. (cf. especially the following issues.) v. 9, n. 54 (2nd ed, 1978)—Story of the Mass; v. 12, n. 71 (Nov.–Dec., 1979)—Sunday Eucharist; v. 13, n. 76 (Nov.–Dec., 1980)—Worship '80: Eucharist; v. 14, n. 77 (Jan.–Feb., 1981)—Sunday Eucharist: II

Notitiae (n. 104), v. 11, n. 4 (April 1975).

[on the "Orans" posture of prayer] "Orant, Orante." *Dictionnaire d'Archéologie Chrétienne et de Liturgie.* Paris, 1936.

Perham, Michael. *The Eucharist.* [Alcuin Club Manual, No. 1] London: Alcuin Club/SPCK, 1978.

Podhradsky, Gerhard. *New Dictionary of the Liturgy.* Staten Island: Alba House, 1966.

Quinn, James, S.J. *The Theology of the Eucharist.* Notre Dame: Fides Publishers, Inc., 1973.

Regan, Patrick, O.S.B. [1]. "Liturgy and the Experience of Celebration." *Worship.* v. 47, n. 10 (Dec. 1973), pp. 592–600.

————[2]. "Pneumatological and Eschatological Aspects of Liturgical Celebration." *Worship.* v. 51, n. 4 (July 1977), pp. 332–50.

Ryan, John Barry. [1]. *The Eucharistic Prayer.* New York: Paulist Press, 1974.

————[2]. "Toward Adult Eucharistic Prayers." *Worship.* v. 48, n. 9 (Nov. 1974), pp. 506–15.

————[3]. Chronicle—Meeting of Societas Liturgica on the Eucharistic Prayer. *Worship.* v. 49, n. 8 (Nov. 1975), pp. 560–67.

Seasoltz, R. Kevin, O.S.B. *New Liturgy, New Laws.* Collegeville, Minn.: The Liturgical Press, 1980.

Sheppard, Lancelot. *The New Liturgy.* London: Darton, Longman & Todd, 1970.

Smits, Kenneth, O.F.M. Cap. "The Eucharistic Prayer." *AIM: Aids in Ministry.* v. 6, n. 3 (Fall 1978), pp. 18–19.

Soubigou, Louis. *A Commentary on the Prefaces and the Eucharistic Prayers of the Roman Missal.* (John A. Otto, trans.) Collegeville, Minn.: Liturgical Press, 1971.

Talley, Thomas J. [1]. "From *Berakah* to *Eucharistia*: A Reopening Question." *Worship.* v. 50 (March 1976), pp. 115–37.

————[2]. "The Eucharistic Prayer: Directions for Development." *Worship.* v. 51, n. 4 (July, 1977), pp. 316–25.

Tegels, Aelred, O.S.B. [1]. Chronicle—"Variety and Uniformity in Eucharistic Prayer." *Worship.* v. 47, n. 8 (Oct. 1973), pp. 501–03.

————[2]. Chronicle—"Creativity in Eucharistic Prayer." *Worship.* v. 49, n. 4 (April 1975), pp. 243–46.

Toporoski, Richard. "The Language of Worship." *Communio: International Catholic Review.* IV (1977), #3, pp. 226–60 (also published in abridged form in *Worship.* v. 52, n. 6 [Nov. 1978], pp. 489–508).

Vagaggini, Cipriano, O.S.B. *The Canon of the Mass and Liturgical*

Reform. Staten Island: Alba House, 1967.

Vischer, L. "Epiclesis: Sign of Unity and Renewal." *Studia Liturgica.* v. 6 (1969), #1, pp. 30–39.

Walsh, Eugene A., S.S. *Practical Suggestions for Celebrating Sunday Mass.* Glendale, Az.: Pastoral Arts Associates of North America, 1978.

"The Windsor Statement on Eucharistic Doctrine." [Anglican/Roman Catholic] (among other places, it may be found in *Worship.* v. 46, n. 1 (Jan. 1972), pp. 2–5).

Word and Action. New York: Seabury Press (SP 57), 1969.

OUTLAWS OF EMPTY POKE

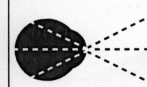

This Large Print Book carries the
Seal of Approval of N.A.V.H.

OUTLAWS OF EMPTY POKE

E. E. HALLERAN

WHEELER PUBLISHING
A part of Gale, Cengage Learning

GALE
CENGAGE Learning

Detroit • New York • San Francisco • New Haven, Conn • Waterville, Maine • London

GALE
CENGAGE Learning·

LIBRARY OF CONGRESS CATALOGING-IN-PUBLICATION DATA

Halleran, E. E. (Eugene E.), 1905–
    Outlaws of Empty Poke / by E.E. Halleran. — Large Print edition.
    pages cm. — (Wheeler Publishing Large Print Western)
    ISBN 978-1-4104-6150-6 (softcover) — ISBN 1-4104-6150-5 (softcover) 1.
Large type books. I. Title.
PS3515.A3818O955 2013
813'.54—dc23   2013017321

Published in 2013 by arrangement with Golden West Literary Agency

Printed in the United States of America
1 2 3 4 5   17 16 15 14 13

Outlaws of Empty Poke

CHAPTER 1

A brassy sun was beginning to lengthen the morning shadows when Vicker saw the wisp of dust on his back trail. He eased the roan around in a quarter turn and squinted hard into the haze that was already turning the valley into a trembling distortion of itself. It was dust, all right. There had been no wandering cattle back there on those barren slopes, and it didn't seem likely that the Apaches would have swung so far to the west.

"Me and my curiosity!" Vicker exclaimed half aloud. A disgusted grimace twisted his stubble of sandy whiskers as he added, "I guess I wasn't as smart as I thought I was. Somebody spotted me."

He stared long enough to make sure that the dust was actually moving toward him, and then he headed east at a pace that would soon put him across the San Pedro and on the main trail to Tombstone. It hurt his pride that his scouting tactics had been clumsy enough to draw attention, but he had seen enough to know that pursuit had to mean something more than mere curiosity on the part of the pursuer.

Beyond the San Pedro, he cut away to the north along the lower slopes of a ridge, keeping well above the almost dry bed of the winding creek. This move should tell him something. If the dust followed him into this land of thorny nowhere, he could be sure that it was actually pursuit and not merely a case of riders happening to be on the same trail as himself.

He even began to feel good about the ruse. He could keep himself in the long shadows of the Mules while the unknown on his trail would be down sun and exposed to observation. Vicker slouched a little more in the saddle, relaxing against the increasing heat and the hint of danger. Here on the border there were no spit-and-polish officers to reprimand a young lieutenant for conserving his energies. In five years of army service, Vicker had never been able to persuade a superior officer that a man could still be alert when he was physically relaxed. Now he could do as he pleased — so he "slouched." In this land, where nature seemed determined to be hostile, a man had to roll with the punches whenever he could.

Twenty minutes later, he knew that he was in trouble. Three riders were coming up at a fast pace, already beginning to edge along the slope where no trail existed. Now there could be no doubt as to their intentions; they were after him. He did not yet know the meaning of some of the things he had been seeing during the past couple of weeks, but the general idea had been clear enough. This was outlaw country. They ruled it as they saw fit, and they would not welcome a stranger who studied their activities.

He knew that there could be no point in trying to outrun pursuit. The roan under him was not much of a horse, having been picked deliberately to seem like the kind of animal a saddle bum might ride. Minimum transportation and part of a disguise. That had been the idea. Not a horse for outrunning well-mounted gunmen, especially after almost three weeks on the poorest kind of graze. For the unshaved tramp in the ancient saddle, there had to be some other answer than flight.

He eased the horse along the yellow slope, picking his way between scattered junipers and around the more bristling mesquite clumps. Somewhere there should be a bit of terrain that might suit his purpose. Before coming into this border country, he had memorized the sketchy maps of the area, so he knew that he was angling away from his goal. His effort to identify pursuit had sent him up along the wrong face of the mountains, into a region that he had not bothered to study because he had not intended to use it.

He noted that the land was not quite as barren as some of the real desert stretches he had seen, but was a ragged sort of wilderness. An occasional shallow draw showed deeper thickets of greasewood, so he hoped that he would find a place where he might set up a desperation defense. Certainly he could not fight three enemies in the open.

For a few minutes, he considered the chances of making a break toward Fort Huachuca, but the idea didn't seem too good. The post was probably closer than Tombstone, but it was still too far away. He had to plan ahead.

The June sun beat down savagely as he continued his slow but steady pace. The blazing rays were coming across the peaks now, and he took an occasional pull at the battered canteen, trying to ease the discomfort of dry mouth and cracked lips. Like the rest of his outfit, the canteen was obviously a discard. It matched the tattered Levi's and the shaggy red whiskers. Vicker had taken plenty of pains to look the drifter in every respect, just as he had studied hard to learn the country before venturing into it. Now he wondered where he had slipped. His disguise had been good enough, so he had to assume that any curious stranger would be subject to the brand of violence that now threatened.

The trio in the rear had closed in briskly during the last hour of riding, making no attempt at concealment, as though aware that their quarry was on a blind trail from which there was no available escape. Vicker studied them over one lean shoulder from time to time, seeing that one man wore the high-crowned conical sombrero of the *vaquero*. Probably it was the same Mexican who had become such a nuisance; during those last few days of watching Ike Marley's wagon. The fellow had made Vicker's job anything but easy, and now it seemed that he must have spotted the fact that Marley was under surveillance by a stranger.

The weary roan was stumbling when Vicker saw the draw that slashed into the eastern mesquite slope. It was clearly a box canyon of some sort, a trap for any man who let himself get caught in it. Still Vicker did not hesitate. He had to gamble on some-

11

thing; time was running out on him.

He reined the bronc into the mesquite that masked the lower end of the slash, riding only about a hundred yards up the first ragged slope and then leading the horse across a series of rock ledges that formed a kind of irregular stairway. He had barely gained the shelter of another mesquite thicket when he saw his pursuers coming around a shoulder of the ridge. He dropped the reins and hurried back down across the ledges, keeping low as he sprinted for the brush that filled the mouth of the draw.

Sweat blinded him by the time he found a place where he could drop to the ground without getting into cactus. There was just time for him to check the action of his forty-five when he heard the stuttering hoofbeats of the pursuit. Almost at that same instant, he heard a shrill yelp in Spanish. "He has gone into the mesquite!" the voice announced. "The man is crazy!"

"Anyhow we got him trapped," a heavier voice broke in, its broad accent suggestive of the southeastern mountains. "They ain't no way outa that pocket. Ya'll spread out and cover it. Don't let 'im bust through!"

Vicker could see them through the brush now. The big man on the black horse was the one giving the orders, the other two ranging out to either side to cover the flanks. When they were in position, the big man motioned them forward, taking the center himself.

There was ample opportunity for Vicker to study the fellow. He saw heavy jowls, a red face, and a straggly mustache. Probably in his early forties, Vicker guessed. A hard man — but a complete stranger. Vicker knew that he was going to kill this man so he didn't let himself think too much about it.

The other two riders were men he had seen not long before. The *vaquero* with the big straw sombrero was the one who had trailed Ike Marley back there below the border, sticking close to the little peddler until he returned to Arizona. And the lanky man coming in toward the draw from the northern approach was the same lantern-jawed, beetle-browed individual who had brought Marley some sort of message just before the store wagon made its crossing of the border. One or the other of them must be the one who had called the turn on Vicker.

The lanky rider turned in his saddle to yell, "Want to take him alive, Moose? Mebbe we oughta find out what he's got to say fer hisself."

"Gun him down!" the big man shouted in reply. "He snooped and run. That's all ah wanta know. Don't let 'im git outa here alive, that's all!"

"It still might be smart business to beat somethin' outa him," the lanky rider persisted.

"Hell with it!" Moose snapped. "That othuh varmint didn't look like much and he turned out to be a revenooer! Jest git him!"

Almost as he barked the order, he raised the Winchester that he had been carrying across his saddle horn. For an instant, Vicker thought that his hiding place had been located, but almost as quickly he knew that the big man was aiming far above him. Either he was shooting wildly or he was a marvelous shot.

Again Vicker got his answer in a hurry. There was a crashing sound up the mountain side, and the big man yipped in triumph. "I got his hoss, boys! Not much trouble about flushin' 'im out now! Blast anything that moves!"

Vicker hugged the stony ground just a little tighter. It would be suicide to let that marksman get an eye on him at this range. In a vague sort of way, he realized that for the first time in his life he was planning to kill a man from ambush — without warning. He supposed it should be worrying him. It wasn't. He was simply glad that he didn't have to meet this fellow out in the open at anything beyond sixgun range.

The other two men were climbing toward the edges of the draw while Moose rode straight toward the mesquite screen. They were not shouting at each other now. The orders were clear. They were to kill the stranger who had seen something he was not supposed to see. The hunt was on.

Vicker's jaw clamped a little more grimly as he eased the Colt into firing position, making certain that no bit of thorny brush was in line to deflect his bullet. Then he eased the hammer back, muffling it against a betraying click. By that time, the big man was close, holding the Winchester so that its muzzle seemed to be sniffing out a trail. Vicker lined his sights on the man's chest, squeezing steadily as the black horse came up the slope. When the gun bucked against his grimy hand, he didn't even wait to check results, but rolled to trigger another quick shot at the lanky man who was just in sight beyond the mesquite on his right. There was a yell of alarm — and perhaps pain — but then the lanky man was whirling his horse to dash back into the open country beyond the draw. He did not try to return the fire, and Vicker saw that he was holding to the saddle horn with both hands as he beat his retreat.

"Darn!" Vicker grumbled under his breath. "I didn't get but one of 'em! I'm still outnumbered."

He hunkered down again after seeing the Mexican ride out to join the wounded man. Neither of them bothered to see what had happened to their surly commander, nor did they make any attempt to catch the black horse when the animal galloped past them. They talked excitedly for a moment or two, and then the *vaquero* rode close to do something to the other man's back. Evidently, that hurried shot had only creased the man. The Mexican didn't even get him to dismount; he simply lifted the other rider's shirttail and applied a hasty pad of some sort.

Vicker used the delay to change his position. In his haste, he had not brought spare ammunition from his bed roll, so he climbed back up the slope to where he had left his horse. The animal was stone dead, shot through the head. An enemy who could make a shot like that was a good one to put out of action. Vicker had to hope that neither of the other pair were as good.

He made no attempt to salvage the bat-

16

tered saddle or other gear, simply unstrapping the slicker roll and taking it with him to a place of better concealment where he might get to the cartridges and the few bits of army hardtack that he had carried as an emergency ration. A shot from the valley warned him that he had been seen, but he decided that the Mexican was not the marksman the dead man had been. This slug had whined off a rock a good ten feet above the target. Moose had made a direct hit at about the same range.

Then another thought came to him, and he didn't feel so good about the way he was figuring things out. He had made another stupid mistake. Instead of worrying over a handful of cartridges he should have dashed out into the open and grabbed the dead man's Winchester.

"You don't deserve to get out of this jam, Vicker," he told himself in fine disgust. "It wasn't bad enough that you had to blunder around and let yourself be spotted on Marley's trail. You had to get extra stupid at exactly the time you should have been using your thick head!"

He eased back down across the ridges, again trying to confuse the enemy by changing position, at the same time hoping that he still might have a chance to try for that fallen rifle.

Then he saw that the enemy was not performing any more brilliantly than he had. They drew apart, the lanky man holding himself stiffly in the saddle, but still able to control his horse. He rode straight back toward the draw, while the Mexican turned north on the trail of the loose horse. It was a bit of bad strategy that Vicker promptly decided to turn to his own account. With only a wounded man close enough to use a weapon, there was still a good chance of getting hold of the fallen rifle.

He scuttled along at a crouch until the mesquite could no longer conceal him. Then he ran straight out into the open. As he had hoped, the lanky rider was taken by surprise. It took him precious moments to see what the intended quarry was trying to do, and then he was slow in using shaky muscles to get his rifle into position. He fired just one shot before Vicker took a headlong dive into the shelter of the corpse. The shot was not even close.

There was a moment of suspense while the Winchester was being pried from beneath the dead man, its action checked for injury or a clogging mass of sand. The weapon proved undamaged, so Vicker blew loose dirt from both muzzle and breech, making sure that a shell was in the chamber and that the sights had not been knocked out of line. By that time, the lanky man was coming in and opening fire as he made the attack. One slug thudded sickeningly into the dead body that had become Vicker's fort, but the others screamed overhead to ricochet up the rocky slope. The lanky man was close when Vicker wiped the sweat from his eyes and brought the captured rifle to bear. There was a moment to steady himself and to try for a gentle squeeze against the unfamiliar trigger pull. In that moment, he saw the lean, hard features that he had noted from a distance, features that were too narrow for the size of the big nose and the heavy black brows that met above that nose. This was indeed the man who had taken some kind of message to Ike Marley.

Then the Winchester barked, and Vicker knew that he had fired low, dragging the weapon's muzzle down just a trifle when the trigger proved to be stiffer than he had anticipated. He could see the lean man's convulsive jerk, and there was a moment or two when the rider fought his horse around in a skidding turn. Vicker could easily have finished the job then, but instead he held his fire. He knew that it was foolish to be squeamish about it, but he still couldn't bring himself to shoot. The man was out of the fight now; there was no need to be a cold-blooded killer just because he happened to be in a country where such men ran the show.

The Mexican gave up his chase of the black horse and came back at a gallop, not quite promptly enough to keep the wounded man from tumbling out of his saddle. Vicker watched as the Mexican dismounted, a little beyond decent range. He saw that once more the wounded man was getting attention, so he turned his own thoughts to the dead man in front of him. It made him feel like a thief to go through the fellow's pockets, but he forced himself to do it. The result was not very important: a few coins, some loose rifle cartridges, a pair of twenty-dollar bills folded together. Vicker took them all, feeling no particular qualms of conscience about it.

By that time, the *vaquero* was helping his wounded companion back into the saddle. The man was moving with evident pain, but he could still handle himself. The bullet that hit him must have been off the mark in more ways than one.

When both men were mounted again, they rode away to the south without even a backward look at the mesquite. Vicker watched them for a minute or two, trying to guess what their next move would be. There would be further pursuit, he supposed, but there was no additional dust anywhere in sight, so he had to hope that they wouldn't come back with reinforcements very soon.

Almost as an afterthought, he slid the forty-five from the dead man's holster, hefting it and looking at its loads. It felt pretty good. Then he saw that it was exactly like his own, even to the cedar butt. The coincidence struck hard at him, and he knew what he was going to find even before he compared the serial numbers on the two guns. They were one digit apart. He did not remember whether his gun had been one number ahead or one behind Ulrich's, but he didn't think it made any difference. This had to be Hal Ulrich's gun. So Ulrich must be the man who had been trapped by these outlaws.

A curious numbness seemed to hit Vicker at the thought. He didn't want to know that Ulrich was dead. He tried to make his mind work on the problem of how the outlaws had known that their victim was a government agent — a revenooer, as Moose had named him. Had they learned that after they had killed him, or had they found means to make him talk? That was even worse than thinking about Ulrich's death.

But this was no time to mourn the loss of a good friend. He had problems of his own. He was afoot in a country that was as savage as the people who lived in it. His only hope was to get out there in that hundred degree heat and catch a horse. Either that or he would soon be just as dead as Hal Ulrich.

CHAPTER 2

Catching the tired-looking chestnut, left behind by the wounded man, seemed like the best bet, but the animal proved maddeningly elusive. The horse never moved very fast, but every time Vicker closed in, there would be a brief spurt and the chase would start all over again. The black kept well ahead of the slower horse, and Vicker paid little attention to him. The important thing was to catch a horse — any horse — before this leg work in the broiling sun could bring on complete collapse. After an hour of it, the heat geting worse by the minute, he was no closer to success than when he started away from the draw. All he had accomplished was to develop blisters on both heels and dried-out nasal membranes that made every breath an effort. His water was gone, and he had thrown away the old canteen.

He kept wondering how long it would take

the Mexican and his wounded companion
to bring up fresh riders. Not that it mat-
tered very much if he could not catch a
horse. A man on foot in this little piece of
hell was as good as dead even without gunmen on his trail.

Then he saw a coiled lariat on the black's
saddle, and it gave him an idea. He had
never gotten within a hundred yards of the
black horse, but several times he had been
within roping distance of the chestnut.
Maybe he could work out a combination.

He moved forward again, trying to ignore
the burning feet and the cracked lips. This
time he followed the black. It took him
twenty painful minutes to get within rifle
range, and when he did so, he sat down, using his knees to support the rifle. Even then
it was difficult to take steady aim. The heat
was beginning to get him.

He sighted carefully and saw the animal
stagger. Levering in a fresh shell, he fired
again. This time the black went down. He
knew a moment of regret at having had to
slaughter so fine an animal, but then he
laughed grimly at himself. The heat must
really be getting to him. He had known no
great qualms at shooting men, but he was
getting finicky about shooting a horse.

The black was dead when he approached.

It took a few moments to make sure that there was nothing in the saddlebags and that there was no canteen on the saddle. Then he took the rope and resumed the painstaking chase of the chestnut. The horse had spooked at the gunshot, so there was now extra distance to make up. Vicker was not at all sure that he would make it.

Actually it required another half hour, but then the chestnut submitted meekly when the loop settled around his neck. Vicker had to rest a few minutes before he could climb into the saddle, but the feel of leather between his knees did something for him. He was mounted once more, armed and fully aware of his danger. A man who lived a generally risky sort of life could ask for no more.

He sent the chestnut into a climb, knowing that his first problem was to get across toward the mesa where Tombstone had come into riotous existence. After that, he must use the remaining daylight hours to hide his trail as much as possible. After dark, he would strike out for the town itself. He could not hope to prevent trackers from learning that he was going to Tombstone, but he would not make things too easy for them.

■ ■ ■ ■

The mining town's night life was in full blast when he wandered past Allen Street's string of saloons. He had abandoned the chestnut as soon as he saw the town lights. Earlier he had dropped the Winchester and the Colt into a ravine. Now there was nothing to identify him with the morning's gun battle. The wounded man had probably seen his face, but a razor would soon take care of that. He wished that he could expect equally prompt relief from his aching feet.

No one seemed to pay any attention to him as he sore-footed it along the hard-packed strip of dirt that served as a sidewalk. He had slipped his sixgun inside his ragged shirt and now seemed harmless enough. People seemed to take him for one of the numerous bums who stuck around the boom town, working in the mines when they could not get drinking money in any other way.

He was only a block from the Border Bar, where he was supposed to meet Naismith, when he almost fled in panic. Not a dozen feet away, coming directly toward him, was Janet Meade. She had been Janet Sebrell for the past five years, but Vicker still thought of her by her maiden name. The lights of one of the larger saloons were directly upon her, and he knew that there could be no mistake; she hadn't changed at all.

He put his head down, hoping that no one had noted his hastily smothered panic. The complete astonishment at seeing the woman had almost been too much for him after the long hours of tension. Just as quickly, however, he knew that he had nothing to worry about. Janet would never recognize him. The man with her — a very young cavalry lieutenant in a bright new uniform — marched stiffly at her side in evident embarrassment. This was the time of night when respectable women left the streets to their professional sisters. The lieutenant seemed to know that. Vicker would have bet that Janet knew it, too. It would be just like her to flaunt convention while pretending to be completely ignorant of what she was doing.

The impression was heightened as he caught her tone. "I declare, Lieutenant, this has been a most thrilling evening! Shocking, I suppose, but interesting. I'm almost glad that our coach connections had to be so bad."

The lieutenant murmured something that

Vicker did not catch. The words were not important anyway. The point was that the young man was annoyed at the way men of all descriptions had come to doorways to stare. Evidently, he was trying to get Janet to see that she was receiving some rather unfortunate attention.

"Nonsense, Lieutenant!" she exclaimed as his murmur subsided. "I'm sure that it is perfectly all right for me to be here, particularly when I am so capably protected."

Then they were past, and Vicker found himself grinning in the shadows. Janet was still at the old game. That young officer — probably not more than four or five years younger than Janet — would go to his quarters thoroughly confused. He would feel that he had spent an adventurous evening playing the knight on a white horse. And he would have a sneaking suspicion that he had made a fool of himself because a pretty woman smiled at him. But he would not think badly of Janet Sebrell. No one ever did. Vicker knew for he had been through the mill.

He hobbled on past the Bird Cage Theatre where a variety troupe was staging a noisy entertainment, but then he left most of the uproar behind as he turned a corner on to one of the streets that catered to patrons with less wealth. Or perhaps less willingness to spend.

The Border Bar was almost out of town. Naismith picked such spots for these meetings. Vicker hoped that his partner would not have made himself too conspicuous. Almost a week had passed since Ben would have had to show up for a possible meeting. In that time, he would have become pretty well known. Tonight's meeting would have to be handled with proper care so as not to involve Ben.

There were six men in the dingy little room when Vicker shoved in through the partly unhinged batwings. None of them seemed too drunk, but they were dirty, sweaty, unshaven, and generally disheveled. Ben Naismith was not quite the dirtiest of the lot. Vicker decided that he could feel completely at home.

Naismith sat with three other men at a rickety table, going through the motions of a cheap poker game in the smoky heat. Vicker knew without looking that there would be small coins on the table and perhaps a couple of small greenbacks. Ben was a genius at organizing games that would allow him to sit for hours at a lookout spot and take no risk of being nicked for much money. He used the device whenever a meeting like this one had to be set up, so Vicker paid little attention to the other men at the table. They would be just window dressing for Ben Naismith — or Benny Smith, as he usually called himself on jobs like this one.

A fifth man was at the bar, trying to wheedle a drink out of a fat, unshaven bartender.

Vicker hobbled to the bar as one of the poker players grunted, "I raise a dime."

Naismith pushed a couple of nickels to the center of the table and said, "See yuh," the deep tone surprising in a man of such meager proportions.

The other two dropped greasy cards face down and sat back in disgust. No one even looked up at the newcomer, but Vicker felt sure that Ben's words had been a cryptic acknowledgment of his partner's arrival.

The man behind the apron was staring unhappily, clearly assuming that he had another bum on his hands. Vicker tried to ease his mind by asking, "Mex money good in heah?" He tried for a broad drawl, but somehow it came out with an alkali rasp in it.

"If yuh got enough of it," the fat man told him. "Silver?"

"What else?" He fished out a peso and let

30

it clatter to the scarred surface of the bar. "How's the beer? Cold?"

"Nothin's cold around here."

"Ah'll take it anyhow."

"Nothin' else?"

"Not right now."

So far as he could tell, he was being ignored by everyone in the place except the bum at his side who kept looking fixedly at the coin. The bartender brought out a bottle and opened it, letting yellow foam run out on the wood as he shoved it toward Vicker. "Grab it," he advised. "Old sponge-gut will, if you don't."

The bum protested in a mutter, but Vicker ignored the byplay. He let some of the tepid beer cut the dust out of his throat, drinking no more of it than he needed to do so. He wasn't afraid of what it might do to him; he simply didn't like it.

Out of the corner of his eye, he saw Naismith push his chair back and get his legs under him. "I reckon I had enough," the little man stated in the heavy voice that always seemed so out of place. "When the cards ain't runnin', there's no point in buckin' 'em."

"You ain't doin' bad," one of the other men snarled resentfully. "Don't try to make nobody think ye're leavin' nothin' in the

31

game. I know darn well ye took a couple o' dollars o' my money!"

Vicker took plenty of time about letting his head swivel around. He didn't want to appear interested, but he knew that Naismith would be giving him his cue. The little man had to call the play now, but Vicker wanted to make sure that there would be no waste of time. A lot of moves had to be made before fresh pursuit could develop.

Ben was on his feet, grinning amiably at the man who had lodged the protest. "I ain't more'n a half dollar to the good — if I'm that, Neddie. If somebody's got yer money, it ain't me."

"Ye're a liar," Neddie snarled, pushing back his own chair to tower a full head over Naismith. "I say ye oughta stick around and give us a chance to git even."

"Don't git proddy. Mebbe if'n yuh lose a buck or two, it might drive yuh back to work."

He started to step around the larger man, but a big hand came out to grab his arm. "I don't like winners hightailin' it out o' the game so early," the man growled. "Set down!"

Naismith tried to shake off the grip, but only succeeded in getting himself whirled back into his chair. By that time, Vicker had put the bottle back on the bar. He grinned amiably at the bum. "I had enough. Help yoreself — if yo' don't think that stuff is gonna rust yore kidneys." He felt pretty good about a couple of things. The drawl had come out better, and he had managed to smile without his lips cracking.

He started toward the door just in time to stumble against the big man who was trying to hold Naismith in the chair. "Sorry," Vicker said politely. "It's kinda hahd to outguess yo' when yo're whirlin' around like that."

The irate poker player was in no mood for jovial small talk. He turned to glower at the bewhiskered tramp. "Don't git smart with me, buster!" he growled. "Jest look where yuh're goin'!"

"I apologized," Vicker said, mildness oozing out all over him. "If yo' were a gentleman — which, of coase, yo're not — theh would be no need to . . ."

He didn't get any further with that particular speech. The big man swung around impatiently, a gnarled fist aimed at brushing aside this frowsy stranger who was interrupting a matter of business. Two things then happened. The first was that Naismith broke for the door and disappeared; the second was that Vicker sidestepped the blow, catching a hairy wrist after the force of the effort was spent. He twisted hard, and this time it was the big man who did a bit of whirling, a yelp of pain sounding as Vicker used the wrist as a lever for tossing the man into a corner of the room.

As the crash died away, Vicker forced his aching feet toward the door. "Just a mite o' politeness woulda saved that," he said in an aggrieved voice. "Makes a man real sorry." It wasn't difficult for him to maintain his pose of pained regret. His feet were providing the pain.

On the street, he paused to let his eyes accustom themselves to the darkness. No one followed him from the saloon, and after a few moments, he saw the small shadow near the corner of a shack across the street. When he moved toward it, the shadow moved ahead of him. Vicker grunted soft approval. Ben was playing it safe, as usual.

There were only a few more buildings on that street, and then the town ended. The noise was behind them, only darkness ahead. Naismith waited in the open where no eavesdropper could approach without being seen. "Sorry about big Neddie," he said in a low tone. "I didn't figger as how he'd git nasty over a couple o' bucks. Yuh're late."

"Almost didn't make it at all. You've got things all set for me to get changed? This time it's real important."

"Yuh don't need to ask, Jack. Ain't I always . . . ?"

"Save it. I'm depending on you to get me through the next hour or so with nobody seeing me."

"Easy. What's up? Somebody on yer tail?"

"There will be. That's why I put on the magnolia and honeysuckle talk. When they start asking around, I want them to get the wrong idea about the man they're trying to find."

"Let's go. I'd better tell yuh that I got a real good idea what yuh been mixin' into. Magruder's in town, and he passed the word that you moved in on somethin' that's none of our business."

"What does he know about it?"

"He ain't told me yet. But come along. Yuh got a room with him at Nellie Cashman's Hotel. He signed up fer both of yuh. That way it'll be kinda confusin' fer anybody what tries to find out when yuh hit town."

Vicker followed in silence. He did not need to be told that something was amiss. Magruder never interfered with the team of

35

Vicker and Naismith when they were making one of their preliminary scouts. To have him getting into the operation at this early stage was significant enough.

They slipped through a couple of dark alleys and then skirted a street where the only buildings were the rough shacks of mine workers. At a corner where lights showed a bit more brightly, Naismith pulled up and held out a restraining hand. "Better stop a bit. I want to make sure that Neddie ain't tryin' to foller me."

"Why should he? For a couple of dollars?"

"I dunno. He's a queer kind of hairpin. Hostler at the OK Corral. It don't hurt none to play safe."

Vicker wasn't going to argue the point. At the moment, safety sounded like the thing he wanted most, unless it was some hot water for his feet.

When they were certain that they were not being followed, they went forward again, hurrying across the lighted street and into another shadow. Finally they halted again behind a long building that had lights showing at several windows. Naismith tried a door to make certain that it was unlocked and then whispered in Vicker's ear, "Stay quiet fer a few minutes. I'll raise a bit o' noise out in front, and then yuh kin slip in.

Magruder's in Room Six. It's the first one to your left after you get through this back hallway. I'll be in later."

Vicker leaned wearily against the wall as the little man disappeared in the night. He was almost too tired to think, but his mind kept coming back to the fact that Magruder was in Tombstone. It had to mean something, and the logical guess was that it was somehow connected with the things he had seen along the border.

He was still puzzling over it when a gunshot sounded from the far side of the hotel. Then somebody yipped in a high, squealing voice, and the gun boomed again. There was a clatter of hurrying feet inside the building, and Vicker eased himself through the doorway. Two more shots sounded, and other voices began to yell alarmed questions. Evidently the occupants of the hotel were rushing to the front to see what was going on.

He saw one man disappear into what he took to be a lobby, but then he was around the corner, aiming for the door that showed the numeral Six in the light of a hall lamp. Before he could grasp the knob, the door opened and a tall man started to come out. There was a grunt of surprise, and then he backed up again. "Inside," he said briefly.

Vicker went in without replying, getting the door shut before both of them began to laugh. Paul Magruder was wearing trousers that bulked awkwardly where he had stuffed a nightshirt into them. The Vice-President of Pacific Mining and Smelting usually hung a lot of dignity on his six-foot frame, but tonight he looked anything but dignified. Instead, he was amused. "Which one of us looks worse?" he laughed. "And what's going on out there?"

"Ben thought I should get in without being seen. He made a small diversion in the front while I came in through a back door."

"Small diversion! It sounded like an Apache raid!"

He pointed to some baggage in a corner. "That's your stuff over there, Jack. Sorry I don't have much water on hand. Looks like you need a lot."

"I'll get along. Better not to ask for more right now. I don't want anybody asking questions." He had dropped into a chair and was prying off the broken boots.

"Trouble?"

"Plenty. It's a long story — and I'm not sure that I know what it all means."

"Maybe I can help on that point."

There was no chance to explain the remark. A cautious tap sounded at the door, and he went over to admit Ben. The little man grinned happily as he saw Vicker in the chair. "Nice show, hey?" he chuckled. "I stir up a real nice fuss when I set about it."

"You're an expert," Vicker told him. "Now shut up and let's get some things talked over. I'll fall asleep before we get it done if we don't make a fast job of it."

CHAPTER 3

Naismith didn't seem to be concerned at the way he had been cut off. "I'll start," he volunteered. "Mostly because I ain't got much to tell. This McLinden gent is more'n he claims to be, but I ain't been able to find no connection with gold. He runs the stage line, and he's got a fist in one or two saloon businesses here in Tombstone. Some folks seem to figger that he might have a couple of other irons in the fire, but it ain't much but gossip."

Vicker splashed cautiously with the water that he had poured from the agateware pitcher. He wasn't thinking too much about McLinden. He knew that Naismith had been sent to Tombstone to see if there might be any gossip about the gold shipments that seemed to be coming out of the Huachucas in two directions. McLinden handled them when they came through Tombstone. Now it didn't seem very important.

"So far as the real job is concerned," he said after a moment, "I can't report much more. The Empty Poke Mine is not only a dead one, it's a fake. Pacific can forget all about it. There's nothing there to develop."

"It took you all this time to find that out?" Magruder asked.

"Not quite. I might as well tell you that I went down there with another bee in my bonnet. Years ago I had a real good friend. Fellow named Hal Ulrich. We were in the army together, and he saved my hide once when we had a brush with some Comanches. Both of us got fed up with it at about the same time. I started this scouting job for Pacific, and Hal resigned his commission to take a job with the Justice Department. They used him on all kinds of border jobs in Texas because he knew the country.

"About three weeks ago I met him in Tucson. He didn't want to do much talking, but I guess he figured he'd have to tell me enough so that I'd know to keep my trap shut about him. It seems that there had been a big mail robbery near El Paso, and the government had reason to believe that the loot, mostly some nice new gold coins, had been taken down into old Mexico. The trail led to this part of the border, so they brought Ulrich out here to do some looking

41

around. The idea was that some kind of outlaw gang must've taken a hand in the gold job, maybe just to keep it hidden until it could be put into circulation a little more safely. Anyhow, this gang was supposed to have some pretty sharp operators running it, and they knew every Federal agent in the area. Ulrich had never worked out here, so they brought him in as a stranger who might have a chance."

He let the final phrase come out grimly, recalling the way he had found Ulrich's gun and what he had heard the gunman say about catching a "revenooer." "I had a hunch that Ulrich had gone into the same part of the country where I was supposed to go for a look at that gold mine. I'm a kind of a greedy cuss, you know, and I got the idea that I might pick up some reward money if I could get on the trail of that gold.

"It was only an idea until I took my first look at the Empty Poke Mine. Then I began to smell a few rats."

"What about this mine?" Magruder inquired. "Why do you say that it's a fake? We know that gold shipments have been coming out of there. That's why we sent you down for a look. Any time a mine is good enough so that its owners divide their shipments, apparently to make it appear that the mine is producing less than it really is, the thing is worth a look."

"Sure. But this fake goes deeper. I found out that the gold comes up from the Empty Poke to Fort Huachuca, handled by a peddler who takes his store wagon down along the border country about every three weeks or so. He sells all kinds of stuff to prospectors, miners, and small ranchers on both sides of the line. When he finishes his loop and heads back to Fort Huachuca, his last stop — like his first one — is always this Empty Poke Mine. He brings in enough washed gold so that it caught our attention. That much you know, of course."

Magruder nodded. "It's at Fort Huachuca that the shipments are actually made, some of the stuff going east to Tombstone and then on to the rail line at Benson in a McLinden stagecoach. The rest of it goes north to Tucson in an army wagon that's supposed to be returning empty from a supply trip to the military post. That part we've run down, although we don't know for sure who settles this division of gold dust before the final shipments are made."

"Easy enough," Vicker told him. "Freight contractor at Fort Huachuca. Fellow named Sam Bunch. He seems to stick strictly to business most of the time, handling his army contracts and getting himself into no trouble. But he's the lad who organizes the gold shipments, I'm certain."

"This peddler?" Naismith put in. "Is that the Ike Marley I've been hearing about?"

Vicker turned to stare. "Who mentioned him by name? I didn't."

"I've been hearing a lot of things. That's why I'm here right now. Get finished with your part of the yarn first, and then I'll tell you mine."

"Right. I decided to follow Marley on one of his regular trips, figuring that he could lead me to the Empty Poke and not make me ask questions around the fort. At first, it was easy. The trail south from the fort runs along the slopes of the Huachucas, and there's cover for a man who doesn't want to be seen. Then the country opens up and it's not so easy. Marley didn't seem worried about being trailed, so I managed."

"Tell me about this fellow Marley," Magruder broke in. "Ben's not the only one who has heard his name mentioned."

Vicker laughed shortly. He had peeled down to bare hide and was trying to use a quart of water to do the work of several gallons. "Seems like Mr. Marley is a lot more important than he looks. He has this big wagon fitted up as a traveling store, and he

44

makes his rounds like I already told you. Mostly he sits up on the seat of the wagon and plays his harmonica while his team plods along. He's a little man — about the same size and shape as Ben — but kinda gray all over. He wears his hair long and has a full beard — both getting plenty gray. He keeps that harmonica going twelve hours a day, mostly with two or three hymn tunes that he plays over and over. You'd pick him to be the most harmless old coot in the world, but I've got a hunch that he's one of the biggest scoundrels along the border." He laughed again and added, "But maybe I'm prejudiced against him. After listening to him play his mouth organ I could be maybe a trifle impatient."

"You have reason to think him a scoundrel?" Magruder asked.

"Let me get on with the tale. I managed to keep close to Marley until he made his first stop at the Empty Poke Mine. It seems to be his first stop after leaving the post and the last one before he gets back to it. This time he was there for only an hour or so. I watched from up above the gulch where the mine shaft is located. Nothing happened. Marley and the other man just talked a bit. Then Marley rolled his wagon on out of the gulch and headed south. I didn't want to follow too close, so I took a chance on dropping in for a visit with the fellow who pretends to be working the Empty Poke."

"A visit!" Magruder exploded. "Are you crazy?"

"Maybe. But he seemed like . . ."

"And why do you say he pretends to be working the mine?"

"Because that's the way it is. And I don't think he pretends very hard. About once a day — so he tells me — he digs out a bit of fresh dirt from a hole in the gulch slope, but then he loafs around and keeps pretty well boozed up. Marley left him a fresh supply of popskull liquor."

"But what's the point of all this?"

Vicker was getting into a nightshirt, enjoying the feel of something other than gritty dust against his skin. "I'll tell you what he told me. You can make your own guesses. This Nate Aylett — that's the old codger's name — was willing enough to talk. I guess he figured I was the same kind of a bum as himself, so he told me all about the soft snap he had fallen into. There is no gold coming out of the hole that they call the Empty Poke Mine. There never was any. According to Aylett there's a man named Dave Norbeck who struck it rich in Sonora, not many miles below the boundary line. Mar-

46

keting raw gold is a bad business in Sonora just now. Between the bandits who really run the province and the crooks who hold the offices, there's small chance of a miner getting his gold out without having most of it taken away from him. So this Norbeck worked out a scheme with Marley. The peddler crosses the border so much that nobody pays any attention to him. No searches, or anything like that. Marely picks up Norbeck's gold and brings it across. Then he hauls it on north and pretends that it's the product of the Empty Poke operation."

"That sounds reasonable enough," Magruder nodded. "It fits with what we know about political conditions in Sonora. It also suggests that there's enough gold coming out to pay for this stage setting they've built up."

"I wonder whether I should shave tonight or wait until tomorrow morning?" Vicker said in a low tone. "Seems a shame to do it twice."

"Stick to business! What did you do after you found out about this fake mine? There was nothing it could mean to us."

"I'd better shave now," Vicker said in the same tone. "No point in taking a chance on having somebody see these whiskers. It could be one mistake too many." He dug into his kit again while Magruder and Nai-smith made unhappy remarks about aggravating people. He was lathering the red stubble when he went on, "I still had that business of Ulrich and the missing gold specie on my mind. Anything that looked a mite suspicious could be mixed up with that deal. And this was suspicious. It seemed like a mighty complicated way to do things. That business of splitting the shipments didn't make sense. I figured that somebody was going to a lot of trouble to hide something, but Nate Aylett didn't worry a bit about telling me what sounded like the truth. So I decided to trail Marley a bit farther."

"On company time!" Magruder growled.

"Why not? There's gold coming in. My job is to locate sources that are worth attention. If the Empty Poke didn't have it, I wanted to find out where it actually was coming from."

This time he drew no reply. "I trailed Ike Marley for ten days. He didn't do anything out of the ordinary — except play that miserable harmonica. Most of the time I was too far away to hear much of it, but I still got mighty tired of 'Beulah Land' and 'Shall We Gather at the River.'

"Marley made what seemed like a regular circle of his customers, most of the time be-

48

ing in Sonora. Then one night three men rode into his camp about dusk. They were Mexicans, I think, although the country was open there, and I couldn't get close enough to make certain. They were with him perhaps twenty minutes and they left some sacks of some kind with him. Next morning Mister Marley had an escort. A *vaquero* rode the hills with him all the time, keeping out of sight but never far away. It made things a lot tougher for me because I had to keep Marley in sight and still not let myself be seen by the *vaquero.* Judging by the way things worked out later, I guess I didn't do so good."

"You think it was gold that these men left with the peddler?"

"Yes. Marley stopped at Norbeck's diggings the next day, and I don't think he picked up a thing there. Norbeck's mine looked a little more like a prospect hole, but I still didn't see any signs of wealth around it. Norbeck may be mining a bit of gold, but he's not sending any such quantity as would account for dividing up deliveries on this side.

"Now comes the funny part. Not comical funny, but odd. After Marley left Norbeck's place, he eased up toward the border along the old trail that leads from Rio Chico across to Fort Huachuca. About a mile south of the boundary line, he just plain stopped. No reason for it that I could see. It was the middle of the morning, but he just pulled up and let his team out to graze where a little trickle of water provided some grass. About noon — after he'd been singing 'Beulah Land' and 'Shall We Gather at the River' for over two hours — a rider came down from the north. Marley seemed to expect him. The two of them talked for maybe five minutes, and then the man — who wasn't a Mexican — headed on down Marley's back trail. The *vaquero* came down from the ridge and joined this other man. Marley harnessed up his team and went north. I followed Marley. He crossed a little later. There was an army patrol not far above the crossing, and he took a few minutes to stop and talk with them. They didn't attempt to search his wagon, of course. Nobody ever does, I'm told."

"Any idea why he waited before coming back into the United States?"

Vicker grunted. "The only reason I could think of doesn't make much sense. I thought he might be waiting until he got word that some particular officer was commanding the patrol. Then I got to thinking that nobody bothers to check on him."

He went on to explain about how he had watched Marley make another brief visit to the Empty Poke. Again nothing had happened. Vicker had felt that his own presence had gone unnoticed, but it was soon after that he found pursuers on his trail. By the time he had told his story of the gunfight, he was clean-shaven, the flat planes of his craggy face shining in the lamplight. He left the sideburns long, darkening them carefully with stain he carried for the purpose. This was old routine now; on many occasions, he had used this same trick to change his appearance for one of the usual mine-investigating jobs. A man with dark hair but sandy whiskers could make good use of that oddity if he played it right. Now that enemies were looking for a bum with sandy whiskers Vicker would make sure to keep himself neat and with some attention to his dark hair. And he would make sure to shave every day.

"One thing," Magruder said when the story was told. "Do you think Marley is tied up with the men who tried to kill you this morning?"

"It looks that way. The whole setup with the two gold mines is an elaborate stage setting. The catch is that there is a double fake. The part about the gold smuggling is as much a diversion as the Empty Poke Mine."

"Diversion for what?"

"I don't know. It could have something to do with the theft of that gold specie. You remember I told you about Hal Ulrich coming down into this country on the trail of that stuff. This morning I heard enough to make me feel pretty certain that Ulrich was murdered. Also I found his gun on the man I shot. There is no doubt about its being his gun."

"You're probably right," Magruder told him soberly. "Now let me put in a few ideas. That's why I'm here, you know. I've got a job for you men in Montana. We've got a lead on a silver strike up there that has all the earmarks of a good one, likely with plenty of copper and maybe some nickel with it. I want the pair of you to hustle up that way and take the usual private look. You can . . ."

"Wait a minute!" Vicker exclaimed. "One moment you're interested in this crazy mess around here, and the next you're proposing to get completely out of it."

"Why not? You said yourself that there's nothing in it for our company."

"Sometimes I like to take a gamble," Vicker said softly. "There could be quite some reward money tangled up in what I've been smelling around here. And I've got a personal angle, too. Hal Ulrich was a good friend of mine. I don't think that I've quite settled accounts for him. Somehow I'd like to do it."

"I thought you hated this heat."

"I do. But I can stand it."

Magruder shook his head. "If you're going to be stubborn, I might as well come right out in the open and tell you that I'm supposed to get you out of this country before you can do any more damage."

Vicker turned in a hurry. "Any more damage! What do you mean by that?"

Magruder laughed softly. "I thought that might shake you up. Actually, I'm not sure what I meant. Maybe you haven't done any damage — yet."

He cut off Vicker's protests with a question. "Do you know Miles O'Fallon?"

"I know who he is. We never met. Big man in the Revenue Service, or something like that."

"Quite a big man. He's chief of investigations for the whole Southwest. About a week ago, he came to see me because he had heard that we had a couple of men working this territory. He asked me to get you out of here."

"Why?"

"Because you might ruin the chances for capturing a mighty dangerous gang of outlaws and smugglers. He explained the set-up, knowing that I'd have to have pretty good reasons for interfering with our regular business. He also asked that I turn over to him any information that either of you should happen to turn up before I could get you out of the way."

"Nice!" Vicker said disgustedly. "Internal Revenue Service or Customs or whoever it is wouldn't mind letting us do their work for them, but they want to tell us when we have to stop working!"

"What's wrong with that? You said yourself that we've got nothing of interest to keep us in this little stretch of sun-baked nothing."

"I told you . . . What about Ulrich? Was he working for O'Fallon?"

"Yes. He's the second man they've lost on this job. Government agents who normally work this territory seem to be well known to the outlaws. Twice they've brought in men from other regions, and each time the agent disappeared."

"How long ago?"

"Your friend Ulrich went south about a month ago, I believe. The other fellow disappeared a fortnight earlier. Why?"

"Because that outlaw mentioned only one

54

officer being killed. It's possible that Hal Ulrich is still alive."

"But you said you found his gun."

"I did. But he could be a prisoner. Maybe they murdered the first one and captured Ulrich. The gunman referred to him as a revenuer. Maybe they knew about that because of their spy service, but there's a chance that they forced Ulrich to talk. If there's a chance that he's alive, I'm going in after him!"

"And that's exactly what O'Fallon wants me to keep you from doing. You could ruin things."

"What things?"

Magruder grimaced. "I suppose I'd better tell you the whole yarn. It might possibly make you think again about getting foolish."

"Give it a try," Vicker invited, stretching himself out on the bed. "One way or another, I'd ought to know what's what."

CHAPTER 4

"How much do you know about the outlaw gang that is supposed to operate along the border here?" Magruder asked. "Maybe I can skip some of the background if you already know it."

"Only the gossip," Vicker told him. "For years there has been a lot of rustling on both sides of the line. The stock thieves steal Mexican horses or cattle and bring them into Arizona where they find buyers who are not too ethical about Mexican brands. Then they steal other stock on this side and peddle it to broad-minded rancheros in Sonora. It was this gang that was supposed to have taken over the job of hiding and handling that stolen specie. I'd guess that Ike Marley is one of their prize operators."

"Then you haven't heard any rumors that the rustler gang has gone into bigger things?"

"Only this crazy gold business."

"And that — as you guessed — is only a cover-up for something else. According to O'Fallon, this crowd has gone into real big business. They still run a bit of stolen stock, but lately they've used their cattle trails for the smuggling of a lot of things. Chinese immigrants — illegal ones, of course — opium, plunder from the pillaging that has been plaguing Sonora, anything that can turn a profit if it's moved from one country to the other.

"At the moment, the big profit for the outlaws has been in jewelry and opium. The jewels — and gold — are the loot from a whole series of raids the Sonora part of the gang has been making. They've looted haciendas, churches, villages. At least a dozen murders have occurred in these raids. The stuff can't be marketed by them in Mexico at any great profit, so they smuggle it across and then have it shipped east where it will bring plenty. The opium comes in at some secret landing on the Gulf of California. Our agents have blocked off most of the old routes, so now the stuff is being shipped across Sonora so as to use this vulnerable bit of border and the available services of the organization."

"If the government knows so much about it, why haven't they moved in on the gang?"

"Several reasons. One is that this information has only become available within the past couple of weeks. They didn't know so much about it when your friend Ulrich was sent down to the border. There are still a lot of details missing — although I think you've just filled in a few gaps for them. Until now they've only found out about shipments after it was too late to intercept them. Now they think there's a good chance to trap the smugglers with some substantial loot. A new administration has taken office in Sonora, and they're pushing hard to clean up organized banditry. Already several thugs who thought themselves above the law have faced firing squads. O'Fallon thinks that there will be an attempt to dispose of all the loot they have on hand before the government down there can find it. We have a pretty good idea as to how it will be handled, so now we're in a position to set a trap."

"We?"

Magruder smiled. "I'm speaking as a patriotic citizen. We — as employees of Pacific Mining and Smelting — are to stay out of the way. We don't want the gang mistaking one of our agents for a government agent and perhaps altering their plans. Now that we have a pretty good idea of how they do things, we want them to keep on doing them."

"I can see the point," Vicker conceded. "But I still think there's a good chance that I could help instead of hinder. The government can't send a man in to watch for last-minute developments. I could do it without arousing any suspicion."

"How?"

"By being myself. Pacific's operations are pretty well known in mining country. You can bet that somebody is already paying a lot of attention to the fact that you're here in Tombstone. Maybe it's also known that I'm registered here with you. If you didn't stir up any talk when you visited with Miles O'Fallon, there will be an easy assumption that you're here to look into some prospect or other."

"I'm sure nobody knew of my talk with O'Fallon. He took plenty of precautions."

"Good. Then somebody is going to expect that a Pacific man will be checking into some kind of mining operation. The Empty Poke has drawn a lot of attention. As a matter of fact, the gang has invited such attention because it's a sort of disguise for their real business. Wouldn't you call it reasonable to suppose that Pacific would be interested — as we really were?"

"But we know . . ."

"Nobody knows that we know. I think that the most natural move for us to make is to go over for a look at the Empty Poke. They might even get suspicious if we didn't. I could ride over to Fort Huachuca and ask some questions about the place. Maybe I'd even go take a look at it. Meanwhile, I can keep an eye on things. It should be interesting to see what the gang will do if they find that their fake mine is to be investigated as a business matter."

"The fool wants to git hisself killed," Naismith growled, breaking his silence for the first time in minutes. "Yuh seen how them polecats shoot first and ask questions later. It'll be suicide."

"I'll have a margin of safety," Vicker said seriously. "Going as myself, with plenty of open talk about it, they won't want to risk any rough stuff. It would draw too much attention. There's a lot of difference between playing a bum and being a known agent for Pacific."

"It might help — if you don't get too carried away with your ideas about locating that Ulrich fellow," Magruder conceded. "O'Fallon could use a lookout. He knows that the gang is under pressure to make a big move, but he knows they've got spies.

He can't put men into the area until he's sure they're where he can grab them."

Vicker turned his face to the wall. "So it's settled," he murmured sleepily. "We'll work out details tomorrow. Ben, you keep your eyes skinned for any tough-looking hombres that seem to be looking for somebody. G'night." He was asleep before Magruder could offer any more objections.

Magruder had to awaken him late the following morning. "Sorry I can't let you get your sleep out, Jack," the tall man said apologetically. "I've got to get on with some plans of my own. Naturally, I want to get back to Tucson and pass your information on to Miles O'Fallon. I think we ought to show ourselves together here in town before I leave. It'll help the impression you want to make — if you're still determined to go ahead with your plan."

"I'm awake," Vicker told him with a crooked smile. "And I think I'll live — if my feet don't make me commit suicide. Those blisters ache all the way to my knees!"

CHAPTER 5

There was no awkwardness in Janet Sebrell's greeting. "Jack Vicker!" she exclaimed
as she caught sight of him. "How nice to
see you! I'd heard, of course, that you were
doing something connected with mining,
but I certainly didn't expect to run into you
like this."

Vicker used the formalities of introduction as a means of keeping his mind away
from things that fought to be remembered.
Janet had not changed very much in the five
years since their last meeting. She still had
her looks, and she still had the knack of
making a man feel that she was interested
in every word he uttered. She used that
knack now, exclaiming over her good fortune in meeting a man big enough to run
one of the famous mining companies. She
gave the impression that she had made a
study of Magruder's career, and for a few
moments Vicker wondered whether his own

presence had been forgotten. Then she turned to fire a volley of questions at him. Where had he been since leaving the army? What was he now doing in Tombstone? Had he seen Fort Huachuca, and what was it like? Weren't traveling conditions terrible when one left the railroad?

Magruder backed away while Vicker was either answering or evading the questions. "Sorry to hurry away," he said politely. "Previous engagement, you know. Take care of those other matters, Jack." His sidelong grin suggested that he was taking himself out of the way, not wanting to be the third party. Five years ago, Vicker would have appreciated the gesture. Now he was not so sure. Janet was still beautiful, but she seemed to have developed a tendency to do a lot of talking. And she was now Mrs. Austin Sebrell.

"I'm only in Tombstone for a couple of days," she explained, breaking in on one of his answers. "Austin is at Fort Huachuca, as you may know, and I'm taking the first coach to the post. I didn't know when I arrived in Tombstone that I would have to wait so long for transportation to the fort. Otherwise I might have asked him to come for me. It's really not so far away, I'm told."

Vicker wasn't at all certain that he liked

the idea of the Sebrells being at Fort Huachuca. He didn't know why he should feel that way about it, but somehow it seemed as though it might complicate matters. Somehow Janet had always complicated life for him. "I'm going to the fort tomorrow," he admitted. "I suppose we'll travel together."

"Of course!" She seemed delighted. "There is only one stage line, and it doesn't seem to run very often. We can have loads of time to talk over old times."

Again Vicker had a feeling that this was not a pleasing prospect. Where Janet was concerned, he would have preferred to forget the past. "Plenty of time," he agreed. "Which means that I should get on with business now. Mr. Magruder leaves town tonight and there is quite a lot we must do before he goes. If you will excuse . . ."

"Couldn't we have dinner together?" she interrupted. "I've had a young lieutenant playing sort of unofficial chaperone to me ever since I met him on the train. He's coming out to his first assigned duty, and he seems to feel that he has an obligation to look after the wife of a superior officer. I haven't found it in my heart to tell him that his superior officer probably will not thank him for the service. Frankly, I don't think

Austin will be at all pleased to have me under foot in such a place."

There was no time for Vicker to find out what she meant by that remark. Out of the corner of his eye, he saw a black-clad figure riding in from the direction of Boot Hill. The peaked sombrero and the dusty black clothing told him all that he needed to know. Pursuit had reached Tombstone without much delay. Now he had to face up to a test that would determine whether he would make any further plans about going to Fort Huachuca. He had to face the Mexican promptly and see what would happen. And he didn't want it to happen with Janet standing by. There was more than a chance that bullets might start to fly.

Then he noticed that the *vaquero* had a couple of companions with him. The other two men were pretending that they paid no attention to the rider ahead of them, but their tense watchfulness was apparent even at the distance. These were the fresh gun-hands brought up to replace the ones who had failed in the first attempt. They would take their cue from the bloodhound ahead of them.

"Let me look you up later," he said hurriedly. "I've really got a bit of pressing business ahead of me. We can . . ."

"Very well," she said, her smile fading. "I didn't know that I would be embarrassing to you. Forgive me." She was turning as she spoke, moving on up the street with a brisk stride that told him of her swift anger.

Vicker didn't look at her again after seeing that she was irritated. It didn't matter. Janet had been irritated before — and when he didn't want her to be. Now he was not particularly concerned about it. For the next few minutes, he had to keep his mind on other things. The man who had ridden guard over Ike Marley was coming straight toward him.

He made himself look as casual as possible, leaning against one of the rough posts that supported a wooden awning. From that position, he could face the open street without appearing to be much interested in the riders who were about to come abreast of him. He had to give the situation a good test without seeming to do so. This *vaquero* was certainly the man who had put those other pursuers on his trail. The man must have seen him at some time. The question was when and how. Had the fellow been close enough to distinguish his features, or hadn't he? The only way to get an answer was to stand there and give the fellow his chance.

At the same time, he knew that he might be defeating another purpose. These trackers might lead him to confederates in Tombstone — but not if they were warned. There was a moment or two in which he considered postponing the test, but he held his position, wondering whether he might not be flinching a little and seeking a way out.

The riders came on steadily, and soon Vicker could see how the black eyes of the Mexican were darting in either direction. The *vaquero* was studying everyone he saw, obviously searching. Then he looked straight at Vicker, getting a calm appraisal in return. Neither man changed expression, and the Mexican rode on. So far as Vicker could tell, the Mexican had given no signal to his companions who halted some yards away.

It was a little difficult to keep the three of them in view without doing some neck twisting, but Vicker saw enough to make him feel that he had passed the crisis. The *vaquero* had seen nothing in the spruce, clean-shaved stranger to remind him of the ragged, sandy-whiskered tramp. And the other two had not halted at any signal, but were going about something that must have been planned before their arrival in town. They tied their broncs at a hitchrack in front of a saloon, but only one of them went in. The other swung away without any exchange of words and sauntered back toward the adobe building that carried the sign, McLinden Stage Lines.

Vicker made a decision promptly. Still loafing along as though not particularly interested in anything, he also moved toward the stage office. He wondered briefly what had happened to Janet, but mostly he was considering what excuse he would use for going into the McLinden place again.

He was inside before he saw her. She must have entered while the gunmen were still in the saddle, and now she was talking to the clerk about the problem of getting her baggage to the coach next morning. Vicker noted that the inner door was closed and that muffled voices could be heard from beyond it. There didn't seem to be much doubt that one of the voices was showing anger. It sounded like McLinden doing what must have been some fancy cursing.

Janet looked around as he entered. "I trust that you completed your affairs satisfactorily," she said, ice in her voice.

"No. I've got a few things on my mind, but I didn't need to be so abrupt. I decided that Magruder could wait while I came along to apologize for the way I must have sounded." That was better than the other excuse he had planned to use.

Her smile came as prettily as ever. "Then you're forgiven. I'm trying to make my plans for tomorrow. I suppose I'll have to prevail on my gallant young lieutenant to take care of baggage for me."

"Good idea," Vicker laughed. "Lieutenants have to be good for something. By the way, what time does the stage leave? I forgot to ask."

"Eight in the morning," she replied, then added, "What about dinner tonight?"

"I've got to get some rest first. I'll look you up later." But Vicker walked away knowing sleep was more important than Janet.

CHAPTER 6

There were four passengers on the rickety stagecoach when it clattered out of Tombstone next morning. Janet Sebrell was pretty enough to have the loungers shooting envious glances at Vicker and Lieutenant Perkins, but she was coldly reserved. Vicker knew that she was letting him know that she hadn't liked his failure to look her up during the evening, but he was content to have it that way. He still had a feeling that the Sebrells were going to prove a complication in an already complex situation, and he made up his mind to avoid both Janet and her husband as far as possible.

Perkins was fussing around like a mother hen, partly over his own baggage and partly over Janet's. He seemed intent on letting everyone know that the army was taking care of everything, but at the same time he gave Vicker the impression that he would have been relieved if someone with at least an oak leaf on his shoulders would come along and give some orders.

The fourth passenger did not arrive until minutes before the stage was ready to pull out. She was a flashy woman of perhaps thirty-five, her blondeness as false as her smile. Careful make-up could not conceal the hard lines at the corners of her eyes, and she made no attempt to conceal the hardness in the eyes themselves. The smile she reserved for her fellow passengers was in marked contrast to the glare she aimed at the men who had brought her to the stage office. In return, they were pretty raucous in letting everyone know that Floss was leaving town by request. Two lawmen and several citizens had formed a committee to make sure that she went. McLinden seemed to be part of that committee.

Vicker gathered that Floss had become a trifle too adept at robbing her clients. Apparently, Tombstone's moral code was loose enough in most respects, but there was a delicate prejudice against fancy women rolling drunken miners for their pokes. Probably that little trick was reserved for saloon-keepers and bartenders, Vicker decided with a half smile. Floss must have violated the rules of the union, so she was being shipped out of town. She was pretty philosophical about it, even managing a smile as she took her seat and looked out at the grim committee.

"So long, you thieving varmints," she called to them with the smile coming back. "Don't think it wasn't nice knowin' yuh — because it wasn't!"

Janet showed no change of expression as the other woman crawled into the coach and took the seat facing her. Lieutenant Perkins entered next and seemed both embarrassed and puzzled. He evidently was not sure whether he should sit next to Janet and have to face Floss, or whether he should risk taking a seat next to the blonde where he could meet Mrs. Sebrell's eyes and understand her wishes. Vicker settled it for him by moving into the seat directly opposite Janet. He had decided that it would be more entertaining to watch the faces of Janet and Perkins as the trip wore along. At the same time, he was curious to see how Janet would react when he took a seat next to Floss.

It was the blonde woman who helped to clear the air of tension as the coach rolled out of town. She aimed a reasonably pleasant smile at Perkins and remarked, "Don't worry about it, sonny. It's all in the game. I've been run out of towns that are a heck of a lot better'n this one. You don't need to feel sorry for me."

Surprisingly enough, Janet laughed. Vicker couldn't tell whether it was a laugh of relief or real amusement at hearing the lieutenant addressed as sonny.

"You think Fort Huachuca will be any improvement?" Vicker asked. "I'm kind of a stranger around here, but I hear that the fort is nobody's bargain as a place to live."

"Hell, I didn't have no choice. They put me on the first stage that was pullin' out. But no matter. Soldiers oughta be good for a stake that'll let me head for some place better."

Janet, stern lines showing around her mouth, had settled back in silence after that first nervous laugh. It was pretty evident that she did not relish being thrown into this kind of company. And Lieutenant Perkins seemed equally shocked.

Floss seemed to accept the other woman's open disdain, but she made an attempt to joke with the young officer. "Don't start lookin' bothered, buster," she advised. "This ain't no part of the country for purty manners. Officers got to learn it just like the other poor devils they badger around."

"Is there much of a town at the fort?" Vicker broke in, trying to ease things a little.

"I don't know a darned thing about it,

mister. But a fort means men. Soldiers need supplies. There's always a wagon camp. And I never seen a fort yet that didn't have some kind of settlement spring up around it. The usual gang of leeches show up to look for loose dollars. I might as well join the crowd."

She had made a point that he had practically ignored. He had seen Fort Huachuca and knew that there were stables and corrals for the freight contractors. He even had his suspicions that somewhere among the freighters were employees of the smuggling ring. He had forgotten about the shady characters who always congregated around army posts. Keeping an eye on so many possibilities was going to be a problem.

Floss kept the talk going in the same vein for a while, addressing most of her remarks to Lieutenant Perkins and clearly getting a lot of amusement out of his blushes. Again, it all made Vicker think of his own career. He had been just as uneasy when he went to the Rio Grande. Maybe he had felt even worse. At that time, he had still been fuming over Janet's marriage to Austin Sebrell.

Somehow the time passed. It was not a long trip to the fort, but the heat and the travel conditions did not make it an easy one. A couple of times he exchanged low-voiced comments with Janet, but for the most part he simply sat and watched the lieutenant's embarrassment as Floss amused herself.

Finally, the coach took on a different tone of creak and rumble as the team began to labor up the long grade of the Huachucas. By looking out of the window, the passengers could see the huddle of whitewashed buildings on the shoulder of the mountain.

"My new home," Janet said in a tight voice. "I don't think I'm much impressed."

"Luck of the draw," Vicker said.

"Not quite. I'd call it the stupidity of a crooked dealer."

Vicker knew that Perkins and Floss were staring, not understanding the hidden meaning. He also knew that Janet was letting her true feelings show. She was letting him know that she no longer had any illusions about her husband. That sort of thing he couldn't afford to encourage.

"He had it coming to him," he told her bluntly.

"I know. And I can't complain. I had my eyes open when I married him."

That wasn't the way he had wanted the talk to go. "We all make mistakes," he said, wondering how to get the conversation into safer channels.

Floss saved the situation by exclaiming, "Amen, brother!"

The laugh that followed was strained and not entirely happy, but it was still all right with Vicker. He used it as a cover to stick his head out and study the first dreary buildings that the coach was approaching.

An army post always seems to start a minor building boom. First come the corrals and the warehouses that civilian contractors and teamsters must use in keeping the post supplied. Then there will be the housing for company laundresses, sometimes on the post itself and sometimes in the fringe settlement. Right behind them come the whiskey peddlers and the harlots. The rowdy suburb is in action almost as soon as the post goes into operation.

The coach stopped in front of one of the outlying adobes, a large, badly built structure that bore a freshly painted sign identifying it as the freight depot. There was a smaller adobe next door that carried a smaller sign with the single word *Whiskey.* Just beyond were a dozen freight wagons backed against the rails of a corral, teamsters lounging in the hot sun as though awaiting orders to move out on their trip north to the rail line. Vicker was mostly interested in the big wooden wagon that stood at the side of the larger adobe. It had a regular roof instead of the common canvas top, and its sides bore the legend, *Ike Marley's Traveling Store. Best Merchandise at Lowest Prices.* Mr. Marley himself leaned against one of the front wheels, his gingery little goatee wagging a slow accompaniment to the tune he was droning on his harmonica. The tune was "Shall We Gather at the River."

"There's Marley," Floss remarked casually. "Him and his hymn tunes! I'm always expecting him to start takin' up a collection!"

Vicker knew a moment of wonder. Marley had not been reported as having worked out of Tombstone at any time in the past. And Floss had claimed to be a stranger at the fort. It seemed a little odd that she should know about the peddler.

The woman was gathering her skirts as she spoke, her words a sort of farewell. The lieutenant moved to open the door for her, but Vicker sat quiet. For the first time, he was getting a closer look at Ike Marley. After having watched the little man for two weeks at long range, it gave him some satisfaction to make such an appraisal.

"So long," Floss called as she moved toward the *Whiskey* sign. "It was real nice meetin' you." Nobody had bothered to give her a hand with the battered valise, and she didn't seem to be expecting any help.

"Tough place for a woman," Perkins muttered.

Vicker nodded. "Tough woman." He was still studying Marley, noting how completely the skinny little peddler gave the impression of being harmless. It was hard to believe that the man was involved with a smuggling gang that made murder a casual part of its operation.

CHAPTER 7

The coach rolled on to the military post and again Vicker noted the usual things. Barracks, officers' quarters, stables, commissary sheds, and the like. Fort Huachuca was exactly what was to be expected of a four-company post at the edge of the desert. Except for a few scattered trees of fair size, it was bare, drab, sun-baked, and generally cheerless.

There was a flurry of activity as the coach drew up in front of a frame building that evidently housed the Officer of the Day. Lieutenant Perkins promptly remembered his training. He came to a crisp salute almost as soon as he was out of the coach, ignoring a couple of troopers who hurried toward the vehicle and speaking formally to an unshaved man in a cotton undershirt who appeared in the doorway of the build-ing. "Lieutenant Perkins reporting for duty, sir. May I present Mrs. Austin Sebrell, sir?

And this other gentleman is Mr. Vicker."

The officer in the doorway looked mildly astonished, but then the name Sebrell seemed to strike him. "Come right in," he invited hastily, disappearing almost before the words were out.

When Vicker followed the others into the dim interior, he saw that the man had slipped into a blue blouse that carried the twin bars of captain on the shoulders. A regular army man, Vicker thought, noting that the mustache was not quite as gray as the stubble on the chin.

"May I apologize for my appearance, Mrs. Sebrell?" the officer asked courteously. "I'm afraid things are inclined to be a bit informal on this post. The heat, you know."

He was still floundering when he introduced himself as Captain Bates. Vicker was inclined to be pleased at the way things were working out. A duty officer caught in his undershirt by a new shavetail and the wife of one of his subordinates was not likely to take too much interest in a mere civilian visitor.

For a few minutes, it worked that way. Bates listened to Janet's account of her decision to join her husband, his confusion not in the least diminished by the obvious fact that he was impressed by her charms.

"You've caught us completely unprepared, Mrs. Sebrell," he told her in that same tone of apology. "Your husband took a patrol out last Tuesday and is not expected back for at least another three days. He didn't say a word to any of us about expecting you, and I rather think he knew nothing about it. The mail is peculiarly unreliable, you know."

"But I wrote to him several weeks ago!"

"He still might not have received your letter. There have been several mail robberies in the territory. But don't worry about it. Mrs. Bates will be only too happy to have a guest for a few days."

"You're very kind, but doesn't my husband have quarters?"

"Bachelor quarters only. But come along. We'll take care of the details later. I'm sure you want to freshen up after that stagecoach ride."

Vicker scarcely heard the latter part of the talk. Bates had given him something else to consider. Austin Sebrell was out with a patrol, had been out for a significant time. It had been on Tuesday that Ike Marley had waited south of the border and then had crossed when he received word that everything was clear. Magruder's guess had been right. Sebrell was the man the smugglers depended on to look the other way. Austin was still up to his old tricks.

He suddenly realized that Captain Bates was talking to him, once more apologizing.

"Sorry to let you stand around like that, Mr. — Vicker, was it?"

"Quite all right. Things get complicated at times."

"And what can I do for you, sir?"

"Advice, mainly. I took one look at the freight depot and decided that I'd ask for a hint or two before I decided where to look for a room. No point in getting into the worst rat's nest if somebody can steer me away."

Janet cut in quickly. "Mr. Vicker is an old friend — of both myself and my husband. They were classmates at the Military Academy."

"Army?" Bates asked needlessly.

Vicker explained his errand, mentioning briefly his military service before joining Pacific. Maybe it wasn't a bad idea to have fort personnel aware of him after all. "In my business I have to live with sources of information, mostly gossip but still information. Sometimes it gets pretty rough, but that's part of the game. I simply hoped that you could steer me toward somebody who might be a little less disreputable than the average."

"We could fix you up on the post. Bachelor quarters."

"Thanks. But business is business. I have to handle it my way."

"Then ask for Sam Bunch. He's probably as complete a scoundrel as any of them in the freighting business, but he knows he can't get along unless he keeps on the good side of the army. Tell him I sent you."

"Thanks again. Probably I'll be seeing you before I leave, Janet."

A wan smile was his reply. "By all means. I'm afraid this isn't going to be a bit better than I was afraid it would be."

He left rather hurriedly then. It wouldn't do to let Janet start bidding for sympathy. Post gossip would undoubtedly make capital of it.

His feet were aching again when he returned to the cluster of buildings beyond the military reservation. He followed the directions Bates had given him and found a dozen loungers, evidently teamsters, clustered around the open door of a sprawling adobe that faced on a side alley away from the other buildings he had noticed. He didn't remember it from his earlier brief visit, but it had to be the right place, a crudely painted sign naming it the office of the *U.S. Forage Agent.* There was a larger sign above a door opening out of the same adobe wall. This one read, *Headquarters Saloon*. Vicker wondered whose headquarters the saloon might be, but it didn't seem like a good time to start asking such questions. Actually his first problem was to answer some.

A much bewhiskered man in overalls looked up from his tilted chair to greet him with a lazy, "Ain't no mine around here, mister. No use lookin'."

There was a general laugh, and the bearded man added, "No offense. Floss passed the word about what yo're aimin' to do around these parts. Seems like yo' picked a heck of a poor place to hunt gold mines."

Vicker pushed his hat to the back of his head and brought out his best grin. "In my line o' work a man has to go to a lot of miserable places and do some fool things. But I get paid for it. Maybe you can tell me where I might find a gent named Sam Bunch. Also you could put me on to a good place to buy a horse and saddle."

"Easy enough. I'm Sam Bunch. Likely I could outfit yo' as well as anybody else. So yo' don't want to talk about gold mines, hey?"

"Sure I do. That's why I'm here — or didn't Floss tell you that much?"

84

He went on quickly, knowing that now was the time to establish his role as he wanted it to be. "There's no secret about how Pacific Mining and Smelting operates. Some of you know that. We want to find anything that's worth developing. We can't do it by hiding our heads in our pockets. A bit of gossip could put us on the trail of just what we want."

"Mines is mostly east o' here," a skinny little man told him.

"Mostly," Vicker agreed. "And mostly they're bought up if they're any good. I got orders to look at one south of here. Claim called the Empty Poke. Somebody's been movin' a lot of gold out of it. We might be interested in making a good offer."

"Who says there's any gold comin' outa there?" Bunch demanded.

Vicker eyed him carefully, but with the smile still showing. "That part I wouldn't know about. The company feeds me the information and sends me out to get more. All I heard was that a man named Marley was bringing out gold from this Empty Poke diggings. Also I understand that it's owned by a gent called Nate Aylett. I want to look at the place, and I want to talk with this Aylett."

Bunch spat into the dust. "Won't do yo'

no good. Nate's a mighty cantankerous critter. I'll give yo' odds he won't sell."

"That's not my problem, either," Vicker told him. "I look and make a report. The company has other men to make the deals. All I want is a place to stay while I find out how to get to the Empty Poke. Then I'll need a horse and saddle, some grub, and the like. Anybody here interested in doing that kind of business?"

"I'm yore man," Bunch told him. "Hear that noise?"

The others fell silent as he held up a gnarled hand. From around a corner of the building came the whining notes of the harmonica. The tune was still "Shall We Gather at the River?"

"Someone in pain?" Vicker asked innocently.

There was a general laugh, and he felt that he had established a place for himself among them. There were now a few nods of approval to replace the previous air of watchful hostility.

"That's Ike Marley," Sam Bunch told him. "Ike's the peddler who's been shippin' a bit of gold for Nate Aylett. Yo' might as well talk to him before yo' decide anything. He's the feller what oughta know the truth."

"Good idea," Vicker nodded. "If I can get

him to start talking, maybe he'd stop torturing that suck-and-blow contraption."

"Not fer long he won't!" Bunch chuckled. "But give it a try. We could use a mite of rest fer our ears." He motioned toward the carpetbag Vicker had been carrying around with him. "Charley kin take care o' the bag for yo'. No point in luggin' it around. Only room I got handy is right in through that door."

A squatty man with big shoulders and huge yellow teeth moved forward to take the bag. Bunch shook his head warningly. "Jest take it in there where the extra bunk is. Don't git nosey and start lookin' through it fer any gold nuggets."

Vicker turned to grin at the joking tone, but then he went on around the corner of the adobe, reasonably pleased with the way matters were developing. He now had a good excuse for speaking directly to Ike Marley, and he had set himself up on good terms with the rest of the gang. Undoubtedly, they thought he was something of an idiot, but that was all right. He liked it that way.

He found Marley perched on a wagon tongue, and the only thing that seemed different about him was his eyes. Vicker was already familiar enough with the goatee and the spare proportions of the man, but it surprised him to find pale-blue eyes peering out of the web of brown wrinkles. They seemed completely out of place.

"Sam Bunch said I'd better talk to you," he announced abruptly, speaking loudly enough to be heard above the harmonica. Marley had cut down on the volume just a little, so he assumed that it was a gesture of listening. "I'm Jack Vicker, agent for Pacific Mining and Smelting. My company wants me to have a look at a prospect being operated by a man named Aylett. They tell me you handle his pay dirt for him."

The harmonica shut off abruptly. There was a long moment in which the pale eyes stared hard at Vicker, something between fear and suspicion showing in them. Then the little man shook his head. "Wouldn't be no point in ridin' out there, mister. Nate wouldn't sell. You'd be wastin' your time."

Vicker shrugged. "It's not my time. Pacific pays me for it. All I do is take a look and make a report. I get paid just the same whether I tell them to get interested or hunt for another hole."

Marley laughed in a nervous cackle. "That's easy then. Set around and rest yourself for a few days, then go back and report. Tell 'em the hole's no good. It'll save you some hot ridin' and you'll be tellin' the truth."

"You mean it's no good?"

"Right."

"Then why won't Aylett consider selling?"

Marley seemed a little confused, but he rallied promptly. "Because Nate ain't got all his buttons, that's why."

"And then I'll have another question to answer. My company knows that Aylett has been shipping gold. If I report that his prospect is no good, they'll want to know where the gold came from. Also I'm supposed to look for signs of other metals. We're not interested in gold alone, you know."

The little man shrugged. "It ain't up to me to tell you your business, mister. Take a look if you figure you've got to." He was almost surly about it, and Vicker suspected that there was a lot of uneasiness behind the gruff manner. Evidently he had decided to stop making explanations before he caught himself up in any more conflicting stories.

"Can you tell me how to get out there?"

"Hard place to find. If you don't mind waitin' around for a few days, mebbe as much as a week, you could trail along with me. It'll be my first stop when I make my next round. But don't expect to find nothin' good."

"Fair enough," Vicker told him, wondering at the unexpected proposal. "Naturally I'll expect to pay you for your trouble."

This time there was no reply. Marley was already wheezing into the opening bars of "Abide with Me."

He took his time about getting back to Sam Bunch, wondering about Marley's remarks. It seemed likely that the peddler had made his final proposal with the idea of keeping Vicker here at the fort until somebody else could make some decisions. It was precisely what Vicker wanted. Now he had the perfect excuse to loaf around and keep an eye on developments.

Bunch showed him the little stall that would be his room. It had a hard bunk and nothing else in the way of furniture, but it was no worse than he had expected. When he was alone, he took a look at the contents of his valise. He had packed it with the anticipation that somebody might search it, so he knew immediately that the search had taken place. The bag contained the riding clothes he had bought in Tombstone, an extra shirt to go with his more formal garb, and three letters of instruction from the company. These orders were the ones

Magruder had written out for him, simply stating what had already been made public. They had been placed there with the idea that someone would read them, but Vicker had placed them between the folds of the white shirt in such a manner that anyone replacing them after reading would find it practically impossible to leave them exactly as they had been.

"So we put Charley on the list," he muttered under his breath. "Sam Bunch was actually telling him to make the search when he pulled that bit of humor about gold nuggets. So now I know something — I hope."

When he went out again, he knew that Bunch was waiting for him to declare himself, waiting to find out whether he suspected that anyone had been into the bag. Accordingly, he put on his best show of good humor. "Now I've got a place to sleep — if anybody wants to call it that. Now what about the horse and the saddle? And I might also remark that I sometimes eat. Anybody run what passes for a restaurant around here?"

"My cook keeps these polecats healthy enough to complain all the time. Eat with 'em if ye ain't squeamish. Meals are cheap."

"What have I got to lose except my sound stomach?"

Bunch laughed. "Then come along, and we'll take a squint at a nag I could let ye have at a bargain. Rent or sell."

The horse was a long-legged chestnut that carried three different brands on its shoulder. Bunch had a bill of sale for the animal, but he was wryly frank in admitting that he suspected possible crookedness in the horse's history. "I bought him honest, and I got what looks like a good paper. That's all I guarantee."

"This an American brand?" Vicker asked, fingering one of the marks.

"Could be. I dunno. In this part o' the country, there's a lot o' border-jumpin' done. Mebbe the nag savvies Spanish. It happens like that."

"Seems like quite a lot happens. This Aylett affair, for example. Everybody keeps telling me that the mine's no good. But it's there, and it's producing."

"No it ain't."

"What do you mean?"

"Heck! Yo' might as well know. Everybody else around here does. Nate Aylett ain't diggin' out no gold. He jest plays possum around a pothole and makes out that he's a miner. Ike's haulin' that gold outa Mexico. Down there a miner has got to pay off a lot of crooked officials before he can put his

92

stuff on the market, so they like to smuggle their color across to this side. Aylett's in a deal with a jasper name of Norbeck. It's Norbeck's gold that Ike brings across, pretendin' that he picks it up at the Empty Poke Mine."

"Then it's true that I'll be wasting my time to look at the Empty Poke?"

"Sure is!"

"Maybe I shouldn't buy the horse."

"Suit yoreself. I kinda figgered yo'd have to see for yoreself. Comp'ny men mostly foller orders."

Vicker laughed. "You're a sharper, Mr. Bunch. Now about the horse? Will you be willing to buy him back when I return?"

"Could be. I wouldn't pay much, though. Bad risk takin' a hoss that mighta been smuggled outa Mexico."

Both of them laughed then. Vicker was beginning to like this man Bunch. He might be a thief — even a murderer — but he was mighty genial about it. For the moment it seemed like a good idea to play up to him. Bunch would undoubtedly boast about the way he was making money out of a crazy man who didn't mind spending company funds. It would help to establish the character Vicker had to play, a character the smuggler crowd didn't need to worry about — or to murder.

An hour later, Vicker had still not made up his mind about Sam Bunch. The evening meal in the rough shed that served as a dining hall for the assorted roughnecks who handled teams for Bunch was in the main about what could be expected. The only part that was at all surprising was that a small table had been placed in one corner, and there Vicker shared his bacon and beans with Floss and Mr. Bunch himself. The Chinese cook gave them a bit of extra service, but the food was the same that was brought in for the others.

At first, Vicker suspected that this might be an occasion for some searching questions — aimed at him — but it didn't work out that way. Floss made the same kind of grim jokes she had made on the stagecoach, and Bunch tossed in an occasional gibe at a man who was spending good money to look at a worthless bit of mining property. The only time that either of them became at all personal was when Floss commented, "I'm kinda surprised to have you around here tonight, Vicker. They tell me your lady friend's husband ain't at the fort right now."

Vicker laughed it off. "You jump to conclusions. There's not a thing between Mrs.

Sebrell and me."

"Don't make jokes, handsome. I saw how she was watchin' you every minute. Don't try to fool ole Floss."

Vicker didn't try. He wasn't going to discuss the subject.

The end of the meal was punctuated by violent thunder as a brief but powerful summer storm swirled down from the Huachuca summits. Vicker took his cue to get some sleep. Even with the hard bunk, he thought that some extra rest might help. At least it would ease those aching feet.

CHAPTER 8

At Dawn, Vicker was awakened by Eddie Bonner, who passed the word that Marley was getting ready to leave. Vicker grumbled sleepily and muttered, "Let him go. I'll catch up."

Bonner hesitated and then disappeared. Vicker took his time about getting into the garb he had bought for the ride, making certain that he left his other clothes as carefully packed as possible. If anybody went through his belongings while he was gone, he wanted to give them the proper impression.

Then he made a big fuss about getting a good breakfast, refusing to be hurried even when a wagoner came in to tell him that Marley's wagon was already a half mile out of camp. "No rush," Vicker told him lazily. "It won't be any trick to follow wagon tracks. I'll catch up with him too soon anyhow. This way I'll spend less time in the heat and have that much less pain in listening to his mouth organ."

When he added delay after breakfast, he discovered that he was making Sam Bunch nervous. The wagon boss didn't try to hurry him along, but it seemed clear that he wanted to do so. Evidently the gang had made some plans that involved this trip and they didn't want Vicker to spoil anything. He was almost tempted to call it off just because it would upset them, but somehow it didn't seem like the smart idea. The gang should be made to feel that everything was going right. There must be nothing to stir them up until the moment when O'Fallon would throw in his men. Vicker just had to hope that the plans involving his visit to the Empty Poke were only such as might be normally expected. It would soon be too late to do anything about other kinds.

He wondered how they were going to play it — always assuming that they still believed him to be Jack Vicker, mining scout. What were they going to let him see at the Empty Poke? Two different stories had already been given to him, not counting the one he had gotten from Nate Aylett on that other trip. It was going to be interesting to see how resourceful a gang of thieves this one might be.

He climbed into the saddle when only vague dust around the bend of the mountain indicated the location of Ike Marley and his harmonica. He passed a few lingering comments with Sam Bunch, mostly because he sensed that Sam was anxious to see him leaving. Then Sam turned away irritably, and Vicker headed out along the wagon tracks. It seemed significant to him that in the hour or so of delay he had not seen either Charley or Eddie Bonner. For that matter, he hadn't seen Floss, but that part was not surprising. In her line of business, early hours were not common.

He overtook the trade wagon a little before noon, slowing his pace deliberately when he noticed that a horseman was riding ahead of the outfit. He hadn't counted on an extra man being along, so he wanted to consider the point a little before he actually joined Marley. He knew quickly that the man was Eddie Bonner, but he couldn't quite guess why the fellow was along.

The explanation seemed casual and easy when Marley and Bonner combined to make it. Bonner's cattle spread was a little farther to the east, but there was always a problem of range cattle drifting. Bonner was making a sweep of inspection as he headed for the home ranch, riding along with

Marley as a matter of sociability until he should reach the part of the country he wanted to cover. It seemed reasonable enough. Vicker just didn't believe it.

"I might even go along for a look at the Empty Poke," Bonner told Vicker with a grin that suggested a bear trap. "In this here country, a man sometimes gits chances to look at minin' claims. I'd kinda admire to see how a expert goes about it. Might learn somethin'."

That seemed like a hint. Evidently the gang was going to play it straight — for a while at least. They wanted him to make his inspection. And that didn't make sense, either. He knew that the place was a complete fake.

Two hours later, they turned in where a gulch broke the chain of rounded summits that made up the Huachucas. Vicker already knew that Aylett's camp and the fake mine was perhaps a half mile back in the notch, but he let Bonner tell him about it. Meanwhile, he kept a watchful eye on the ground. The hard clay wasn't showing much in the way of prints, but it was pretty clear that at least one rider had been in and out lately. Probably Charley.

Both Marley and Bonner turned silent as they approached the bend where the supposed mining shaft was located. Then, Bonner suddenly began to chatter. He didn't make much sense, but it was clear that he was determined to hold Vicker's attention. Maybe the hawk-nosed man had seen the tracks and wanted to keep the visitor from paying any attention to them. It didn't seem important since such tracks might have been made by Aylett himself.

Marley swung his team in beside one of the rock piles that had become silent monuments to Aylett's faking. Vicker rode across to a fringe of trees, tying his horse with a little extra care while he let his mind work on what he was seeing. Aylett wasn't as bleary-eyed as he had been before, and he was actually doing some work. There were other changes, some of them significant. The main one was that the place now began to look like a mining claim. A wheelbarrow Vicker had not seen before was obviously being used to bring out ore. A neglected sluice had been repaired and showed signs of having been used. New piles of gravel appeared along the tiny brook that wandered through the gulch. Somebody had gone to a lot of trouble to make the place look like an honest operation.

Suddenly Vicker knew why the change seemed so startling. Aylett was not even working the same shaft. Behind a screen of bushes, he could see the shallow hole that had been the center of the earlier bit of lazy faking. There was no sign that anything in the way of gravel had been removed from it since his earlier visit. Now there was a new shaft, a gaping scar between two boulders where the loose gravel had been removed and hauled out to the stream. Vicker wondered if a sort of miracle had happened. Maybe Aylett had actually found real pay dirt so close to where he had set up his original fake. In the gold-mining business, stranger things had happened.

He felt a twinge of uneasiness as he turned away from his horse and went to join the others. There was a chance that Aylett might recognize him. On the earlier visit, he had not yet acquired much of a stubble, and the day's ride had given him the beginnings of a shadow on his chin. He wished that he had been smart enough to ride out here in the black frock coat and white shirt. Switching to more comfortable clothing had partly ruined his disguise. He could only hope that Aylett had been as drunk as he had appeared on that other visit.

He watched the old man's face closely, but could see no sign of recognition. Aylett was probably in his sixties, but looked older

— a white fringe framing a pink bald spot, straggling white whiskers stained with tobacco juice adding an extra frame for the red nose. Today, Aylett simply looked scared. Vicker guessed that the old man missed his liquor, having been ordered to stay sober for the occasion. There was also a good chance that his part in the deal was rather an innocent one. He had been hired to act like a miner when such acting meant nothing. Now he was getting into something he didn't quite understand, and he was sober enough to be afraid.

Still he had been well coached in his part. He shook hands stiffly and announced that he had heard of Mr. Vicker and Pacific Mining. Then he plunged right in, inviting Vicker to take a good look at the property. "We hit it big this time," he boasted. "Fust off, we thought we had it, but the vein petered out. Then we struck pay dirt in there between them two layers o' country rock. Mostly loose gravel mixed with chunks of rock. Plenty o' workin' room, and the vein real easy to work because we got rock walls on each side of it."

He blurted it all out as though he'd memorized it well. Then he waved a hand toward the piles of gravel near the sluice. "Take a look at some of the stuff I brought out already. Some of it's had the color washed out, but that one pile next to the sluice ain't been worked yet."

Vicker nodded. "I might as well get right at it," he said quietly. "Seems like it might be real good."

The attitudes of the other two men told him that this was the way they had planned it. He was being invited to take a look, and they were going to stick around while he did the looking. After that . . . he didn't dare guess. The hole that McLinden and Aylett had said was a fake was not being worked now. There had to be some reason why the change had taken place. Maybe they had decided to try a bit of fraud and had switched the scene of digging operations because they knew that he had already been told that the original shaft was no good. Or maybe . . .

He stopped guessing and walked across to stare at the pile of gravel Aylett had indicated. There was some good-looking color showing in it, definite flakes of gold. Also there were some odd-looking lumps of ore that didn't seem to be of the same type of rock that he had seen in this gulch. Except for those lumps, the pile reminded Vicker of other examples of deliberate salting that he had observed. Probably somebody had loaded a shotgun with fine gold and had blasted away into the gravel pile. It was an old trick, but it was as good as any. Adding those lumps of legitimate ore was something else. There were real veins of yellow in some of the stuff, enough of it so that samples would assay pretty well. And those veins hadn't been planted with a shotgun or anything else; they were really part of the ore.

He made no comment, but turned and walked across to the hole that had been dug between the rock surfaces. Everywhere there were signs of work, pick and shovel marks, the wheelbarrow track, and footprints. Maybe Aylett had worked himself sober on this setup.

The formation was exactly as Aylett had described it, a six-foot vein of gravel between rock walls. Again he could see the glint of color in the gravel.

He took plenty of time, thinking as much as looking. His guess was that the shotgun had been used again at this point. Some of the flecks of gold seemed just a little too clear. Then he noticed that nowhere in this lot of gravel were any of those lumps of ore. There weren't even any bits of rock that looked like the ones in the pile by the creek. Someone had gone to a lot of trouble to salt this mine. They had not only pulled the old shotgun trick but they had brought in the lumps from some distant point. Why?

At first glance, the explanation seemed fairly simple. McLinden had made some moves when he learned that a Pacific agent was determined to have a look at the place. The gang had not wanted Vicker to see a complete fake so they had arranged to set up a more elaborate one. Then they had fixed it so there would be a delay at Fort Huachuca while their stage setting was being prepared. When everything was ready, their messenger — Charley — rode back to the fort and passed the word. At that point, Marley was told to get on with his part of taking the mining man to the property.

It all seemed to work out, but it didn't explain anything. What was the point of it? Was this what it appeared to be, an attempt to salt a worthless bit of property to sell it to an unwary buyer? Did somebody among the smugglers think that there was a chance to pick up a little extra profit? Vicker didn't think so. McLinden would have done some investigating. He would have found out about Pacific Mining and about Jack Vicker. He would have learned that Pacific was thorough about such things and that Vicker was a hard man to fool, a man who had never yet put his approval on a piece of poor property. Any mining man would know that an expert would never be fooled by a salting job such as this one. That foreign ore would be a dead giveaway. For some reason Vicker was supposed to spot the fake.

The same question came back to him. What was the point of it? What did anybody stand to gain by this crazy stunt? For a few minutes, he considered putting on a pretense of being fooled. If the gang didn't expect to fool him, it would throw their calculations out if he didn't do what they expected. Then he tossed the idea aside. He would only arouse suspicions — and that was exactly the thing he did not dare to do. He had to play it their way.

The three men outside the shaft were watching him narrowly as he came out of the shallow hole. He could only hope that Aylett would not look so carefully that he would begin to see a resemblance to an earlier visitor in the present one. That would undoubtedly prove fatal. The others would quickly realize that the ragged man who had visited Nate was the same one who had trailed Marley and fought that battle on the mountainside.

He decided to use the bold attack with Aylett as his target, hoping that the altered voice might keep the old man from getting any wayward thoughts about the saddle bum. "Who's the joker who scrambled this mess of eggs?" he demanded angrily. "Nobody ever took enough gold out of that scratch hole to cap a tooth!"

Aylett started a halfhearted protest, but Vicker cut him off with the same anger ringing in his voice. "I don't know what you thought I'd swallow mister, but this is as clumsy a job of mine-salting as I've ever seen — and I've seen a few. I should have believed that fellow McLinden over in Tombstone when he told me that this was a worthless claim. Heck, it's not even a claim!"

By ignoring Bonner and the peddler and with the reference to McLinden he hoped to confuse them a little, but it didn't seem to make a bit of difference. He got his reaction so promptly that he was taken completely by surprise. Bonner's voice snapped, "Reach, mister! Get them hands up and keep 'em there! Nate, slide in and take his gun. Careful now!"

Vicker turned his head and saw that he was looking squarely into the muzzle of a Colt forty-five. "What . . . ?"

"Get 'em up there!" Bonner urged. He eased a little to one side so that Aylett could pick up Vicker's gun without getting in the line of fire. Without turning his head or easing his glare at Vicker, he shot another order. "Ike! Get on that wagon and get out of here. Forget what you just saw."

Vicker took some slight comfort from that final order. Bonner was trying to make him think that Marley was not a part of the game. Apparently they weren't intending to murder him or they wouldn't bother to think about what kind of story he would tell or whom he would implicate when he got back to civilization. It was about the only good point he could find in the mess. He still didn't know why they had rigged an elaborate hoax that they clearly expected him to recognize. What was perhaps worse, he was likely to be tied up — literally or otherwise — just when he should have been available to give information to O'Fallon's men when they moved in.

"What's the point of all this?" he asked Bonner in an aggrieved tone. "You can't hope to sell a salted mine like this. A lot of people know that I came down here to look at it. Nobody will even consider it while I'm missing. You couldn't find a buyer now even if the salting job was a good one — and it's mighty clumsy."

"Behave yerself and yuh won't git hurt,"

Bonner growled. "There ain't no use in askin' questions. I ain't tellin' yuh nothin' exceptin' that we ain't lettin' yuh go back and tell nobody what yuh seen here."

Vicker felt a little annoyed at himself because he wanted to laugh. There wasn't anything funny in any part of it, but it still seemed oddly ridiculous that he should go on playing the bewildered mine scout while Bonner continued pretending that he was worried about a mine-salting game that had gone awry. He could only hope that Bonner was as ignorant of Vicker's pretense as Vicker was puzzled about the reason behind the crazy mess.

"Use your head, man!" he snapped. "What could I tell anybody? That you salted a mine? It's been done before. Nobody ever does anything about it. My company wouldn't bother to prosecute. We simply drop the whole thing. There's no point in holding me."

For an instant, he thought the beak-nosed man might rise to the bait and boast of what the operation really meant. Then the moment passed, and Bonner ordered, "Over this way, mister. And don't try no cute tricks. I ain't aimin' to shoot if'n I don't have to. Just don't make me waste a slug. It wouldn't mean no more'n that to me."

Vicker obeyed the order, knowing that Bonner had spoken simple truth finally. He heard the man tell Aylett to get something from the saddlebags and then he went on trying to figure out some answers. This thing had clearly been planned out ahead of time. Bonner was following careful orders.

There was a delay until Aylett came back with a pair of handcuffs. At Bonner's curt command, he sidled around behind Vicker and snapped them on the prisoner's wrists.

"Now tie his feet," Bonner continued. "Better sit down, mister. It'll be easier than havin' me knock yuh down. Easier fer yuhrself, I mean."

There was nothing to do but to submit. Bonner not only held the gun with a steady hand, he had it cocked all the time.

CHAPTER 9

The pair disappeared down the gulch, and left Vicker on the ground for a good hour. The captive tried to work himself around so that the manacled hands could get at the knots that held his ankles, but he never could quite make it. Twice he managed to get finger tips almost into position, but the well-tied ropes would not yield to his fingernails, and he could not maintain the position long enough to really work on them.

Then his captors returned. Aylett resumed drinking, but Bonner came over to check on the ropes. "Sorry about this," he said, his grin showing nothing that even approximated sorrow. "I got my orders, so I do what I'm supposed to do."

"Whose orders?" Vicker asked.

"Don't ask me no questions, and yuh won't git told no lies. Just rest comfortable like."

"Sure! With my hands cramped up behind me and my legs tied! Thanks!"

"No need to git sarcastic. I could make it a lot worse."

When Vicker made no reply, the man stretched out in the shade of a pine and went to sleep.

Gnats buzzed around the prisoner's face. An ant explored inside the collar of his shirt. The sun was hitting him directly now, the temperature of the gulch close to the hundred mark. Bonner snored and Aylett began to sing dolefully between hiccups. This was quite a musical gang, Vicker thought with forced humor. Marley played the harmonica and Aylett sang.

After a while, he forced himself to forget personal discomfort and irritation. It was clear that they did not intend to murder him. Assuming that sooner or later he would be turned loose, he wanted to get the picture as clear in his mind as possible.

From the beginning, there had been one puzzle after another. Now it occurred to him that he still didn't know the answer to that first puzzle, the one about why Marley had waited south of the border. One guess had been pretty obvious, and he had accepted it, particularly after learning that Austin Sebrell was involved. Now it didn't seem quite convincing that Marley would have timed his move so that he would have a friend in command of the army patrol on the border. The army didn't actually patrol the border, and the army didn't work for the Customs Service. There had been no alert against smugglers. It seemed likely that most of the garrison of the fort knew about the gold deal that Marley was operating. The whole thing was open gossip around the stables, so it would be well known in barracks. No one seemed to see anything wrong in it. Then why should Marley wait for Sebrell or anyone else?

The only answer that came to him wasn't completely satisfactory because it was a matter of sheer guess He wished that he had been able to check on dates and times when Marley had made his northbound trips, comparing that information with the roster of patrol duty and the government records of smuggled goods appearing on the American market. Possibly there would be a pattern there. When Marley was bringing in gold — from whatever source — he would have moved without taking particular precautions. Maybe the spread of the gossip had been deliberate. No one was going to bother about such a matter, so nobody tried to keep it a secret.

On the other hand, when there was something else being carried by the little peddler, the gang didn't take chances. They made certain that their confederate — probably Sebrell — was in position to protect them against chance inspections. It would have been an added precaution, since army patrols didn't bother border traffic anyway.

He knew that the theory was weak, but he couldn't think of a better one, and he had a hunch that it might be correct. Knowing Austin Sebrell as he did, it seemed like the sort of thing that would appeal to him. More than likely Sebrell had known of the gold shipments before the gang approached him. He might have assumed that he was being paid to guard a secret that was no secret at all. That would appeal to his pride as an accomplished schemer. Maybe he didn't even suspect that he was conniving at something really important.

Unable to go any further with that line of thought, he turned his mind to other, more important problems. Why had he been led into this deliberately planned salting job? Somebody had hurried out here to plant the gold. Then he had been led to the spot, the plotters knowing perfectly well that he would call the turn. Now they held him prisoner. Why? As he had explained to Bonner, there was nothing the salters had to fear. The mine was a fake, but nobody ever suffered prosecution for salting. Nor would publicity hurt them any; they had let it be known from the beginning that Aylett was playing a game with a fake mine. It didn't make even as much sense as the Sebrell affair.

He patiently reviewed the facts. So far as he could judge — and hope — he was known to the gang only as a mine scout. Bonner's attitude seemed to prove that point. So he had to assume that all of this was intended to keep him out of the way. He had become an inconvenience, but because he was well known to a lot of people, the gang could not risk murdering him as summarily as they had tried to do with an unknown saddle tramp.

The logical guess was that they had not wanted him prowling about the Empty Poke in the first place. Both McLinden and Sam Bunch had tried to discourage the trip. When they learned that they could not talk him out of it, they made plans, rather elaborate plans, that still required a lot of explanation before they would make sense.

He tried to puzzle it out. What would be the difference between a barren hole and a salted mine in the eyes of a legitimate mine scout? It didn't seem to make any difference at all, but then he began to wonder how such a mining scout — with no other knowledge of the situation — would have reacted in each instance. If such a scout had seen the Empty Poke as it was — as he had seen it two weeks earlier — he probably would have gone back to town with some pretty disgusted remarks about the place and some sharp questions about where Marley was getting the gold that he was bringing in. Word of the gold-smuggling would have spread, and the government would have gotten interested. The harmless little secret known to teamsters and soldiers might not have seemed quite so harmless when it became known at a distance from the border.

On the other hand, a report of deliberate mine-salting would have produced a different reaction. There would be no need to mention Marley. Fraud and not smuggling would get the attention. This idea fitted with the attempt Bonner had made to let his prisoner think that Marley knew nothing of what was happening. The gang didn't mind being accused of mine-salting, but they were taking pains to keep people from getting too much impressed by rumors of smuggling.

It still didn't explain why Vicker should be taken prisoner. Why hadn't he been permitted to denounce the attempted salting fraud and go back to Fort Huachuca? Somehow it seemed that the brain behind the smuggling ring seemed to become unnecessarily devious at times. That bit about using Sebrell — or some other officer — when critical shipments were coming north was the same kind of added complication as this kidnaping. The gang seemed to get a bit edgy when big moments arrived.

That must be it! The big smuggling attempt was to be made sooner than had been originally planned. The mine-salting had been for the purpose Vicker had figured out. But then word had come along that the Mexican half of the gang was on the way north. Vicker had to be kept out of the way while the big move was being made. It all made more sense when he considered it from that angle . . . and he had to recognize that he had put himself exactly in the wrong place. Probably the gang didn't even suspect that they had trapped the one man who could tip off federal agents to their plans.

He dozed out of sheer weariness and disgust, waking with sharp aches in his muscles and an ant in his ear. His threshings brought Bonner to him. The gunman said nothing, but dragged him unceremoniously to a shady spot and dropped him there.

At dusk, the beak-nosed man opened a couple of cans and produced what passed for a supper. He ate what he wanted and then unlocked the handcuffs for Vicker to clean up the leavings. During the time that the prisoner was unshackled, Bonner sat back beyond possible leaping range, his gun held ready. He made no comments and refused to reply when Vicker tried a couple of questions on him.

It seemed that there might be a chance for a break when the time came for Bonner to replace the handcuffs, but the gunman didn't take any needless chances. He simply went across to the mouth of the shaft and kicked Aylett awake. The casual brutality of the kicking seemed to cause no ill feeling. Bonner simply used the method that was best suited to getting some action out of the befuddled older man.

"Cuff him again, Nate!" he snapped. "Hustle it up, you old soak! This time, leave his hands in front. He'll sleep easier."

It seemed like a strange bit of consideration to come from the man who had just kicked Aylett. Vicker decided that Bonner was a pretty cold bit of work. He was carrying out his orders with no particular feeling one way or another. He could ease a prisoner's discomfort as casually as he could shoot him. Vicker didn't like to think of how the man's mood might change if he should discover that his prisoner was the man who had shot his brother.

As darkness settled over the gulch, Vicker had an added worry. In another day, that sandy stubble would begin to get pretty ugly. Nate Aylett might begin to remember an earlier visitor. If Aylett talked — and Bonner listened — and Bonner began to add up a few things, there would be no more talk about prisoners being made easy for sleeping.

He moved cautiously, testing to see whether he could now get to the ropes that bound his ankles together. Perhaps he could make a break under cover of darkness. Maybe he could even get away with one of the horses. With Aylett in a drunken sleep and Bonner . . .

The dream didn't get very far. Bonner growled some orders at his companion, and the pair of them proceeded to kill off any of the chances Vicker had been considering. They did it simply by tying another rope around the prisoner's waist and fastening the cuffs to it. Aylett did the work, and Bonner checked the knots after it was finished.

"Fer a drunk yuh don't do bad, Nate," the gunman chuckled. "A man would have to be a contorshener to git outa that rig."

Aylett nodded, pleased with himself. He even tried to ape the other man's good humor. "Sleep purty, Mister Vicker," he said with a low bow that almost caused him to fall across the prone man.

Bonner reached out to grab a shoulder and haul the older man away. Then he planted a hard foot at the seat of Aylett's pants and started him back toward the mine shaft. "Back to yuhr bottle, Nate. It don't seem like one good job means that yuh gotta act cute."

For Vicker the night was a succession of aches and pains. Cramped muscles kept waking him, but then he would sleep again, exhaustion claiming its toll. He knew vaguely that there had been some kind of movement around the camp on one of his first waking spells, but he had assumed that Bonner was going out to do a little scouting. Later, he found the gulch so silent that he spent a few minutes trying to loosen his bonds, but without any trace of success. When he awoke at the first light of dawn, he couldn't recall the sequence of events or much of anything else.

Then his thoughts began to take on a semblance of sanity, and he heard heavy snoring not far away. As the light strengthened, he saw that it was Nate Aylett who was doing the snoring. Bonner was nowhere in sight.

An hour later, Aylett stirred and sat up, rubbing bloodshot eyes and stretching mightily. It took him a long time to get his wits about him, but finally he turned to aim a crooked smile at Vicker. "Darn yuh," he said without any particular malice, "now I gotta figger how to handle yuh."

Vicker understood then that Bonner had left the gulch during the night and would not be back very soon. "Easy enough," he told the old man with a grin that was at least as twisted as the one he was watching. "Just cut me loose and get back to your loafing. No reason for either of us to be bothered."

Aylett shook his frowsy head. "It wouldn't work out. Not when I got orders from this crowd."

"Which crowd?" Vicker didn't need an answer, but he wanted to see whether Aylett would give him one.

The head wagged again. "It wouldn't be no healthier fer me to tell yuh than it would be to turn yuh loose." He stared for several moments, the bleary eyes narrowing a little.

"Say! Ain't I seen yuh somewhere before? Seems like yuh look a heap more familiar than yuh done yestiday."

Vicker swallowed hard. It was a bit of irony that for the moment his greatest source of danger was his own whiskers. "You're getting used to me," he laughed, trying to make it sound like a joke. Then, trying to get the old man's thoughts away from a dangerous topic, he asked, "Where's my dear friend Bonner?"

"Away. And don't yuh be gittin' no ideas on that account! I kin git jest as tough as anybody." It was clear that the old man was blustering to maintain his own courage. He was not too sure of himself, and he was scared green at the thought of what might happen to him if he didn't carry out his orders. In a way, that made him doubly dangerous.

Still it seemed to Vicker that there was now a chance of escape. Bonner had set a pattern in taking off the handcuffs at mealtime. If Aylett did the same thing, there might be an opportunity to make a break. He watched silently while the pretended miner brought out a coffee pot and frying pan before fussing around to get them set up and stir the fire. The old man did a lot of blundering. His reactions were not very fast in the first place, and heavy drinking had made him shaky. Vicker grew hopeful.

Neither of them spoke again while Aylett cooked and ate his meal of flapjacks, bacon, and coffee. Then Vicker inquired mildly, "Don't I get anything to eat in this hotel?"

Aylett turned a thin smile toward him. "Yuh wouldn't be countin' on gittin' the cuffs off so's yuh could make a break, would yuh? 'Cause it ain't gonna happen. I'm leavin' the leftovers and the coffee pot right here on this flat rock. Then I'm gonna set me down over there in the shade and keep a gun aimed right smack at yer guts. Wiggle over and feed yerself as best yuh kin. It'll be a mite awkward, but yuh don't need to hurry none. Time is somethin' we both got lots of. Try any other kind o' wigglin' and I plug yuh!"

It didn't help a bit to know that Aylett was still scared. The old man wasn't going to take any chances. Actually he might be more dangerous than Bonner would have been. Simply because he was unsure of himself and inclined to be unsteady, he might shoot for no reason at all.

With that threat in mind, Vicker took a good hour to get the food and the coffee. With his hands lashed at his waist, he could only inch around and place things where he could then get his mouth to them as an animal might. And he had to do it with the knowledge that Aylett was getting extra courage out of a bottle all the time. The bottle and the gun didn't make a happy combination for a prisoner.

At least it took all morning to get breakfast over. By that time, Vicker was weary enough so that he didn't want to do anything except lie quiet for a while. By rolling to keep out of the worst of the sun's glare, he found a little more comfort than he had been able to get on the previous afternoon, but it wasn't much of an improvement. The gulch was stifling, with no air stirring. Twice he asked Aylett to ease up on the ropes so that he might get rid of muscle cramps and fight off the insects, but the old man paid no attention. When Vicker tried cursing him, the result was the same. Aylett had reached the singing stage now, and he wasn't even looking at his prisoner.

By noon the man was once more quite drunk, so Vicker began to work at the ropes that held his wrists to his body. It was slow toil, but he kept rubbing at the rocky ground until he was sure that some of the rope strands were beginning to fray. He was beginning to have hopes when Aylett stirred and looked around suspiciously. For a moment or two, it seemed that he might come across to take a look, so Vicker pretended to be struggling with a cramp and asked again to have the ropes eased. That seemed to settle it. The old man wasn't going to get himself mixed up in any dangerous operation like that. He simply rolled over and went to sleep.

They ate again just before dark, practically duplicating the ritual of the morning. This time Vicker had to be more careful, keeping his body at an angle so that the frayed rope would not show. It was no more than halfway through, but he didn't want to waste such painful efforts. Nor was he sure that Aylett would even try to renew the lashings. With his fears, the old man might simply decide to shoot his prisoner rather than risk getting too close.

As night came on, he tried to get Aylett to tell him why he was being held and for how long. Earlier he had been content to avoid the old man's scrutiny. Now in the darkness, with those telltale whiskers invisible, he could risk fishing for information. The only answer he received was one he guessed was the truth. Aylett simply didn't know.

"Might as well stop proddin', mister," Nate grumbled. "I ain't runnin' this business. I take orders and get paid. No more.

Somebody will be along in a day or two. Yuh'll find out soon enough."

That was hint enough for Vicker. A day or two. It meant that the gang was actually moving for a quick crossing of the border. It also suggested that no other gang member would be in the gulch for some time. With any luck, Vicker might hope to get free during the night. Then there would still be time to get back to the fort with the information he had gained. He didn't let himself worry about how he would manage Aylett. Even handcuffed, he should be able to take care of a drunk.

Chapter 10

Aylett seemed wide awake after his afternoon nap, so Vicker had to be patient. He worked cautiously at the ropes, but mostly he tried to think out the problems that had shown themselves. One answer that had not seemed too smart at first gradually became convincing to him, mainly because it fitted with everything else. The Empty Poke Mine had been picked as the spot for some kind of transfer of the goods coming up out of Mexico. The gang knew that Ike Marley had been tailed by a man who had gotten away from them. They could no longer depend on Marley as a safe means of handling their stuff. This time Marley would be a red herring. He would go through his regular routine, maybe to the extent of handling a bit of gold, but the real loot would come across at some other point and by some other means. With so many miles of unguarded border, that part would be no problem.

It seemed like a good bet that the plan had been in the making when McLinden learned that Jack Vicker was determined to have a look at the Empty Poke property. The gang didn't want him to be there. Ostensibly, they made him a prisoner, to keep him from exposing that fraud, but actually to keep him out of the way while the smuggling business was completed. When they turned him loose, he would report the fraud, but would not suspect the other part of the plot. Aylett and Bonner would disappear into Mexico for a while, and there would be no suspicion of the real plotters. Pacific wouldn't press matters if they got their agent back safely.

He could find no flaw in the reasoning, but it made him all the more certain that time was now important. A couple of days, Aylett had said. The smugglers were planning to make their move while the government forces were smugly waiting for Ike Marley to return. It had to be that way.

When Aylett finally took a couple of long swigs from his jug and stretched out under a tree, Vicker went to work on the ropes in earnest. He wondered what Bonner might be doing. Probably he had gone to report or to pick up fresh orders. Or perhaps he had gone back to Fort Huachuca to relate that the mining man had passed up the Empty Poke and had gone on to look at some other bit of mining property. That would keep people from asking questions until the gang could make its move.

The thought made him work a little harder, forgetting the raw places on his wrists and knuckles. It took all of his will power, sore muscles reluctant to do his bidding. Several times he had to stop and rest, working the cramps out of his twisted body, but finally he knew that his manacled hands were no longer fastened to his waist. He guessed that the time was a little past midnight.

It took some time to get circulation going, and then he set to work on the knots at his ankles. Stiff fingers proved clumsy, and again it seemed as though the job would never end. Once he had to stop and lie quiet while Aylett stumbled out into the bushes. The old man didn't come near him, however, and renewed snoring signaled for more work.

Then the ropes fell away. He lay flat to start moving his legs, fearing that he would fall flat if he tried to stand up too soon. It would be fatal to take a fall and have those handcuffs clatter on a rock. He had to use plenty of caution, and he had to plan every move. There must be no foolish scruples about handling Nate Aylett. Probably he would be able to hold the man, but there would be little chance of getting him tied up while he was himself hampered by the handcuffs.

By the time he was ready to trust his legs, he knew what he was going to do. He took a few cautious steps, making sure that he was steady enough for the purpose. The numbed feet didn't want to do his bidding, but he didn't want to delay any longer. Aylett might wake up again. Even a drunken man was dangerous when he had both hands free and was armed. Aylett had to be knocked out quickly.

Vicker chose as his weapon the heavy iron skillet that had been used for making the flapjacks. It was the only thing with a handle that a manacled man might wield with any accuracy. Aylett's gun had not been in evidence during the evening, so Vicker didn't know where it was. Better to use the skillet than to risk hunting for the gun.

He picked it up carefully, making sure that the handcuff chain did not jingle. Then he had to steady himself again. A wave of dizziness had hit him as he stooped over, but the threat passed and he assumed that it was just a matter of slow circulation. He could see the dark form of the old man, and he could hear the snores, so there was no trouble in locating his target.

Aylett did not move as Vicker closed in. He was on his side, his head pillowed on one arm. Vicker did not hesitate even though he felt some of the revulsion that had hit him when he'd shot the gunman from ambush. It didn't seem decent to hit an old man while he slept, but there was no other way. He simply swung the skillet hard, and Aylett uttered one soft but explosive grunt. That was it.

Vicker moved swiftly after that, finding energy he didn't know he had. Locating the ropes that he had so recently dicarded, he clumsily but effectively tied up the new prisoner. Working in handcuffs wasn't easy, but he was grim about the job. Aylett wasn't going to cause any trouble for some time to come.

When the man was completely helpless — and still unconscious — Vicker began his search for the handcuff key. He tried every pocket in the old man's faded garments, but all he found was a plug of tobacco, some crumpled papers that he guessed in the darkness would be paper money, and a big pocket knife.

That left him in something of a stew. Probably he could get a saddle on a horse and get himself into it, but it didn't seem like a good risk to head out into open country so handicapped. Even assuming that he could find Aylett's gun or his own, he would be in mighty poor position to use it in any kind of running fight. The handcuffs were turning out to be more of a problem than he had anticipated.

He decided to rest for a few minutes. There was not much point in trying to search the camp in darkness, so he postponed the effort. Maybe Aylett could be persuaded to talk when he regained consciousness. A little persuasion ought to suffice with such a man.

Relaxing from his long hours of discomfort and stern effort almost wrecked his plans. He fell asleep while he tried to figure out what move he should make next. It was full daylight when he opened his eyes again. His legs had stiffened badly, and both hands were so stiff and sore that he could scarcely move his fingers. He managed to get on his feet, staggering a little before he knew that he actually could stand up. Then he saw that Aylett was glaring angrily and fearfully at him.

"Morning," Vicker said with a wry smile. "Looks like the good fairies came during the night and changed things around a mite. Funny, eh?"

Aylett's unhappy grunt suggested that he didn't see anything very humorous in the situation. Vicker let him scowl and began a search of the camp. It didn't take long to find a cache of personal property in a cleft of the rock wall where Aylett had kept his cooking utensils. His own gun and belt were there along with a rifle that he passed up because he knew he would not be able to handle it. He made sure that it was unloaded, tossing the shells back into the brush. A box of extra cartridges went the same way. There was no sign of a handcuff key.

"Where's the key to these things, Nate?" he demanded as he went back to stare down at his prisoner. "You might as well tell me now instead of having me knock it out of you the hard way. I won't be soft, you know."

"Gimme a drink," the old man croaked, jerking his head toward the jug. "I got a headache."

"Likely," Vicker agreed. "Maybe two headaches. One out of the jug and one out of a frying pan. Or ain't that funny, either?"

Aylett still didn't react. He simply kept his

bloodshot eyes on the man he evidently feared. "How'd yuh git loose?" he quavered.

This time it was Vicker's turn to ignore a question. He went back to the fire, stirring it up a little and adding some light wood. Then he picked up a cup that looked as though it had not been washed for weeks and took it across to the jug. "I'll make you a trade, Nate," he offered. "A drink for the handcuff key." He got a good smell of the stuff he was pouring into the cup and added, "No need to claim frying-pan credit for that headache of yours. This stuff would do it all alone. Smells like it ought to be poured back in the cesspool. Where's that key?"

Aylett tried to sit up as the drink was poured, but then he sank back again. "I ain't got it. Honest. Bonner took it with him. He don't trust me."

Vicker felt sure that the old man was telling the truth. He wanted the drink too badly to waste time with a lie. "So go ahead," he muttered. "Have your poison anyway. I should have expected this."

He held the cup to the prone man's lips, watching as the stuff went down. There wasn't even a sputter. Aylett swallowed it in a couple of gulps and settled back again.

Vicker had to do some more thinking. If

Bonner had kept the key, it was evident that he would be coming back before long. Maybe he could still get clear before that would happen. On the other hand, he didn't want to be caught helpless in the open.

"When is Bonner due back?" he asked.

Aylett opened one eye. "I still think I musta seen yuh somewhere before. Are yuh sure . . . ?"

Vicker took a step as though to launch a kick. "Answer my question! When do you expect Bonner?" He had to know, and he had to keep Aylett's mind away from that matter of recognition.

The old man shut his eye as he saw what he thought was a kick coming. When nothing happened, he opened both eyes. "I dunno," he said finally. "He had to pass along a message and git some orders."

"Pass what message? Talk!" The foot threatened again.

"Got to let . . . somebody know about yuh bein' here."

"Who?"

"I dunno. Honest I don't."

"Don't lie to me, Nate. I think you know. And I think you'd rather tell me than get your guts kicked out!"

"So it's Sam. Sam Bunch at the fort. I reckon he ain't the one what gives the orders, but he's the one what passes 'em on. It was him Bonner went to see."

"Who gives orders to Sam?"

"That part I don't know. Yuh can't make me tell yuh somethin' I don't know. Not even by kickin'."

Vicker reached for the jug and held it up where the old man could see it. Then he tipped it and began to pour the raw liquor out on the ground. "Maybe I won't kick you," he said quietly. "But neither will this stuff if I pour it out. Start talking, and I stop pouring."

Scarcely a cupful had gone out of the jug when Nate began to pour out a mixture of protest and story. Vicker turned the jug upright again and listened. Aylett had been hired by Sam Bunch. He was to pose as a miner for the gold-smuggling deal that everybody seemed to know about. A few days ago, he had been warned that he would have to handle matters a bit differently. He was given a new story to tell and warned to get ready to lend a hand in holding a prisoner. He didn't know why the prisoner was to be held. He still didn't know. As long as he received his wages and plenty of pop-skull whiskey, he didn't ask questions. He knew about Ike Marley and the Bonner brothers, but no other names seemed to mean much to him.

Vicker prodded him three times with small pourings from the jug, but finally decided that Aylett knew no more than he had told. The man wasn't enough of an actor to hide his feelings too well. He simply didn't know.

After a while, Vicker left him alone, taking the jug to a safe distance. There was still a possibility that Aylett might work up a few extra memories if he got thirsty enough. Meanwhile he might sober up enough to think of a point that he would want to trade for a drink. It didn't make much difference now that a sober Aylett might start thinking about sandy whiskers. Vicker as a prisoner had had to fear that possibility; now it didn't seem to be much of a threat.

He went through the camp equipment in hopes of finding a file or some other tool that might be used on the handcuffs. He knew that a man who was handy with simply tools could open almost any pair of handcuffs, but the knowledge was not much good to him. He wasn't the man who could use the tools, and anyway he couldn't find anything that looked hopeful for the purpose. It was a shame that Ben Naismith was back in Tombstone keeping a fruitless watch on McLinden. Ben had the talents to make short work of such a job.

After an hour of searching, he gave up and began to put a saddle on his horse. It was clumsy work, and he had to make several attempts before he could get the cinch tightened to his satisfaction. Finally he was ready to go, but he still had not made up his mind as to how he would try to escape. There was a chance that he might make Fort Huachuca without being spotted, but Bonner would be coming back from the fort soon and there was a risk of running into him. Making a detour along the top of the mountain didn't sound like a smart way to handle the matter. It would be bad enough getting chased out in the open. In strange country, it would be even worse.

Then another thought came. His escape would probably put the smugglers on the alert. The chance of catching them unaware would be lost. What he needed to do was to keep the gang unaware of his escape until it was too late for them to change plans. Then he had to reach Fort Huachuca in a hurry so as to pass the word to the men who could do something about it. For a fellow in handcuffs, it wasn't going to be easy. He had to trap Bonner and keep him quiet for the necessary time. Even without the handcuffs that was not a simple problem.

Climbing painfully into the saddle, he

rode down the gulch, alert for the chance that Bonner might have left some unknown sentry on duty there. When he found the passage clear, he took a few minutes to study the nearby hills and the flat country to the east. It was a dreary view, with its yellow gravel and dusty clumps of mesquite, but it looked harmless enough. No dust trailer marked a movement of any sort. Which was as it should be. Army patrols would be farther to the east on the alert against the Apache alarm. Marley was down in Sonora. The rest of the gang would be busy with their preparations for the big move. Seeing the dreary land bare in front of him, he could feel that he had made a few correct guesses.

Which gave him something else to consider. If the gang actually planned to use the gulch for some kind of transfer of smuggled goods, there should be some sort of hint as to how the transfer would be made. A wagon or pack horses should be arriving before long. The stuff would have to be handled in some manner that would not attract attention.

After a few minutes, he saw a wisp of dust in the northeast. It seemed to him that the dust was on the rough trail along the mountain, so he guessed that this would be Bonner coming back from Fort Huachuca. The time element seemed right.

He moved back into cover and prepared to wait. It seemed like the only chance. Bonner had the handcuff keys and had to be put out of action so he could not spread an alarm. There would be plenty of danger in trying to take the man, but the risk had to be run.

An hour later, he was still sweating it out in the mesquite, but now he knew that there was a rider under that plume of dust, a rider who was coming straight toward him. In another twenty minutes, he knew that it was Bonner who was heading in toward the gulch entrance. Somehow he had to find a way to capture the man. Shooting him from ambush would be the safest, but Vicker knew that he would not do it. A conscience was a mighty unhandy thing to have at times like this — but he had one, such as it was. The only possibility was to catch Bonner unaware and hold a gun on him until he could be persuaded to disarm himself and to give up the key. If the gunman tried to resist . . . well, in that case, conscience wouldn't have much to do with it. Vicker could almost hope that Bonner would try something. It would simplify things a lot.

He tied his horse in a deeper clump of

mesquite and took up a position close to the trail, but where he would be well hidden until he chose to show himself. Almost as an afterthought he checked the loads in his sixgun. It would have been a grim joke on him if his captors had unloaded the weapon after taking it from him. Fortunately, they hadn't done so. He managed to get a sixth cartridge from his belt and slipped it into the empty chamber. For the moment, he wasn't going to worry about a safety measure; it would be a lot safer anyway to have that extra bullet available. Now he was ready, his spot on the right-hand side of the trail giving him a chance to catch Bonner from an angle that would make the gunman turn his body awkwardly before he would be able to bring a gun to bear. Even a man with handcuffs could get in a shot before his enemy could make that kind of a move.

Bonner was just coming up the easy slope into the mouth of the gulch when a voice spoke almost in Vicker's ear. "Drop the gun!" The exclamation point was provided by the click of a hammer. Then the voice added softly, only a slight accent suggesting the nationality of the speaker, "Please do nothing foolish. Drop the gun."

Vicker didn't even try to turn around.

Disgust at his own carelessness mingled with a bitterness of failure. He should have known! All the time he had been telling himself that this gulch was to be a focal point for whatever was to happen. He had wondered why none of the gang had appeared to make preparations. But he hadn't listened to his own thoughts. He knew that the gulch must have another entrance, an entrance that would let the smugglers bring their stuff in without crossing the line at a suspected point.

The gun dropped from his hands as the thoughts went through his mind.

CHAPTER 11

Behind him the voice ordered, "You will please to come this way, *señor.*" The politeness in the words was all on the surface. Vicker turned and saw that he was under the gun of the same *vaquero* who had turned up so frequently in the past couple of weeks. At a distance, the man had looked like just another rider. In Tombstone, he had seemed keener, a little more grim, but still just a gunhand. Now Vicker had a hunch that he had underestimated his man. This fellow was an important cog in the smuggling machine. Worse than that, he was a man who might get ideas about the sandy stubble that was getting so prominent on Vicker's chin. If Aylett didn't get his sodden memory to working, there was a good chance that this sharp-eyed outlaw might call the turn.

For the moment, the man seemed content to accept things as they seemed. Evidently he knew about Jack Vicker, so he didn't look for anyone else. He simply ordered Vicker along while he eased in behind him to pick up the discarded gun. By that time, Bonner rode up; the Mexican hailed him, telling quickly how he had found Aylett tied up and the prisoner missing. He had trailed the escaped captive and surprised him just as he was laying an ambush.

Bonner stared down from his saddle. "Goin' to gun me from the brush, hey?" he growled.

"No," Vicker replied as steadily as he could manage. "Somehow I never got around to being much of a hand at drygulching. I just wanted to make you turn over that key." He raised his manacled hands in explanation. This time he knew that he needed to convince the gunman. Bonner no longer looked disinterested. His glare was completely personal now.

"Get movin'!" Bonner ordered after a moment's hesitation that suggested he had been toying with the idea of shooting the prisoner. "We'll see what Nate's got to say fer hisself."

The *vaquero* laughed. "He is very thirsty, that one. He told me." Then he added, "He is still tied up. It seemed like the proper thing to leave him that way. Small punishment for his carelessness."

"Right. And he won't be so liquored up when we git him to tell us what happened. That skull varnish keeps him stupid most o' the time." He looked around as he asked, "This varmint have a bronc?"

The *vaquero* pointed. "I bring it. Perhaps we let him walk for a time. It should use up some of his troublesome ambition."

Bonner seemed to like that style of humor. He laughed aloud and motioned for the Mexican to get the concealed horse. "Yuh're a smart one, Chico. But I know somethin' that's gonna take a lot more o' the ginger outa this polecat. Wait'll I tell him what's goin' on back at the fort."

He rode silently behind the stumbling Vicker until the Mexican came up with the horse. Then he said, "Seems like yuh ain't well thought of by folks back at Huachuca, Mister Vicker. They got men out lookin' fer yuh. Seems as how they got it all worked out that yuh bushwhacked a officer gent name of Sebrell. That's a joke on yuh, ain't it?"

Vicker half turned. "What happened to Sebrell? Where?"

"He got hisself killed over in Greasewood Canyon yestiday mornin'. He was comin' through with a patrol, and somebody gunned him from the brush. A couple of his men tried to ride down the killer, but they never even got a look at him. Mighty rough country over there."

"But why should they think that I did it?"

Bonner laughed again. He was evidently enjoying himself hugely. "I reckon I kin claim a mite of the credit, but they was already doin' a bit o' thinkin' along that line. Seems as how folks knowed that Mrs. Sebrell was an ole flame o' yourn. Sebrell stole her away from yuh, and yuh wanted to git her back."

"That's a lot of nonsense!" Vicker blurted. "I haven't . . ." He cut it off. There was no point in protesting to Eddie Bonner. Maybe there would be little point in protesting to anyone else. He had actually come to Fort Huachuca with Janet. Several people had heard them talking together, and Janet had certainly made some statements that were open to misinterpretation.

Bonner wasn't going to let him drop the subject. "I kin see why yuh feel a mite worried. When I heard how they was talkin', I almost felt sorry, seein' as how I could give yuh a real clear alibi. Then I got to thinkin'. Yuh're kind of a nuisance to me, Vicker. I'd be in a lot better shape if'n I didn't have to figger that yuh'd stir up a fuss about me when yuh git back — and assumin' that yuh do. So I passed the word about how yuh rode out here to the Empty Poke, but didn't seem much interested in the place. I told 'em that yuh rode out again like yuh had somethin' else on yuhr mind. Right away folks got to workin' out the time, and it seemed to them that yuh coulda jest made it over to Greasewood Canyon in time to bushwhack the husband of the woman yuh was itchin' to git. Now that I find yuh waitin' to gun me down, I'm kinda glad I fixed things up all nice and neat fer yuh."

Vicker didn't trust himself to reply. Not only had his fine plans for escape exploded in his face — or rather behind his back — but he was in more trouble. Making another escape was still his immediate goal, but this time he would have to take a prisoner with him, a prisoner who could be made to talk. It wasn't cheering to know that his alibi for the Sebrell murder depended upon two men who were enemies to him. For the moment, he almost forgot that he had a bigger and closer worry. If either Aylett or Chico should begin to get ideas about those sandy whiskers, there would be no problem of clearing himself of a murder charge. He would never get back to face such a charge.

As they were nearing the prospect hole,

the *vaquero* rode forward and exchanged a few cautious words with Eddie Bonner. Vicker heard only a little of it, and what he heard was cryptic. Something about another two days and that Marley would stay clear. It seemed to fit well enough with his earlier guesses. The gang was making its move, would be at the gulch in two days. They knew that Marley was no longer of use to them, so they would keep him in Sonora until it was over. If the Customs men kept an eye on Marley, the job would be over before any government trap could be set.

He wondered whether Sebrell's murder might not be part of the big plan. If Sebrell had been taking pay for his dubious part in the game, he would be considered dangerous by the gang. With Marley out of it, there was no point in using Sebrell. In a situation like that, it was quite likely that Sebrell would be eliminated. This crowd didn't take unnecessary risks. And that was another source of concern. How long would they continue to keep a prisoner who might prove dangerous to them? It was just possible that the Sebrell killing was a preliminary step to the murder of Jack Vicker. Probably they could work out some kind of a game in which Vicker's death would appear as the killing of a fugitive from justice.

The grim thought led to another. Whoever had ordered the murder of Austin Sebrell must have known about Vicker's relationship to the couple. Perhaps that would account for the whole crazy business of showing a fake mine and then capturing the man who could expose it. That had been just an excuse to keep Vicker a prisoner while the Sebrell frameup could be put into operation. It seemed like quite a stretch of the imagination, but it was also the kind of planning that the gang's leader seemed to like. Bonner's quick return to Fort Huachuca could then be considered as having been planned ahead of time. Bonner hadn't given evidence against the absent suspect simply out of petty malice; he had had his orders all the time.

Laying aside the wilder guesses, there was one point that stood out. This thing had been planned from Fort Huachuca. McLinden would not have been in sufficiently close touch with developments to keep the proper orders going out. Only at the fort would there have been a person who could properly judge times and movements so as to set this complicated development into action. Sam Bunch was beginning to look like a far more important fellow than he had appeared at first.

By the time Vicker had progressed that far with his guesses, they were back at the fake mine site, and he had other painful matters to distract him. Bonner held a gun on him while the Mexican moved in to fell him with a surprise twist. Then both men held him down and tied his feet together again. After that, Bonner unlocked the handcuffs and replaced them after twisting his arms around behind his back.

"Mebbe that'll hold yuh a mite better," the gunman growled. "And there better not be no next time on this bustin' loose business. From here on I shoot yuh down on mighty small excuse, orders or no orders."

He turned away and wandered idly across to where Nate Aylett was still lying helpless. The old man had been cursing steadily since seeing help arrive, and now he ripped out another string of complaints. "Yuh took long enough to git here! I been tied up since last night!"

Bonner didn't bother to reply. He simply untied Aylett and hauled him to his feet. Then he knocked him down again with a hard right to the mouth. "That's fer gittin' careless," he said in a low voice. "Now stay away from that jug and rustle up some grub. Me'n Chico's hungry."

Aylett struggled to his feet, wiping the

blood that came from broken lips. Then he did as he had been ordered, muttering under his breath. No one else spoke until Aylett had brought out a hasty meal of bacon, beans, and coffee, adding to it some fragments of army hardtack. Then Bonner snapped out new orders. "Pack everything, Nate. Git it on a couple o' broncs. We move out right away."

Aylett started to protest, but Bonner stared him down. "Do what I tell yuh! We got orders. Yuh know what that means."

Oddly enough, he swung to explain those orders to Vicker. "Yuh're still in a lot o' trouble around here, mister. It was bad enough when all I had to do was to keep yuh outa the way fer a spell. Now yuh've got a killin' hangin' over yuhr head, so I got to git yuh clear. Likely somebody's gonna come out here to make sure yuh done what I said yuh done. So yuh got to be somewhere else." He was checking the ropes as he spoke, evidently getting ready to put the prisoner on a horse that the Mexican was bringing.

Minutes later Aylett's belongings were on a pack horse, and the little party moved out, headed west in the direction Vicker had only partly scouted when he had been in the gulch earlier. He knew that the west end of the passage swung around toward the south, and he could guess that it led to the border. Now he had to do some more guessing. Were they intending to take him into Sonora, or was the move a shorter one that would clear the gulch in case someone did come looking for the suspected killer?

He found it hard to keep his mind on the question. He was more curious about those orders that Bonner kept mentioning. Who had given them? Why had Bonner been so deliberate about getting back into the gulch and then getting out of it again? He seemed to know exactly how much time he had for the moves. Certainly he was not worried about an army patrol moving in on him unexpectedly. The outlaws knew exactly what to expect and when to expect it.

The ride was not one that Vicker could enjoy. His feet had been tied under the horse's belly, the ropes so tight that he was forced into a position that quickly brought acute agony to thigh muscles. He couldn't wipe the dust or sweat away from his eyes. He couldn't brush away the flies that kept settling on his face. And he kept growing more and more conscious of what the dust might be doing to his stubble. It seemed to him that every mile made him look a little more like the bum who had skulked through this miserable country earlier. Twice he noticed that Aylett was staring hard at him, and he had an uneasy feeling that the old man was remembering now. But Aylett gave no sign, and Vicker began to hope that Bonner's brutality would keep the old man from talking, out of spite if for no other reason.

When they broke out of the gulch, Bonner swung to the left. Before long, Vicker felt sure that they were not going on into Mexico. The move was becoming a big half circle that would take them around the mountains south of the gulch. As nearly as he could figure, they would come back east not far from the trail Marley was accustomed to using. There would be a certain amount of risk for his captors in that area, so he couldn't guess why they were not continuing on toward the west where there would be less chance of meeting an army patrol.

After a while, he wondered if the purpose might not have something to do with a diversion. If the smugglers proposed to use Empty Poke gulch in the handling of their illegal goods they would want to keep attention elsewhere. Perhaps the fellow who did such elaborate planning had figured out a way to use a prisoner in making some sort of false trail.

At that point, Vicker's imagination seemed to leave him. He couldn't figure out what moves were to be made, and he couldn't guess how his own situation would affect any of it. The smugglers had a problem of getting their plunder through an open stretch of country — even after it was safely across the border. They knew that some sort of alarm must be out. Marley could no longer be used. Yet they were going ahead with their plans. Evidently they had things figured out.

Bonner called a halt in late afternoon, having reached a spot that Vicker judged was four miles north of the border and not more than a mile west of the trail that Marley commonly used. The crossing, where Sebrell's patrol had failed to search Marley's wagon, would be almost due south.

Bonner and Chico exchanged a few words, and the Mexican rode northeast across the slope of the mountain, heading in a direction that would almost complete the circle. Then Bonner ordered Aylett out of the saddle and came across to untie Vicker's feet. With a quick motion, he grabbed one loose foot and heaved, tumbling the prisoner hard to the ground on the opposite side of the horse. "Time to stretch yuhr legs, Mister Vicker," he announced with mock good humor. "Take it easy and I won't have to tie yuh up fer a spell."

Vicker didn't even try to get up. He couldn't imagine himself trying a getaway now. Both legs were completely numb from the way they had been tied under the horse. And now he was aching in a lot of new places. He knew that both elbows had been badly skinned when he tumbled from the horse, and he suspected that his left shoulder had been wrenched. Perhaps it was only a bruise; it didn't seem to be worth the effort to think about it.

"Git yuhr eyes open, Nate," Bonner ordered. "I'll take a nap while Chico's havin' a look around. This time don't let him git near yuh." He jerked his head toward the still-prone Vicker.

Aylett muttered something and pulled a gun. In a matter of minutes, Bonner was snoring and Aylett was beginning to take a few nips from a flask he had produced. Vicker managed to get himself to a sitting position, inching against a tree where he could ease himself back without having the manacled hands in his way. He wondered what chance he would have in persuading Aylett to help him. The old man evidently harbored a grudge for the earlier escape, but it was just as clear that Bonner was the

155

object of more hate. With the right kind of . . . Vicker shook off the thought. What was the use of trying to make any plans that would depend on Nate Aylett. He wasn't to be trusted no matter how things worked out.

Suddenly Vicker knew that he had been asleep. Dusk was closing down on the lower slopes, and Chico was riding up the slope toward the temporary camp. Bonner climbed to his feet and went to meet the Mexican, again the pair of them conferring in whispers. Evidently the *vaquero*'s report was satisfactory, for Bonner said, "We kin move in another hour. Jest time for a bite o' grub."

Then one of Vicker's earlier fears began to prove itself. For the first time, Chico seemed to take a good look at the prisoner; black eyes narrowed as he studied the growing crop of sandy whiskers with their coating of alkali dust. "I see you before, *señor*?" he asked in a voice that was almost a hiss.

Vicker had an answer ready. He had been expecting this moment. "Sure you did. In Tombstone. You and Bonner and another jasper rode in while I was there."

"He was there, all right," Bonner agreed carelessly. "Stop dreamin' and git yuhr belly full fer a long ride."

"It is not the same," Chico replied in that

156

same low tone. "There is another time that I think I see him." He spoke rapidly in Spanish, explaining how he had spotted the man who spied on Marley. It had been a distance look, but he had seen him again during the fight in the valley. The man had come into the open to get the rifle of the wounded man, Spottswell. Both times Chico had seen the reddish whiskers. The prisoner was the right size, and the stubble was beginning to look familiar. He could be the same man.

He went over it twice, Bonner's Spanish evidently not being good enough to follow the first rapid explanation. Vicker understood perfectly without the repetition. He was in big trouble now.

They exchanged a few comments on what it might mean, and then Bonner shrugged it off. "We'll soon find out," he said, his slow Spanish still good enough for the purpose. "My brother saw the man who shot him. He spoke of red whiskers. I don't think this man can be the same one, but Moose will know." Then he added in English, "The varmint that gut-shot Moose will have one heck of a time, and I don't care what kinda orders I got!"

Vicker kept his face expressionless. He guessed that Bonner had dropped into

English partly as a test, but he was ready for it. Having steeled himself to give no indication that he understood the Spanish, he was ready for the rest of it.

It didn't even make much difference when Bonner went into Spanish once more to tell Chico, "There is Apache trouble. No one will know if this man is found properly butchered. The Apaches will be blamed. Maybe it will be well to get rid of him that way no matter who he is." For Vicker the only idea worth considering was that he had to make his escape. Moose Bonner would identify him at once, even if another day's growth of beard didn't have Aylett adding to the Mexican's suspicions.

CHAPTER 12

There was an uneasy half minute while Bonner stared hard at him, but then the hawk-nosed man turned away to follow his own advice about getting a bit of food in preparation for the journey, a journey to the Circle D, judging by what he had said. Vicker had a little time alone with his physical aches and his worries before Aylett came over to bring him a drink of water. Evidently no one was going to bother about feeding him.

As the old man held the canteen for him, he whispered hoarsely, "I kinda had a hunch yuh was the same feller."

Vicker paused between swallows to ask, "What do you mean?"

There was a movement of one bleary eye that was probably intended to be a wink, then Aylett muttered, "I kin savvy a bit o' Spanish. They got it all figgered out that yuh been around these parts before. Mebbe yuh're the hairpin what shot Spottswell and Moose Bonner. Yuh want I should tell 'em yuh was prowlin' around the gulch a fortnight ago?"

"Would it make any difference?"

"Nope. Seems like they got yuh dead to rights — and I shore do mean dead!" He went away with the canteen then, leaving Vicker to do some more guessing. Aylett was not showing his hand, if he actually had made up his mind about anything. There was one ray of hope. He hadn't yet said anything to Bonner about his private suspicions.

Ten minutes later, Vicker was forced to climb to the saddle and be lashed fast once more. Then they moved into the east, every step the horse took adding an extra twinge of pain to legs that seemed to be all aches anyway. At midnight, they halted for a breather, but then went on again, Vicker getting no respite but no longer expecting any. A couple of times he had fallen to one side, momentarily losing consciousness. Each time the added strain on one leg brought an extra jab of agony, but he managed to pull himself erect. It annoyed him in a vague sort of way. A man ought to be able to lose some of his misery in unconsciousness, but he couldn't have that much luck. He complained in a mutter — but then he would realize that he was letting himself become irrational. He had to keep his head. There might still be a chance.

They halted again at dawn, this time taking a completely helpless prisoner from his horse. Aylett built a fire and made coffee. Bonner produced some more of the broken hardtack; that was breakfast. At first, Vicker tried to refuse both the biscuit and the coffee, but Aylett grunted something in his ear that brought him to his senses even though he didn't actually hear the words. He had to keep himself going. Food, even this kind of food, might be important to him later.

It was while they were resting that Chico yelped an alarm. A rider was coming in from the northeast. Bonner and the *vaquero* promptly took cover, guns ready, Bonner shouting for Aylett to keep a close watch on the prisoner.

The rider came on without slackening his pace and after a few minutes, Bonner snapped out a relieved, "God! He scared daylight outa me!"

By that time Vicker could recognize the hard hat. He wondered what Sparling's presence might mean. Obviously Bonner had not been expecting to meet the army scout in this part of the country.

It brought an uneasy thought. Sparling was supposed to be loyal to the army. The gang would have taken pains to keep him clear of any open involvement with the smuggling plans. Then why was he coming into a camp where the gang was holding a prisoner? It didn't make any difference that Bonner had partly made up his mind to disregard orders about that prisoner. The idea certainly had been that Vicker was to be released at some later date. The gang leader must have issued those orders. Sparling would know about them, but he would not know about Bonner's private plans. Then why was he showing himself? It all seemed pretty confusing, but Vicker was mildly pleased with himself that he had thought it out. Maybe he wasn't as far gone as he had believed himself to be.

The scout came in at a gallop, ignoring the drawn guns of the two men who stood up in the mesquite. If he saw Vicker he paid no heed. "Apaches on the loose, boys," he announced grimly. "I got to pass the word and . . ."

"Come off it, Milt," Bonner jeered. "I ain't no outsider. They told me about how they was goin' to stir up a batch o' talk about the Injuns bein' on the warpath. Sorta keep the army interested in some place besides where we don't want 'em moseyin' around. What's the truth?"

Sparling gave him a wolfish grin. "Ye're smart, Bonner. Stupid-smart! This ain't no fake like we planned to tell folks about. It's the real thing. Old Geronimo has got some of his young hellions on the loose again. Some of his crowd rode right down into Mexico, but then they doubled back to take a crack at our side of the line. We turned in a false alarm that turned out to be too true fer comfort."

"So what? The troops oughta be in the right spot to hit 'em. And it suits us perfect."

"Would I be hightailin' it over here if it was workin' out that way? Mebbe I was wrong; yuh're not stupid-smart — jest plain stupid!" He swung to the ground stiff-legged, wiping his face with the big yellow handkerchief. "What I'm tryin' to tell yuh is that the Apaches is likely to bust up the whole plan. I was out with a patrol huntin' fer this man Vicker, and we got word about the Apache alarm. I knowed we was fakin' it, so I didn't think much about it when I got a message to lead the patrol south from Tombstone. Bates was takin' a couple o' platoons over east o' Tombstone where the fake reports claimed the Apaches had been raidin'."

"Jest like we figgered," Bonner growled.

"That's what I thought. But it ain't like that no more. I was out ahead of the patrol, makin' fancy moves like I was huntin' Injuns, and all at once I wasn't huntin' no more. There they was — or anyhow there they'd been. A war party had burned out the old Meyer place, leavin' Meyer and his old woman staked out on ant hills fer the vermin to finish. They was dead when I found 'em. I broke up the patrol in a hurry, makin' messengers outa the men to find the rest of the troops. Me, I swung over toward Circle D to warn the boys there. Then I hightailed it west. The rest of the gang has got to know that this fancy fake we dreamed up turned out to be the real thing."

Bonner had stopped grinning. "Yuh figger Circle D's in danger?"

"Could be. The varmints was headin' in that direction. Not direct, o' course. I got around 'em to warn the boys at the ranch."

"How many men at the place when you was there?"

"At Circle D? Two, not countin' yer brother. I don't reckon as how he'd amount to much in a fight."

"How many Apaches?"

Sparling shook his head. "Hard to say. They fool yuh when yuh try to read their

164

sign. Never kin be sure when yuh're lookin' at the trail of jest part of a war party. I'd say six, mebbe eight. All warriors."

Bonner snapped a quick order at the Mexican. "Get ready, Chico. We got to give the boys a hand over there. Mebbe . . ." He broke off to stare perplexedly at Vicker. "Wonder what we oughta do about him? Might as well shoot him, I reckon. He already seen too much."

"Not here," Sparling interrupted as Bonner started to pull his gun. "Yuh got orders about him. Remember?"

"To blazes with orders. I'm figgerin' he's the varmint what killed Spottswell and gutshot Moose."

The scout stared in surprise. "Kinda havin' bad dreams, ain't ye, Eddie? This jigger was in Tombstone when that happened."

"I don't believe it. I want Moose to take a look at him. Then . . ."

"Easy. Don't go doin' nothin' yuh'll be sorry fer. Orders is orders."

"We'll change the orders. Like I said, he's been seein' too much. Seein' yuh ride in here and talk like this, fer instance."

Sparling started another warning about carrying out orders, and Bonner suddenly climbed into his saddle. "I'm ridin' fer Circle D. It ain't no time to talk like a

165

lawyer. If'n yuh think he's got to stay alive, yuh kin take charge of him. See how yuh like it!" He started to wheel his bronc, but then halted to add, "Jest keep him where I kin find him again when I git ready. If he's the polecat I think he is, I'll make him wish it was Apaches what picked him up!"

He was on his way out through the mesquite with that final cheering note, Chico hard on his trail. Sparling watched them for a moment, and then turned to gaze half whimsically at Vicker. "Yuh ain't among friends, friend," he observed. "Climb up on that hoss. We got to make some tracks back the other way." He added, "On second thought, I'm leaving you with Aylett and heading out west again — but we'll ride together a spell. Aylett better watch you real good after I'm gone."

CHAPTER 13

They led the horses into the thickest of the brush, Aylett tying them up. Then both men climbed to the rim of the little valley, studying their surroundings. To the west were the flats across which Milt Sparling was forcing his jaded horse. His dust trail seemed almost halfway to the first slopes of the southern Huachucas, but they knew that the distance would be deceptive. Sparling still had a long way to travel. There was no other dust showing in that direction so they could assume that the scout was not going to have any immediate problems. There were no army patrols along the distant mountains, so far as they could guess. Suddenly they spotted a lone rider to the north.

"Wonder who that polecat is?" Aylett worried. "I ain't likin' this none."

Vicker didn't bother to reply. He had a feeling that Aylett was ready to help him, but was still fearful of gang vengeance.

While Vicker still wore handcuffs and there was a strange rider hanging around, possibly a spy of the smuggling ring, Nate wasn't going to commit himself. For Vicker the uncertainty was, of course, even worse. Possibly the unknown had already swung north away from this particular stretch of thorny nothing, but there was also a chance that the man might be watching the fugitives from cover. Why he was watching would be largely a matter of why he was in this country in the first place. Perhaps the man might even be Hal Ulrich, in which case he would continue to be an unknown quantity because he could have no way of knowing who was who or what was actually happening now.

They went back to the hollow, and Aylett built a fire for brewing coffee. Both of them decided to risk using the water in order that they might have the stronger beverage. Traveling at night they would not need water so badly, and they would not be moving into strange country. They knew where water could be found, whether they headed for Fort Huachuca or the gulch country.

Aylett was still fighting an almost visible fight with himself, trying to decide whether he should risk taking Vicker to Fort Huachuca. It was clear that he still held a strong fear of the men who employed him, but it was just as clear that he had been impressed by the near panic that Milt Sparling had displayed. If the gang was in trouble, Aylett was about ready to abandon them.

The pair of them made two more trips to the rim during the afternoon, but could see nothing of other riders in any direction. The bleak, dreary landscape was shimmering with little heat devils, but it was the same landscape that it always seemed to be. Nothing was happening.

Vicker let a wry grin come to his dusty lips at the thought. Nothing was happening? How wrong could a man get? To the southwest, the smugglers must be getting across the line and into the western part of the hills with their products of murder, pillage, and general lawlessness. To the east, army patrols would be blundering around in the straggling hills, watched by both outlaws and Apaches. Or perhaps the army had already met some of the hostiles in one of those running combats that always seemed to develop when pursuing troops took an Apache trail, the sort of combat that scarcely annoyed the Apaches but became a maddening frustration for the army. In the southeast, there would be the threat to Circle D. Maybe there had already been a fight there, with or without Eddie Bonner and Chico. Nothing was happening!

When it was beginning to grow dark, they made a third observation trip to the rim of the little basin. This time Aylett snapped a hasty warning. "Watch it! There's somebody in that clump o' juniper. I seen the branches move."

"Easy," Vicker cautioned. "Don't draw fire. I can't give you any help, you know."

"Back up. Easy. Mebbe we kin draw him outa there. Ease down the slope like we was goin' back to the hosses. Then git behind a bush."

Vicker followed orders, watching the junipers until he could no longer see across the rim of the hollow. He saw nothing, but he was willing to believe that Aylett had not been fooled. The old man was pretty sober now, and there was still that unknown rider to account for. Probably the man had moved close to take a look at them.

He hoped that the reason for the other fellow's curiosity was good. Reason assured him that it was more than likely that way. One of the gang's hired guns would not have felt it necessary to keep out of sight of Sparling, but this fellow had done so. It was better than an even bet that the man in the junipers would be friendly to the prisoner.

They waited for several minutes, and then Aylett eased up the slope for another look. "Darn!" he growled. "Varmint didn't git sucked in on that one. Let's git back to the hosses."

They went back down the slope, the darkness closing in on them. Aylett had to make his decision rather quickly now; in a matter of minutes, it would be time to move. Vicker was about to prod the man a little when Nate dug into his saddlebags and came up with a battered but well-oiled forty-five.

"Better take this," he told Vicker shortly. "I don't figger as how yuh'd try to use it on me. It ain't my choosin' that got yuh into this. Mebbe yuh could help out a mite if'n we was to git in trouble."

"You figure good," Vicker told him, hiding the small triumph in his smile. "Shooting you wouldn't get me out of these irons. But what do we do now?"

Aylett shook his head. "I still dunno. It's a risk either way."

"Then let's move west while it's still light enough for that fellow in the bushes to see us start. We'll let him think we're on our way to the Empty Poke. As soon as it's dark, we can cut north and pick up the regular wagon trail into Fort Huachuca. It would let us get to the fort before daybreak. With

171

a little luck, we can get under cover without any of the gang knowing. I'll risk the charges they'll put against me as long as I've got you to back up my story."

"Supposin' some itchy sentry . . . ?"

"We're safer in the dark than we'd be in daylight. No sentry is going to recognize me until after I've let them know that I'm coming in."

Aylett seemed relieved at having the decision taken away from him. "I reckon yuh got it figgered good," he said with a gusty sigh. "Yuh want I should give yuh hand up on the bronc?"

Vicker's grin was broader now. He had played it right. Aylett was not only persuaded, he was trying to make himself liked. Vicker let the old man boost him into the saddle and then hand him the gun that he would have to hold awkwardly behind him. He didn't think that he would be much good in any kind of fight, but it was still a good feeling to have that gun in his grasp.

It was when Aylett was climbing wearily into his saddle that a man came out of the brush behind them, a sixgun raised warily. "No wrong moves!" he snapped before either of them knew that he was there. "Git yer paws up and keep 'em there!"

Vicker turned his head, staring hard in

the gloom. "Ben! What are you . . . ? Was it you that rode along north of us today?"

"Sure. What about this old coot?" He waved his gun cautiously in the direction of Aylett. "Trust him?"

"I think so — now."

Naismith let his gun sag. "I had a time figgerin' this thing out. He's got yuh handcuffed, but it didn't look like he was actin' real nasty nor nothin'. I couldn't make up my mind until he handed yuh the gun. Then I figgered it might be a good idea to move in. What's goin' on anyhow?"

"This is a friend of mine, Nate," Vicker said quietly. "I think we'll get through all right now. Ben, this is Nate Aylett. He's the fellow who pretended to be the miner at the Empty Poke. Now he's fed up with getting kicked around by the gang, and he's going to help me get back to the fort." It didn't seem like a bad idea to throw in a reminder to Aylett about the bad treatment he had received from Eddie Bonner.

Aylett sat silently on his horse and stared. It seemed clear that he didn't intend to make up his mind about anything any longer. It was beyond him; all he could do was to hope that sooner or later he would have some time alone with a bottle.

Vicker swung a foot over the saddle horn

and slid to the ground. "Got light enough for a bit of lock-picking, Ben? I've been wearing these things so long that I'm afraid they'll grow fast to me."

"I'll give it a try," Naismith said, fumbling in a pocket to bring out a pocket knife that sprouted an amazing assortment of odd gadgets. "Who put the irons on yuh?"

"I'll tell you about it while you work. What's more important than who put them on is what we can do when you get them off. First, tell me how come you're rambling around here?"

Naismith chuckled and went to work. "Hurry-up message from Magruder. He said you was missin' and suspected of havin' bushwhacked one of the officers from the fort. He told me to find yuh before the army did. He must think I'm a bloodhound what was crossed with a fortune teller!"

"Nice combination," Vicker observed with a chuckle. "Maybe he was right. You did it."

"Dumb luck. I had a hunch that mebbe yuh'd moved down into Mexico again, so I figgered that the best way to get onto yuhr tail was to find this gulch and start from there — like woulda happened in yore case. I was cuttin' across country to look fer the gulch when I spotted three riders what didn't look normal somehow. I was a little

174

ahead, so I holed up and took a good look while they rode past. I still wasn't real close, but I could see that one of 'em was our missin' bright boy. And he was all tied up. First off I took the other two jaspers to be lawmen, and I figured they'd picked yuh up fer that killin' Magruder told me about. I wasn't sure so I jest eased and looked."

He grunted in triumph as one of the cuffs came loose. "Come in right handy to be a slippery character," he crowed. "A man never knows when his talents is goin' to pay off."

Vicker swung his hands around to the front, easing the shoulder muscles. "You're wonderful," he agreed. "Not to mention gabby. Now work from this side."

"Thanks. Nice to git appreciation like that. Anyhow, when I seen one o' yer guards ridin' off alone, I kinda got some doubts about who it was that had yuh tied up. Fer a spell, like I already told yuh, it didn't make sense, but then I took a chance after the old timer handed yuh the gun."

"You played it smart," Vicker told him briefly. "Now let me fill you in on some of the things you don't know about." He ran over his part of the account swiftly, getting it completed just as Naismith removed the second cuff from his chafed wrist.

175

"Now we have to decide on a couple of points. Nate's ready to throw in with us and lend a hand. He never was mixed up in any of the real crime, so I don't think he'll need to worry about being arrested. I can do a little lying for him when the time comes." That was tossed in just to keep Aylett from having any doubts as to what he'd better do. "Anyway, we've got two possible courses. We can ride north during the night and try to get into Fort Huachuca without being spotted by any of the gang's scouts — or getting shot by a sentry. Likely it's the safest plan. At that point, I can pass on to the Customs men the things I know. They could still have a chance of catching the smugglers over there at the Empty Poke. If the gang should get wind that I've escaped, they might hide out so that the government men would lose their chance of making a big capture, but that wouldn't be my fault. I've got no real responsibility for any of this."

"Get on with the second scheme," Naismith laughed. "When you build up the first one so big, I know darned well yuh ain't figurin' to use it. What kind of a cockeyed mess are yuh plannin' to stir up now?"

"Don't be so smart! Our other choice is to get into the hills near the gulch and watch what happens there. I'm pretty sure that I've guessed right about the smugglers and their general plans. We could do ourselves some good in the matter of reward money."

"And what else? Seems to me I remember that you were itchin' to help out a feller named Ulrich. Still got that stuck in yer craw?"

"In a way. I can't find a trace of him. Maybe he's the one that was murdered. Or maybe he's in that hot spot at the Circle D. I want to be in a position to give him a hand if there's a possible chance. I don't figure I could do it if I had to stick around Fort Huachuca and get all tangled up in murder investigations and the rest of the tangle."

"So we start fer the gulch. I'll split the deal with yuh. While yuh're lookin' out fer Ulrich, I'll handle any part o' the game that might show a profit. Now tell me one more thing. How come yuh're so sure the gang is goin' to use that gulch? I follow yer guessin' about how they won't put no stock in Marley, and I'll go along with the idea that they'll use Marley to draw off the Federal boys, but how do yuh know they won't run the stuff across somewhere else? There's a lot o' this border that ain't guarded."

"I could be wrong — but think about it a little. Nate, how long before I showed up at the Empty Poke was it that your smuggling pals brought in that load of ore?"

"A day."

"Tell me just how they did it. I know the general idea, of course, but a few details might be helpful. Who brought it? What did they tell you when they arrived? How long did they stay? That sort of thing."

They were talking in complete darkness now, and Aylett's silence made Vicker wonder. Was the old man trying to figure out a lie, or was he still too scared to talk. "Out with it, Nate," he urged. "You're with us now."

"Sure. It ain't that. I was kinda drunk about then, and somehow it ain't too easy to remember things. I know I was loafin' around like always when a wagon come in from the west. Mex drivin' it. Lanky man with a shotgun ridin' behind him. I started to tell 'em the yarn I was supposed to tell anybody what wandered in . . ."

"The same yarn you told me when I visited you three weeks ago?"

Aylett's chuckle came easily. "Nope. I was drunker'n usual that time. Yuh sure had me fooled when yuh showed up all fixed up purty. I didn't suspect that yuh was the same feller I'd seen before. Then the whiskers got to growin'. By the time Chico

178

started talkin' suspicious like, I knowed, but by that time I wasn't so sure I wanted to help Chico."

"Good. But get on with the story. What else do you remember?"

"Lemme think. The Mex unloaded his cartful of ore and gravel. Then the lanky man blasted a load o' gold filin's into the pile. Made a joke about shootin' eagles. Told me they'd filed up a bunch o' brand new ten-dollar gold pieces that they'd picked up in a stagecoach robbery about a year ago. They didn't dare try to spend the money because there was a new mint mark or somethin' that they knowed gov'ment men would be watchin' fer. They'd been grindin' 'em up a few at a time and lettin' Marley haul 'em in as raw gold. Gold's jest as good one way as another, so they wasn't losin' nothin', and it was a heap safer way to git rid of it."

"The devious mind at work again?" Vicker suggested to himself aloud.

"What's devious?" Naismith asked.

"Don't worry about it. I was talking to myself. While I was at it, I should have mentioned that the government should work up an interest in the party that bought Marley's gold. If the stuff he was hauling back from Sonora was what Nate says it was, there should have been enough alloy in it to make an honest buyer wary. But go on, Nate. What happened next?"

The old man grunted before replying. "Kinda feels like that storm we seen a spell ago might be workin' toward us. Coolin' off mighty fast."

"Good. I wouldn't mind getting soaked. What happened after the Mexican blasted the gold bits into the gravel pile?"

"He looked around a bit and seen that crack between the bits o' solid rock. He made me dig out what would look like the openin' of a shaft, and he fired another couple o' loads of gold filin's into it. Then he told me about how I was to fix up the story about findin' a new vein that had good stuff in it. In the meantime, the Mex — and, by the way, you got it wrong about the shootin'. It wasn't the Mex what done any o' what I'm tellin' yuh about. It was the skinny jasper. Anyhow, the Mex took the wagon back into the woods and hid it. Then the pair of them went back into the gulch the way they'd come, the Mex ridin' one o' the hosses what had been pullin' the wagon. It was after they left that I seen how they'd put them lumps o' good ore into the gravel."

"And all of this happened just one day

before I came along with Marley and Bonner?"

"Right. Less'n a full day when yuh figger it out close."

"I'm figuring close," Vicker told him grimly. "I'm figuring that at the time this gold was being planted at the Empty Poke, they were still sticking to the story at Fort Huachuca that the whole thing out here was a fake. About that time, Milt Sparling started passing along some messages and they changed yarns. Marley began to get ready for his trip, and I was more or less invited along. The time works out kinda funny."

Naismith put in a suggestion. "Somebody passed the word when the two men with the wagon started fer the gulch. By the time they were doin' their saltin' the message got through and the gang at Fort Huachuca knowed that they had to change yarns."

"I think you're right. This was planned some time ago. Sparling simply brought word that the planning was working out."

"What difference does it make?"

"Maybe a lot. I've been thinking all the time that they did it as an elaborate plan to get me all tangled up, maybe as a good excuse for holding me prisoner until the big move could be made. Then they'd turn me loose, not wanting to get a big stink made over messing around with a man who had the influence of a big company behind him. I would be turned loose to tell a yarn about a mine-salting job, but I would not suspect the real truth. Even when I complicated matters by almost escaping, they still seemed to be working along that same line. Now I know that they must have had it planned before I started making loud noises about taking a look at the Empty Poke. Those complications were not set up on my account; they just used them for an extra purpose when I began to bother them."

"I hope yuh know what yuh're talkin' about," Ben grumbled. "It don't make much sense the way I hear it comin' out."

Vicker ignored him to fire a question at Aylett. "You're sure that they left that ore wagon in the gulch, Nate?"

"Yep. Mebbe a dozen rods from the diggin's but back where the woods was thick."

"Then I know what we've got to do. Nate, you don't need to start worryin' about that alibi you're going to give me. I think we'll forget the fort just now and have a try at handling a few things on our own account. It's just possible that we might make expenses out of it."

"It's gittin' real cool now," Naismith said

in an odd voice. "So it can't be that the heat's affectin' his head. Must be somethin' else."

Vicker laughed. "Let's ride, gents. Stay close and I'll tell you how I figure things. You might need to know before it's over."

CHAPTER 14

It took some careful scrambling to reach the narrow ledge Aylett had mentioned, but then they were in good shape until they began the actual descent. After that, they had to move with every possible bit of caution so as to avoid noise. Once Naismith almost fell headlong, but he banged into Vicker, and at that moment Vicker happened to be well braced. The moment passed, and presently they could see the open area where Vicker had spent those hideously uncomfortable hours as a prisoner. The first look was something of a shock. There were five horses in sight. The odds were going to be long.

Then it became apparent that the first look hadn't told the story. Two of the animals were heavy beasts wearing collars, undoubtedly the draft horses that were to haul the ore wagon. The other three were saddled, all of them carrying the usual slicker rolls, saddlebags, and extra canteens.

"I wonder how they plan to guard Nate," Vicker whispered in Ben's ear. "They'd want him to drive the wagon, but they wouldn't be trusting him with loot that ought to run into maybe six figures. Somebody has to be set up to watch him."

"Who'd they have that could go along without it lookin' suspicious?"

"Bonner. But he's not here. I'd guess that it's to be a little more tricky than that. Maybe men in relays. Always at a distance, but close enough to move in if anything goes wrong."

He dropped down another twenty feet, knowing that now he had to be extra careful. The camp was not far away now. He might easily be spotted even if he didn't make a sound. It took some doing, but he finally managed to find a spot where a break in the timber let him see the opposite end of the clearing. There were three men lounging there, one the Mexican who had talked to Milt Sparling. Neither of the others could be identified, their faces turned away as they lay sprawled on the ground. Vicker had a notion that one of them was the fellow they called Charley. At least he was of the same squatty build.

"I think we can do it," Vicker breathed as

185

Naismith slid in beside him.

"Do what?"

"Take 'em. My guess is that the Mex is the relay man. He'll ride off to pass the word to his part of the gang when the move begins. The other pair act as guards, maybe all the way to the fort. One of 'em hails from there, I think."

"How do we do it?"

"Let's wait and see how Aylett shapes up. If we can take over from these fellows, we can go through with their regular plan, only it'll be the two of us who try to act like guards. At a distance, other gang members will think nothing's wrong. If we don't fool 'em . . ." He let the thought drift away. Ben didn't need any second-hand guesses on that point.

"Neat," Naismith whispered. "We steal the ore wagon. Got any idea how yuh'll work things out when yuh git to the fort?"

"No. Right now all I'm thinking about is how we'll get the wagon out of this gulch." Neither of them had bothered to comment that the wagon was ready. It stood near the spot where the gravel pile had once been, already loaded and waiting.

"Let's take 'em while they're off guard," Ben suggested. "We kin do it."

"No. Wait for Aylett. He'll be along ac-

186

cording to our plan. I want to hear what they tell him. It might save us a mistake or two."

The minutes dragged past. Vicker knew that there was a very real danger from Sparling. The man might have picked up their trail and realized that the presence of an extra man in their party was a threat to the outlaw plans. In that case, he would come back to the gulch in a hurry. Waiting was adding to the risk of what was ahead, but it still seemed like the thing to do. They simply had to gamble that Sparling would not swing to the south and find the tracks.

Then Aylett appeared, riding along as though he didn't have a care in the world. The Mexican rapped an order at the loungers, and they came up quickly. One was Charley, and the other looked vaguely familiar. Vicker had a notion that he had seen the man at Fort Huachuca, but he couldn't be sure. It didn't make too much difference.

After that, events moved at a fast pace. The Mexican snapped his orders, and the man Vicker could not name set about the business of harnessing the team that was to haul the ore wagon. Charley took over the business of letting Nate know what was expected of him, his instructions more than a little confused by the way the Mexican kept shouting questions about the delay. The outlaws seemed to assume that Sparling had taken charge of Aylett's prisoner, for they didn't even ask about him. All they wanted was to get that load of ore on the trail.

Aylett played his part well enough, although Vicker suspected that he wasn't having to try very hard. What was actually happening was confusing enough for him; he didn't have to do much acting to seem pretty well mixed up.

And that was the way the three men seemed to accept it. They did not try to explain or to ask; they simply gave him his orders. Everything was fitting in with Vicker's guesses, so far as he could tell. There was no hint as to whether or not he had been right about concealed guards following the wagon.

He waited until Aylett was actually on the wagon, hoping for a little more in the way of information. The Mexican turned away then, firing a brief "You know what to do. Be careful," at the other two.

"Get ready," Vicker murmured. "Take the Mex, but don't move until I give the word. I want to catch that other pair just as they start for their horses. We'll take 'em alive if we can."

It was a good plan, but it didn't work out. Just as he grunted the order to Naismith and jumped out into the open, the Mexican turned back as though remembering something he hadn't told the others. It put him in position to see Vicker, and he yelled a quick alarm. He was digging for his gun when Vicker went into a crouch that almost became a headlong fall, sore muscles not quite ready to do his bidding. Two gunshots boomed almost together, and then a third one made Vicker's ears ache. Ben had taken a hand quickly.

By that time, the other two men had swung into action. Vicker did not dare look to see what had happened to the Mexican. Ben would have to handle that part of the fight. He had to cut down on the pair who were so much nearer to him. Their slugs were already whining around his ears.

Without thinking about it, he knew that Charley was the better gunhand, so he made him his first target. It took two shots to do it, but then he had only the one enemy. A split second later he had none. It was over so fast that he couldn't quite believe it.

"Watch the Mex," Ben warned dryly. "He ain't dead."

Vicker reloaded without changing his

position. It came as a surprise to discover that he had only one live shell left in his gun. He wasn't quite sure how he could have fired so many times without even knowing it. But then he wasn't too clear about most of the rest of it. Nate Aylett still sat on the wagon seat as though he hadn't even had time to look around.

"Darn fast fight," Naismith said in that same dry tone. "Cover me while I take a look at the Mex."

Some of the numbness left Vicker then, and he went about the cleanup with some of his old efficiency. Taking a position that would let him see the Mexican without completely losing sight of the other pair, he held his gun ready while Ben ran across to take the *vaquero*'s gun. Without looking around, he shouted an order at Aylett. "Get going, Nate. We'll be with you in a jiffy. If anybody stops you, tell 'em you didn't see anything wrong back here."

"Hold it," Ben called across. "This polecat's alive. Hurt bad, but I reckon he'll make it if'n we git him to a sawbones before too long. Mebbe he'll do some talkin'."

"Hold it, Nate," Vicker shouted. "You're going to have a passenger."

They worked fast then, first making sure that the other two outlaws were dead. Naismith showed considerable skill in plugging up a hole in the Mexican's right shoulder. It was a bad wound, low enough so that it might have touched a lung. The man was unconscious and probably would stay that way for some time to come. They bandaged him as carefully as possible, then rolled a tarp around him and lifted him to the top of the ore, pushing enough of the fake stuff off the wagon so that there would be a hollow. Then they sent Aylett down the gulch trail, remaining behind only long enough to secure what food and water they could find in the camp, refilling canteens at the brook.

Examination of the dead men's pockets as well as those of the Mexican told them nothing, so they could only go along with the plan they had discussed. The other guesses had turned out to be good ones, so they would act on the assumption that the rest of it was equally accurate. Those final instructions issued by the Mexican seemed to fit.

"Take extra horses," Vicker said when they were ready. "No telling how tough this will get. Ours are in bad shape, so we'll be ready to swap off if we need to."

They overtook Aylett while the ore wagon was still in the gulch. Vicker repeated his instructions. "Just drive this load to Fort

Huachuca. The gang is going to be watching, but they'll expect to see two riders flanking you. With any luck, nobody will notice that we're not the riders they're expecting. If there's trouble we'll be on hand in a hurry."

They let him draw ahead once more, using the brief wait to make a change of horses. The outlaw's mounts seemed to be in much better condition than the ones they had been riding, so they changed over, taking their own along with them for emergencies. There was no point in skipping any possible precautions when there were so many other risks that they could do nothing about.

They kept to the mountain slope above the wagon, riding in the edge of the brush and not making any particular attempt at concealment. If there were smuggler sentinels watching the wagon, they would expect to see guards. The important matter was to make sure that no one came for a close look. The big danger was that Sparling would have sounded some kind of alarm.

It was hot, the sun barely past its zenith, as they hit the open country beyond the first stretch of hilly trail. Vicker wondered whether the wounded man would survive his ordeal, but he didn't let it worry him too much. There was no reason for him to feel any pity for the outlaw. Undoubtedly, the man had committed his full share of murders among his own people. That was the way this gang had operated.

He could see that Nate was hunched on the wagon seat, looking like a lump of gray clay in the distance. The old man was letting the horses set their own pace as though he had long since given up all hope of taking any active hand in what was happening. Vicker was satisfied. So long as Nate followed his instructions — and remained alive long enough to furnish that alibi — he didn't care very much about anything.

Ben seemed to have been thinking along the same line. He laughed shortly and remarked, "I wonder if that old coot has figgered it out that he's settin' darn near on top of enough loot to buy up every hired gun in the southwest?"

"Don't say it like that," Vicker begged. "You'll have me thinking that I guessed wrong about how many men the gang might put on this detail."

They worked their way north for a little over two hours, no sign of trouble showing anywhere. By that time, the wagon trail had swung out into flat country at the base of the range. Any sentries posted by the smugglers would be on the mountain, since there was no place of concealment for them east of the trail. Vicker accordingly moved across to the trail itself, not wanting to get too close to a concealed watcher on the slopes. Ben had been riding a little to the right of him, so the move forced both men to converge on the wagon. Aylett pulled up to rest his team for a few minutes, and they talked things over, first taking a look at the still-unconscious Mexican. The man was breathing, but he had continued to bleed quite a bit.

"We'll stick with you on this next stretch, Nate," Vicker said when they were ready to move once more. "No decent cover, so we'll gamble that it's the right thing to do."

Another sweltering half hour passed, and then they could see two lots of dust in the distance, one almost due east and the other a little to the north of it. They studied it for some minutes as they rode out ahead of the wagon and presently Naismith chuckled. "We're like a couple o' kids tiptoein' past a graveyard in the dark. A man ain't supposed to sweat much in this dry country, but I'm wet all over."

"It'll keep you cool," Vicker told him.

"I sorta want to shiver a bit."

"What do you make of that dust on the

right? It seemed to be closing in on us, but now it seems to be swinging away."

"Likely one o' them scouts. He rode in to take a long look at us, but now he's headin' on to join the other party. Mebbe he thinks the game's goin' like they planned it."

"I'd like to know what Sparling did. He's the lad who can throw the hooks into our act."

"How does this trail run? Seems like we'll be climbin' up the shoulder of the mountain before long."

"That's right. We wind around the mountain and come down into Fort Huachuca."

"Then we might git away with the fake. If anybody comes along while we're out here in the open they're bound to get smart about what's happened. If we make the mountain all right, we kin stay out in the brush more. Nate kin pass inspection good enough."

"I hope you're right — but I still wonder about Sparling. If he passed the word that Nate disappeared, they'll have the wind up."

The ore wagon seemed to lag interminably. The horses had been hauling for a long time under that broiling sun, and nothing more than a walk could be expected of them. With the trail beginning to wind uphill, the pace would be even slower. And every extra minute increased the risk that word would be passed to the distant watchers that something had gone wrong with the plans.

Vicker began to calculate the amount of daylight remaining. If they did not make the fort by dusk, they were really in trouble! The trail went through mesquite thickets on the edge of the slope, and it would be a simple matter for the gang to close in without being seen. Maybe some of their gunmen were already posted in ambush ahead. It seemed like a likely possibility.

At a guess, there was still six miles to go, most of it across the brushy shoulder of the mountain. Six miles with tired horses.

"Dust gittin' closer," Ben growled, pointing into the northeast. They could see it more plainly in the slanting rays of the late afternoon sun, and there seemed to be little doubt that the two dust spirals had merged into one. At least two of the watchers had joined up and were moving across to climb the mountain ahead of the wagon.

"I'll bet the first dust was Sparling's," Vicker said glumly. "He's been keeping an eye on us, but didn't know what to think about it. Then he picked up another outpost, and they're going to take a close look."

They moved into the shadow of the mountain then. It was cooler, but physical comfort no longer meant much. The trail curved around a bulge of the hill, and they could see that there were two men making the dust ahead. Then they had a clearer look along the slope to the north. There was more dust there.

"Could be more trouble — or it could be a patrol out of the fort."

"More graveyard antics," Ben jeered. "Yuh ain't tiptoein' now; yuh're whistlin' in the dark. Them clouds o' dust are fixin' to join up."

Vicker didn't argue the point. It seemed all too likely that the sentinels who had started to come in from the east would know that other gang members would come down from the fort to meet the wagon. It was the kind of precaution that would naturally be taken.

Aylett was still letting his team plod along without paying much attention to them. Now Vicker dropped back to ride beside the wagon. "We're in for it, Nate," he said simply. "Be ready for a bluff if we can work out a way to handle it. Otherwise . . . just keep your gun handy."

He repeated the idea when he moved up beside Naismith once more. "I don't think they know yet that their plunder has been hijacked. Maybe they won't come in too close because they won't want to have anybody seeing them ride in with the wagon. If they try to go on with the scheme of having this look like a surprise development that involves nobody but Aylett, we've got a chance to get through."

"And if they don't play it that way?"

"No choice. We'll try to catch 'em by surprise and shoot it out."

"I just wish I could git one look at whatever's under that gravel. I might git a mite more enthused about fightin' fer it."

"Forget it. If we can pull this thing off, we'll have claims on a fistful of reward offers. Fight for that."

"I'm feelin' more like a fight already."

"Don't get carried away. We've got to keep them guessing until the last minute. You know why. They'll have us cold if they get a chance to pick us off while we try to get the wagon through."

They lost sight of the enemy for several minutes, the shadows lengthening rapidly. Vicker was just beginning to fear that the outlaws had taken to the mesquite when he saw them ahead. There were three of them, and they were riding slowly along the wagon trace as though in no particular hurry to meet the oncoming wagon.

"Take your hat off, Nate," Vicker called back to the old man. "Give 'em plenty of chance to identify you."

"I get it," Ben muttered, pulling his own hat brim low. "We keep shady and let 'em study Nate. Then we open up when they git close. Right?"

"Right. We gamble on a close-range fight. It's the only way we stand a chance. If they have time to bring up more men — or to use rifles — we're done!"

The distance dwindled rapidly in spite of the slow pace. "No mercy," Vicker reminded his companion. "we get 'em cold here or they'll have us by the neck."

"Kinda frightenin'," Ben said. "Like waitin' fer a killer to draw when yuh know he's too fast fer yuh."

"Shut up! You scare a man."

Ben laughed aloud. "Hell! Yuh don't scare that easy. I know yuh."

It didn't make too much sense, but it eased the tension a little. When Vicker spoke again, his voice was cold and calculating. "The one on our right is Milt Sparling. I'll take him. Sam Bunch is in the middle. He's yours. Keep your head down until I give the word. Then don't miss! That third man could be fast with a gun, so we don't have time for any second shots at the others."

CHAPTER 15

The next move seemed somewhat ridiculous. Sparling raised his right hand as though preparing to parley with hostile savages. The theatrical gesture told Vicker something. The men ahead were nervous. They knew that they were meeting guards who had been ordered to shoot at any sign of trouble. With darkness closing down, they wanted to make sure that no mistakes would be made. There was grim humor in returning the signal and guaranteeing the mistake that they clearly didn't suspect.

"Keep 'em off guard a little longer," Vicker murmured to his companion. "Get Sparling if I miss. He's got a rifle in the scabbard."

The trio halted then, apparently satisfied. Judging by the way they eased their ponies to the side of the trail, they intended to let the wagon pass so that they might fall in behind it. They looked relaxed, talking among themselves as though certain that the big risk was past.

The distance closed as the light dwindled. Vicker wondered how close he dared to get. He could recognize both Bunch and Sparling. How long would it be before Bunch would realize that neither of the riders ahead of the wagon was as burly as Charley?

"Watch 'em!" Vicker snapped in an undertone. "Sam's saying something to Milt now. Maybe he's getting suspicious."

Seconds later the scout yelled, "Who's that with yuh, Nate? Where's Charley and Joe?"

He was digging for his gun as he shouted the questions. It was Aylett who made the real surprise move. The old man snatched up the sixgun that had been in his lap and opened up with both speed and skill. Vicker was ready, but his gun had not yet cleared leather when Aylett started shooting.

For an instant, Vicker ducked, thinking that Aylett might have changed sides again and was trying to do some back-shooting. Then he saw that the old man's slugs had knocked Bunch out of the saddle. He recovered himself and opened up at Sparling, knowing that the scout was returning the favor. The roar of gunfire erupted, climbed to a frenzied peak, and died away as quickly as it had started. Like the fight in the gulch,

202

it was over so fast that it was hard to believe that it had happened. For Vicker, the convincing part was the blood that was running down his left arm. It didn't hurt much, but the blood warned him that he had been hit.

He controlled the bucking horse with an effort, finding that he was so far off the trail that he was down the hill a little. It made it difficult to see what had happened, but there was no more firing. For the moment, he was content with that.

"Move in and take a look. Careful now," he told Naismith. "I got a nick in my upper arm that needs a bit of attention. I can handle it. Just make sure that we're not going to get any more trouble from those three."

He used a few seconds in rolling up his left sleeve, finding that he could use the left arm reasonably well. The slug had ripped across the fleshy part of the outer arm, but evidently had not injured muscles or hit the bone. He used the rolled sleeve as a makeshift compress and then ignored the trickle of blood that continued to run down his arm. He was a lot more worried about Nate Aylett. The old man had fallen sideways on the wagon seat, blood streaming from a head wound.

Vicker slid from the saddle and made a

quick examination. Like his own injury, this one was superficial. Nate's scalp had been creased, and the blood looked pretty messy in his unkempt white hair, but he was not badly injured. It was a bit of trouble to get a bandanna tied on as a bandage, particularly with blood from the arm wound making the whole operation slippery, but the job was done when Naismith rode back to announce that only one of the enemy still breathed. Both Bunch and Sparling were dead. Aylett's first volley had practically riddled the freight boss.

"The other jasper's got a busted leg and a bad furrow along his ribs. He's afraid he's goin' to die, so I told him we'd take care of him if'n he wanted to tell all he knows."

Vicker grinned in the thickening twilight. "Go scare him some more. I'll get Nate comfortable and start driving the wagon. We'll load all the wounded on the gravel. The team can take the extra weight if we don't hurry 'em too much."

He handled his chore clumsily, the wounded arm beginning to throb now, and drove the team on to where Ben crouched beside the groaning outlaw. "We'll take him in to the doc if he tells us a few things," he said grimly to Naismith. "Otherwise we leave him here."

The gruff tone was convincing enough, for the fellow began to promise all kinds of things. Vicker cut him off. "Save it for the law! All I want to know is who killed Lieutenant Sebrell and what happened to a man named Ulrich who was working this country about a month ago?"

"I kin tell yuh about the Sebrell part," the gunman whined. "But I never heard o' no Ulrich."

"Let's hear it!"

"Bunch figgered as how Sebrell might git ornery, so they decided to kill him off. It was Sparlin' what done it. I heard him tell Sam about it."

"Who planned to blame it on me?"

"Sam, I reckon. Anyhow he was the one what told Eddie Bonner what to say when he was here at the fort. I never did figger out why he done it."

"And you never heard of Hal Ulrich?"

"Nope. Honest I didn't. Yuh're goin' to git me in to the doc, ain't yuh?"

"Maybe. What about some other killings that this sweet little outfit of yours engineered? Maybe a couple of government agents, for instance?"

"I dunno fer sure. I drove a wagon for Sam. The rest of it wasn't none o' my business."

"But you've heard that a couple of strangers were murdered because the gang took them to be spies!"

"I heard." The man seemed resigned. "I never heard no names."

"When was all this?"

"I ain't so sure. Could be the killin's were a spell before I ever heard any talk about 'em."

"But about how long ago?"

"Fust one was mebbe two months back. Then it happened again about three or four weeks ago. Mebbe that last one coulda been the gent you put a name to. I didn't hear no name either time."

Vicker knew a sense of frustration. He wasn't sure what he had actually accomplished, but it seemed pretty certain that his original objective had been lost. Ulrich had fallen victim to the gang, just as he had feared.

"Load him on, Ben," he said shortly. "Leave the others where they are. Plenty of time to pick up dead men when this is over."

Twenty minutes later, they were challenged by a picket out of Fort Huachuca. The challenge was only the minor part. Even as the trooper bawled his order to halt, he also fired his carbine. Evidently the skeleton

206

garrison now holding the post was in a bad state of nerves.

For a few minutes there was a bit of confusion, but then a sergeant and three other men arrived in answer to the gunshot. Vicker evaded the demand for identification, stressing that there were wounded men who demanded quick medical attention. The soldiers moved in warily as though expecting some kind of treachery, and Vicker kept talking, intent on getting a couple of ideas across.

Finally the sergeant seemed willing to take matters at face value. He sent a trooper hurrying ahead to alert the guard officer and the surgeon. Then he asked curiously, "What's been goin' on out here?"

"Plenty," Vicker told him. "Now do me a favor. Get us into the post as quietly as possible. Don't ask questions, but take my word for it that you'll be doing the right thing. I want this wagon put under strong guard just as soon as we stop using it for an ambulance."

"Seems like you git real free at givin' orders, mister."

"Sorry. Humor me. It'll pay."

The non-com snorted angrily, but didn't argue further. They eased in past the outer buildings of the military post without attracting much attention, evidently because there were few men left on duty there. Then two men with lanterns approached, escorting an officer. It was Captain Bates.

Vicker didn't wait to be recognized. "Jack Vicker here, Captain. Have any civil authorities moved in on you yet? I want to get in touch with federal officers in a hurry."

Bates grunted. "No more than they want to find you, mister."

"So I hear. What about it? Anybody around?"

"Six of them rode in just before dusk. Revenue man and some deputy marshals. But the army's got first claim on you. We don't . . ."

"This is important, Captain. I didn't kill Sebrell, and I can prove it. Take my word for it so we don't waste time now. I'm not going to run away."

"Spell it out," Bates snapped, unconvinced but withholding judgment.

Vicker filled in most of it as they followed the wagon to the surgeon's crude hospital. Lights had come on in several places, and the flurry of activity indicated that the wounded were going to get quick attention. "I'll wait," Vicker broke in on his own account. "But I'd better get down a while. I'm not feeling up to the mark. Loss of blood, maybe."

Bates snapped a couple of orders, and the uncertainty was over. Vicker was taken along to the adjutant's office where Bates himself put a temporary bandage on the wounded arm. By that time, two men who looked like cattlemen came in.

Again Vicker had to start from the beginning. He was getting pretty tired of that part of his story. "Save it," he said after a few minutes. "I don't think I'll get through it all right now. Just keep things quiet if you can and don't let anybody get near that ore wagon. And don't let any of that gang around the freight stables get away from you."

He didn't get around to telling them why. Continued strain, the days of fatigue, and the wound simply added up to more of a total than he could handle. His last conscious thought was that he didn't have to tell them all of it. Ben could fill in enough.

When he opened his eyes, he thought that he had been unconscious for only a matter of seconds. Bates was still standing over him, and the two civilian officers were in the same spot near the door. Then Bates came forward with a tumbler in his hand, nodding to the orderly who stood at one side. "Lift his head again, Brannigan. We can get the rest of it down him now."

Vicker took a good swallow of the stuff that was in the glass and sputtered, "Holy Smoke! The army must get its whiskey from the same place Nate Aylett does!"

Two other men came into his field of vision at that moment, and he was amazed to see that one of them was Paul Magruder. Pacific's top field man was grinning happily. "He's ready to talk. I can tell by the bellyaching."

"What are you doin' here?" Vicker demanded. "I don't think you can mind your own business any more than I can."

"I don't get shot doing it," Magruder retorted. "This is Mr. O'Fallon. You know about him. We've got most of the story from Naismith. Aylett bears him out on everything. We know what the gang was doing and we know that Sparling murdered Lieutenant Sebrell. Now let's have the rest of it, the part that Ben didn't know."

"You searched under the ore in the wagon?" Vicker asked.

"You bet! It's the biggest haul the Treasury boys have made in many a moon. Jewelry plundered from haciendas and churches all over Sonora! Enough opium to supply the San Francisco market for months. Several thousand dollars in specie, almost certainly

210

the remains of that mail-coach robbery. It's big!"

O'Fallon moved in then. "We're still mixed up as to who was the real boss in this gang, Vicker Naismith thinks it was Bunch or Sparling. They're both dead, he tells us."

"They're dead, all right, but neither of them bossed the show. Call them the ram-rods, but not the boss. And the same goes for McLinden. You know about him, of course."

"We'll have him in custody in a matter of hours."

"Maybe he'll talk. Or you could get a confession out of some of the gang at Circle D."

"You're wrong on that point. The Apaches killed them all. Our patrol found the re-mains. Both Bonners and three other men. At least we think the Bonners were in-cluded. It was pretty hard to tell after the Apaches finished with them."

Vicker thought for a moment. His head was clearing rapidly and he remembered that now was the time for him to put in his claim for possible reward money. "Let me tell you how I worked it out," he said slowly. "It ought to be right because I used the same kind of figuring to let me grab that load of plunder — for which an honest citizen like me ought to receive much remuneration."

"Stop blowing off steam!" Magruder snapped. "You'll get what's coming to you."

"As I started to say, I tried to figure out how it happened that a whole series of orders for gang operations seemed to come out of Fort Huachuca. I didn't think Bunch was the man issuing them because in one case he didn't even know about what was happening. When I first came over here, he told me the old yarn about gold smuggling from Sonora. But at that very time the mine-salting operation had been started. The fake ore was being collected. He didn't know about the change of plan until after he told me the old yarn. I figured that the scheme had been ordered from Tombstone."

"Why Tombstone? Because of McLinden?"

"Not entirely. Because it was in Tombstone that the gang first got word about my first trip down into the border country. All at once they knew that Marley had been trailed by a spy who got away from them. They also knew that they had lost Spottswell and one of the Bonners. Almost at the same time, they discovered that they were going to have me looking around the Empty Poke. That was when they had to improvise something that would allow them to bring in their plunder without using Marley and without having to worry about what a mine scout might see."

"But McLinden couldn't have made some of these last decisions," Magruder protested. "He was too far away."

"Who said it was McLinden? I crossed him off my suspect list for the very reason you mention, along with some others. At first, I wasn't so sure. Before I started away from here with Ike Marley, there was a lot of tearing around! Charley rode south on some kind of an errand. A bit later, Bonner had a chore. Then Sparling turned up and things got more excited than ever. For a while I thought Sparling had brought orders or was giving some. Then things stalled. It seemed like he'd brought information and somebody was doing some hard thinking before deciding what to do about the news. Then everything got active again. Marley started loading his wagon, passing me the word that he would be leaving for the Empty Poke at dawn. Not many hours earlier he'd said that he didn't expect to leave for a week. It wasn't hard to guess that somebody had put out some new orders.

"Then Austin Sebrell was murdered and the gang saw their chance to foul up the picture by blaming the killing on me. Again the orders came out quickly, giving Bonner a story to tell that would make me look bad. Bonner admitted that much to me. That was when I gave up figuring that it could be McLinden. And it wasn't Sparling. He wasn't here. I don't think the rest of the gang even knew he was the guilty man at that time. They didn't know they were protecting him when they accused me."

"Great!" Magruder interrupted. "You've now figured it all out so that nobody is boss of this mob."

Lieutenant Perkins appeared in the doorway at that moment, his tone as apologetic as his words. "Excuse me, sir, but Mrs. Sebrell wants to come over and take care of Mr. Vicker. She seems to have the impression that he was wounded while a fugitive from an unjust charge."

"Darn it, Perkins!" Captain Bates snapped. "Stop interrupting! Tell the lady . . ." He broke off to stare quizzically at Vicker. "Maybe I'd better let you send the message. There seems to be something in all this that I don't understand."

"Not a thing," Vicker assured him. "If you'd been willing to see the facts as they are, you'd never have fallen for that yarn that I killed Sebrell to get his wife."

Bates was showing a little red behind the ears. "You've got to admit that it looked . . ."

"Only to people who needed a fresh subject for gossip, Captain. But forget that part. I don't need the lady's assistance as a nurse, and I'd rather not start any fresh gossip. I'd take it as a favor if the lieutenant would inform her that I'm leaving for Montana at daylight tomorrow morning. I won't have time for any social affairs or farewells. I have a job for the company that must be handled without delay."

Magruder laughed grimly. "It's in Nevada, and there's no hurry."

"You tell it your way," Vicker growled. "Let Perkins tell it mine."

O'Fallon interrupted with a show of impatience. "Get back to the other story. I'm sure there's more important business here than a matter of lying to a lady."

"It's pretty important," Vicker retorted, letting the smile come back. "But we'll get on with the smuggler story. Where was I?"

"Dangling," O'Fallon told him. "You'd just explained why none of the gang could have been boss of the outfit."

"Not exactly. I explained why three main lieutenants were only lieutenants. There was one person — and only one person — who could have made a quick decision that day in Tombstone and another decision here at Fort Huachuca. Actually, there were four people who were in Tombstone on the day that emergency orders had to be given and who were also here at Fort Huachuca when Sparling brought word that the Mexican part of the gang was moving into action with the salting operation. I was one of the four. I eliminated me without much struggle because I really didn't think I was the one."

"A comedian!" Magruder exploded. "Stop smirking and get on with it."

"Patience, boss. Anyway, the other three were Lieutenant Perkins, Mrs. Sebrell, and a lady I know only as Floss. For a whole lot of reasons I could forget the first two. They had just arrived in Tombstone, and they hadn't been in this part of the country before. So . . ."

O'Fallon snapped an order at one of the men near the door. Then he looked down at Vicker again. "You're not joking, I suppose?"

"Not at all. Maybe you'll remember the report that the gang you blamed for the big gold robbery was supposed to have a woman in it. I think she must have been the boss. When they hustled their gold into Mexico in getting away from the law on this side of the line, I imagine she saw her chance to link up the old rustler gang here with the bandit operations in Sonora. She could control the whole outfit so that it could serve a lot of criminal purposes. By posing as a dance-hall tart, she could be in touch with everything and still never be suspected of the game she was actually playing. When she wanted to make a quick move from Tombstone to Fort Huachuca, she simply had McLinden pretend to be driving her out of town. It all seems to fit."

"I suppose it does," O'Fallon said almost gloomily. "You seem to have been right on all counts."

Vicker grinned. "Now you sound like Mister Magruder. He fails to appreciate my true worth. Anyhow, I'm not coming out of this with everything I hoped to get, you know. I started snooping in the first place because I had hopes of getting a friend of mine out of trouble. The smugglers got to him first. Killing a few thugs is not much of a return for losing Hal Ulrich."

A new voice broke in then. Vicker hadn't seen Naismith come into the room, but the little man was making himself quite at home. "We lost on another matter," he announced, stressing the *we* with some significance. "Them polecats what got theirselves killed by the Apaches. Could be we mighta

217

collected some bounty on 'em if'n the red-skins hadn't got 'em first. Now it looks like the only one with any price on his head is the Mex we hauled in from the gulch. He's dead, but that don't make no difference. There's still a thousand pesos offered fer him by the Sonora governor."

Vicker let his head go back. "A thousand pesos," he murmured. "Hardly enough to pay his fare in from the mine. And how's Nate?"

"Gittin' drunk jest as fast as he kin make it."

The much harassed Lieutenant Perkins appeared in the doorway once more. "Sorry, sir," he said to Captain Bates. "Mrs. Sebrell keeps insisting. She wants to see Mr. Vicker."

This time he didn't get a reply. A disturbance behind him forced him to step aside, and a woman stumbled into the lamplight. It was Floss, her big hat tilted precariously to the back of her overdone curls. A deputy came in behind her, obviously having just pushed her through ahead of him. "We nailed her just in time," he told O'Fallon. "She was all packed up and gettin' a saddle on a bronc."

Floss straightened the hat and snarled at O'Fallon, "You ain't got a thing on me, mister!"

Vicker raised his head long enough to aim a crooked grin at her. "I'll give you odds that McLinden gives them all they need. That weasel will talk to save himself. Want to bet?"

When she refused to reply, he added, "I think that's why you tried to run. You know he'll squeal like a stuck pig."

This time he drew fire. She raged at him. "I wish I'd let Bonner kill you when he wanted to. That way we'd . . ."

O'Fallon promptly began to bombard her with questions, trying to capitalize on the slip she had made. She cursed him energetically, the pair of them setting up quite an uproar. In the midst of it, Lieutenant Perkins began to press for an answer about Mrs. Sebrell, shouting to make Bates hear him above the other voices.

Vicker had closed his eyes after baiting Floss into her admission, but now he reopened them long enough to get Naismith's attention. "Get a couple of broncs ready for a move at dawn, Ben," he pleaded. "Maybe it'll be a bit more peaceful and quiet up there in Montana or Nevada or wherever it is we're going. I can't stand all this excitement."

ABOUT THE AUTHOR

E. E. Halleran was born in Wildwood, New Jersey. He graduated with a Bachelor's degree from Bucknell University in Lewisburg, Pennsylvania, and did postgraduate work at Temple University Law School, Rutgers University where he earned a Master's degree in Education, and the University of Pennsylvania in Philadelphia. He worked as a teacher of social studies at Ocean City High School in New Jersey from 1928 until his retirement in 1949. Halleran began publishing Western stories in magazines, with stories in Wild West, Western Story, and feature articles about Western American history in Big-Book Western. His first novel, *No Range is Free,* was published by Macrae Smith in 1944 and had both commercial and critical success. It was followed that same year by *Prairie Guns* (Macrae Smith, 1944). *Indian Fighter* (Ballantine, 1964) won a Spur Award as Best Western Historical

Novel from the Western Writers of America. Halleran's Western fiction is meticulously researched with notable accuracy, both as to the period in which it is set and often populated by historical personalities, while the stories are filled with suspense and fast-paced drama. Among the characters in *Prairie Guns* are Wild Bill Hickok, while he was still a U.S. marshal, and the Indian chieftain Roman Nose. His characters, both fictitious and historical, appear against backdrops of documented historical events through which the historical characters actually lived, and without any overt attempt to create legends or myths. His descriptive and narrative talent is always such that a reader is instantly swept up by the events of the story and becomes deeply involved with the characters. Among his finest books — always a difficult choice with this author — are *No Range is Free, Outposts Of Vengeance* (Macrae Smith, 1945) set during the time of the war with the Miami Indians, and *Winter Ambush* (Macrae Smith, 1954) concerned with the attempt by the U.S. Army to quell a Mormon uprising.

The employees of Thorndike Press hope you have enjoyed this Large Print book. All our Thorndike, Wheeler, and Kennebec Large Print titles are designed for easy reading, and all our books are made to last. Other Thorndike Press Large Print books are available at your library, through selected bookstores, or directly from us.

For information about titles, please call:
  (800) 223-1244

or visit our Web site at:
  http://gale.cengage.com/thorndike

To share your comments, please write:
  Publisher
  Thorndike Press
  10 Water St., Suite 310
  Waterville, ME 04901

DATE DUE

WC			
ME			
DN "18"			

Demco, Inc. 38-293

CPSIA information can be obtained
at www.ICGtesting.com
Printed in the USA
FFOW05n0904150813

9 781410 461506